THE WOMEN OF THE ALL-AMERICAN
GIRLS PROFESSIONAL BASEBALL LEAGUE

THE WOMEN OF THE ALL-AMERICAN GIRLS PROFESSIONAL BASEBALL LEAGUE

A Biographical Dictionary

by W. C. MADDEN

McFarland & Company, Inc., Publishers

Jefferson, North Carolina, and London

I dedicate this book to my wife,
Janice Darlene Madden,
and the players of the AAGPBL

Front cover (*clockwise from top left*): Gloria "Tippy" Schweigerdt (right), Pauline "Hedy Crawley, Lillian "Bird Dog" Jackson.

British Library Cataloguing-in-Publication data are available

Library of Congress Cataloguing-in-Publication Data

Madden, W. C.
    The women of the All-American Girls Professional Baseball League :
a biographical dictionary / by W. C. Madden.
        p.   cm.
    Includes index.
    ISBN 0-7864-0304-7 (library binding : 50# alkaline paper) ∞
    1. All-American Girls Professional Baseball League.   2. Women
baseball players — United States — Biography — Dictionaries.
I. Title.
GV875.M34   1997
796.357'092'2 — dc21   97-9158
[B]   CIP

Manufactured in the United States of America

McFarland & Company, Inc., Publishers
    Box 611, Jefferson, North Carolina 28640

Acknowledgments

The idea for this book originated back in 1993 when I was completing my first book, *The Hoosiers of Summer*. I ran into former player Nancy Rockwell DeShone, who said I should include the Hoosier women of the league in my first book. Then I thought about writing another book of baseball biographies about the women's league.

I have to give a lot of credit to my wife, Janice. She helped me with some of the research and interviews. I would also like to thank my daughter Randi Madden for drawing pictures of players of whom we were unable to obtain photographs. I received a lot of help and cooperation from the AAGPBL Players Association. Dottie Collins and Wimp Baumgartner cleared the way for me to do interviews with the former players and helped me with research.

The Northern Indiana Historical Society was of great help in providing some of the information for this book. And Tim Miles of the National Baseball Hall of Fame was quick in providing information they had on the league.

Finally, the former players are to be thanked for their cooperation in allowing me to interview many of them —190 to be exact. Some players sent me the only photograph of themselves that they owned and other valuable information about the league and its players.

Contents

Introduction

For a dozen years during the 1940s and 1950s perhaps as many as 700 women played baseball professionally in the All-American Girls Professional Baseball League. They were paid much more than a normal job could have paid them for a game that most would have played for free.

Many of the women of the All-American Girls Professional Baseball League were superb athletes and had excelled at many sports before they joined the league. They attained some records unequaled by their male counterparts, such as 201 stolen bases by Sophie Kurys in one season, and a 20-2 pitching record by Jean Faut one summer. While the last Major League Baseball player to hit .400 was Ted Williams in 1953, Joanne Weaver accomplished the feat in 1954 with a .429 average. Joanne Winter hurled 63 consecutive scoreless innings for six shutouts in a row; the Major League record is 59 innings in a row by Orel Hershiser.

When you look at the statistics, you may notice low figures for home runs and extra base hits. The first 11 years of the league was played with a larger ball that was not conducive to hitting home runs. However, the league went to a Major League sized ball in 1954 and extra base hits became more prolific. So 1943–1953 should be considered the "dead-ball era" in the league. Also, understand that games in the first three years of the league were played with underhand pitching much more like softball. After the 1947 season, the underhand delivery was forbidden.

The league kept good statistics only on players who played more than 10 games in a season. So statistics on some players are unavailable. While Major League Baseball considers only players who played in a game, the AAGPBL Players Association considers anyone who signed a contract as a player in the league. Some 700 players signed contracts with the league, but no complete record has been compiled on those contracts. The league did not keep accurate records on all players who played or were signed to contracts. This book does not include information on players in which only partial names were uncovered during research. This book does account for more than 600 of the players who signed contracts. Some of them, admittedly, never played in a game in the league.

Most of the players came from the United States or Canada, but a few players came from Cuba or other countries. There were nine sets of sisters who played in the league, including one trio — the Weaver sisters.

The league and players did not attain much recognition for their achievements until the National Baseball Hall of Fame in Cooperstown officially honored the league in 1988. Only one player from the league — Dorothy Schroeder — is eligible to be inducted as a player in the Hall of Fame, but the AAGPBL Players Association does not want individual recognition. Then in 1992, the movie *A League of Their Own* was released. It told the league's story to the country with a cast of first-rate movie stars, including Tom Hanks and Geena Davis. Some of the actual players of the league appeared at the end of the film.

The renaissance of recognition of the league came at a time when many of the players reached retirement or had passed on. This book hopes to capture some of their memories and statistics, so they will never be forgotten.

A Brief History
of the AAGPBL

The idea for a women's professional baseball league came in 1942 from Philip K. Wrigley, the owner of the Chicago Cubs National League baseball team. With the support of Branch Rickey and Paul V. Harper, Wrigley sent his scouts out to scour the country and Canada for players for his new league, which was first called the All-American Girls Softball League. Tryouts were held in various cities and some 280 finalists were invited to Wrigley Field in Chicago for the final selection process. In all, 64 women were selected to play on the first four teams in the league: South Bend, Indiana; Rockford, Illinois; Kenosha, Wisconsin; and Racine, Wisconsin.

Before the season began, softball was dropped from the name of the league, because softball rules had been discarded in favor of baseball rules. However, underhand pitching and a 12-inch softball would be used. An All-Star Game was held at Wrigley Field — the first night game at the stadium — in the middle of the first season. The All-Star Game was abandoned for the next two seasons before it was resumed in 1946. Racine won the first championship, which was called the Scholarship Series because a $1,000 scholarship went to the winning city.

The initial success of the first season — 176,000 fans — led the league to add two more teams in 1944: the Milwaukee Chicks and the Minneapolis Millerettes. However, Minneapolis failed to draw fans and the team was put on the road the remainder of the season. Both franchises were moved the following year: the Chicks went to Grand Rapids, Michigan, and the Millerettes were moved to Fort Wayne, Indiana, and renamed the Daisies. The championship series was renamed the Shaughnessy Playoff Series and Milwaukee won the title. The league drew some 450,000 fans in 1944, yet Wrigley decided he had seen enough of his experiment and sold the league to advertising director Arthur Meyerhoff. Max Carey was named as the president of the league. Teams were set up much like major league franchises with each club handling its own affairs.

After the war ended in 1945, the league shifted more toward baseball rules. In 1946, the ball was reduced to 11 inches in circumference, the base paths were lengthened to 72 feet and sidearm pitching was introduced. The league increased to eight teams and attendance rose to 750,000. Underhand pitching was ended after the 1947 season; only sidearm or overhand pitching was allowed. This led many of the whirlwind pitchers to abandon the league for the rival Chicago National League.

The league reached its zenith in 1948 as a total of 10 teams were formed to compete. A month into the season, the Springfield (Ill.) Sallies franchise had not developed and became a traveling team, much like Minneapolis in 1944. The league brought in Cuban players, which was a result of holding spring training in Havana in 1947 and exhibition games in 1948. The league drew nearly a million fans on the season.

Poor financial management finally caught up to the league in 1949 and it began to slide.

The departure of several good players robbed the league of some of its best talent. Spring training was turned over to the teams to conduct. The Chicago and Springfield franchises were turned into player development teams in 1949 and 1950 and went on barnstorming tours of the country to recruit new talent. The ball was further reduced to 10 inches and the distance from home plate to the pitching mound was lengthened to 55 feet. Max Carey was replaced by Fred Leo as president of the league.

The Muskegon (Mich.) Lassies folded halfway through the 1950 season and was moved to Kalamazoo. The Belles also moved to Battle Creek, Michigan, at the end of the season and Racine called it quits. The clubs rid themselves of the management corporation and Meyerhoff after the season, too.

Kenosha (Wis.) and Peoria (Ill.) folded after the 1951 season. Fred Leo turned in his resignation as league president and he was replaced by Harold Van Orman. By 1952, the league was down to six teams and attendance was continuing to dwindle. The Muskegon franchise folded after 1953, leaving the league with five teams.

Nineteen fifty-four saw drastic changes in a last-ditch effort to save the league. The ball was reduced to major league size, the pitching mound was moved back to 60 feet—just six inches shy of the majors—and the base paths were lengthened to 85 feet, which was five feet short of major league baseball. The game was now very close to its male counterpart. The women started knocking out home runs like never before. But with attendance continuing to decline and debt continuing to mount, the league closed its doors after the season. The wartime replacement to men's baseball managed to survive 12 seasons, which was longer than some had predicted.

Abbreviations
Used in Statistics

A	Assists	HR	Home Runs
AB	At Bats	IP	Innings Pitched
BA	Batting Average	PCT	(Winning) Percentage
BB	Base on Balls (Allowed)	PO	Put Outs
BL	Bats Left	R	Runs (Allowed)
BR	Bats Right	RBI	Runs Batted In
DP	Double Plays	SB	Stolen Bases
2B	Doubles	SH	Switch Hitter
E	Errors	SO	Strike Outs
ER	Earned Runs	TL	Throws Left
ERA	Earned Run Average	TR	Throws Right
FA	Fielding Average	TB	Throws Left and Right
G	Games	3B	Triples
H	Hits (Allowed)	W–L	Won–Loss Record

THE PLAYERS

Abbott, Velma

**Born: May 29, 1924, Regina, Saskatchewan, Canada. Died: Date unknown. 5'2",
110, Infielder, BR, TR. Kenosha Comets, 1946; Peoria Redwings, 1946; Rockford
Peaches, 1946; Fort Wayne Daisies, 1947.**

Flora Velma Abbott was a light-hitting utility infielder for four different teams in two
seasons. She played with the Alameda Girls in California, twice world champions in amateur
softball, before joining the league. The brown-haired Canadian wore number 6 with the
Daisies and called Pismo Beach, California, home when she played in the league.

G	BA	AB	H	2B	3B	HR	SB	BB	SO	R	RBI		PO	A	E	DP	FA
						BATTING									FIELDING		
149	.155	438	68	2	4	1	33	38	43	42	20		187	239	51	16	.893

Evelyn "Tommie" Adams

Acker, Fredda

**Anderson, South Carolina. Pitcher.
South Bend Blue Sox, 1947.**

Fredda Acker was in the league for one season and used mainly for publicity purposes.

The attractive woman was named Mrs. America in 1946. The league hired her in 1947 to assist in a charm school and fashion show at the spring training camp in Havana, Cuba. After spring training, she was signed to a contract by South Bend and joined her sister, Viola Thompson, on the team. However, the pitcher never appeared in a game that season.

Adams, Evelyn "Tommie"

**Born: Nov. 16, 1923, Richmond, Virginia. 5'3", 110,
Shortstop, SH, TR. Fort Wayne Daisies, 1946;
Grand Rapids Chicks, 1946.**

Evelyn Adams spent a season in the sun with two teams and quit because of a lingering illness.

"Tommie" began playing baseball when she was 14 with the only girls baseball team in Virginia. She was their star pitcher. The Freckles would play against men's teams, sort of like the modern-day Colorado Silver Bullets. Then she began playing softball two years later.

The baseball experience is what helped her make the AAGPBL in 1946. She was not selected as a pitcher, however, and was turned into a shortstop.

"I hit a triple and brought in the winning run," recalled Adams of her one season with the league. Her greatest thrill was playing in the Shaughnessy Playoffs.

Tommie became sick and had to quit. "They thought I had malaria, but it turned out to be bronchitis," she explained. Because of her professional status, she couldn't play amateur softball for a while, so she took up coaching cadet nurses. Later, she took to playing softball again and golfing. She went to work for A&P Tea Company and retired in 1984 after 34 years with the company.

She was named to the Richmond Softball Hall of Fame in 1974. Today she lives in Richmond and still plays slow-pitch softball, although admittedly she doesn't like it. She was honored to throw out the first pitch in a game the Silver Bullets played in Richmond.

				BATTING									FIELDING				
G	BA	AB	H	2B	3B	HR	SB	BB	SO	R	RBI		PO	A	E	DP	FA
39	.140	86	12	1	1	0	4	6	20	6	1		12	22	8	1	.810

Ahrndt (Proefrock), Ellen "Babe"

Born: Nov. 8, 1922, Racine, Wisconsin. 5'4", 120, 2nd Base, BR, TR. South Bend Blue Sox, 1945.

The All-American league wasn't for everyone, including Ellen Ahrndt, who only played in three games in a season with South Bend.

Living in the country near Racine, Ahrndt played organized softball at age 14 with a town team. A business associate—Marnie Danhauser—played in the league and her coach approached Ahrndt about playing. She accepted, went to Wrigley Field for a tryout and made the league. She saw action in three games during the season.

Once when the team came to Racine, they decided to honor her with a homecoming night. "They started me, but took me out," she said. "My old coach was steaming."

The next season she wasn't offered a contract. "It wasn't my kind of life," she admitted. Instead, she married William Proefrock in 1947 and they raised two children, Kipp and Kurt. Now they have two grandchildren. Retired and living in Brodhead, Wisconsin, the couple travels and fishes together.

Ellen "Babe" Ahrndt

BATTING

G	BA	AB	H
3	.000	3	0

Albright, Ellen

Pitcher, 3rd Base, 2nd Base. Chicago Colleens, 1948.

Eileen Albright was primarily an infielder for the expansion Chicago Colleens for a season. She also pitched four games, which were all losses.

PITCHING

W–L	PCT	ERA	G	IP	H	R	ER	BB	SO
0–4	.000	2.46	4	22	17	11	6	19	10

BATTING | FIELDING

G	BA	AB	H	2B	3B	HR	SB	BB	SO	R	RBI	G	PO	A	E	DP	FA
65	.141	142	20	3	0	0	9	19	24	9	4	65	90	114	20	8	.911

Alderfer (Benner), Gertrude "Gert"

Born: Sept. 21, 1931, Telford, Pennsylvania. 5'7", 155, 1st Base, BR, TR. Springfield Sallies, 1949; Chicago Colleens, 1950; Kalamazoo Lassies, 1950.

Gertrude Alderfer spent most of her two seasons in the league on the traveling teams. The all-around athlete lettered in eight sports in high school. After baseball, she married and had two daughters and a son. At last count she had four grandchildren. She retired in 1992 after working 43 years in a machine shop.

BATTING

G	BA	AB	H	2B	3B	HR	SB	BB	SO	R	RBI
54	.236	212	50	3	3	1	9	22	24	38	24

(1950 Chicago Colleens statistics only)

Allard, Beatrice "Bea"

Born: July 10, 1930, Muskegon, Michigan. 5'4", 130, Pitcher, TR, BR. Muskegon Lassies, 1949.

Beatrice Allard's pitching career was cut short by a dead arm after the manager changed her delivery.

"Bea" played a little sandlot ball when she was a youngster. She became a big fan of the Muskegon Lassies and decided one day to go to one of the tryouts to help a friend get into the league. She had no intention of playing in the league, but she had a good arm and Max Carey spotted the potential pitcher, so he signed her to a contract. "I got into the league on a fluke," she admits now.

In the season opener in Muskegon, she was called to relieve in the ninth inning with the bases

Beatrice "Bea" Allard

loaded and nobody out. She struck out the first two batters and the third popped out to preserve the win and earn her a save.

Her pitching was going along fine until manager Bill Wamby decided her delivery needed changing. Her arm got sore as a result, but she didn't complain. She finally decided to go to a doctor, who told her the arm was no good anymore and her playing days were over.

She joined the Army as a cryptographer for three years. Afterwards, she filed for unemployment and ended up working in the Grand Rapids Employment Office for the next 31 years. She retired in 1991 and now follows the Auburn University women's basketball team.

Allard went to Cooperstown when the league was inducted into the National Baseball Hall of Fame in 1988. "That was the most emotional 48 hours of my life," she said. Now she lives in Lillian, Alabama.

PITCHING										BATTING			FIELDING			
W–L	PCT	ERA	G	IP	H	R	ER	BB	SO	BA	AB	H	PO	A	E	FA
2–2	.500	2.75	19	59	48	26	18	49	15	.200	20	4	4	14	2	.900

Allen, Agnes "Aggie" L.

Born: Sept. 21, 1930, Alvord, Iowa. 5'3", 120, Pitcher, Outfield, TR, BR. Springfield Sallies, 1950; Kalamazoo Lassies, 1951–53; Battle Creek Belles, 1951.

If the league would have handed out most improved awards, Agnes Allen would have received one. After two poor seasons, she came back with a winning record in her last season. In all she played four years with the league.

Being that her father was a semipro player, she took up baseball the first day she could catch the ball. Her father and two brothers were all pitchers, so they taught her the trade. She didn't start playing organized softball until high school.

Allen read about the league in a newspaper and conned her dad into taking her to a tryout in Cedar Rapids, Iowa. The scout liked what he saw and invited her to Wrigley Field for another tryout. She was taken by the traveling Springfield Sallies in 1950 for more seasoning. Her biggest thrill was pitching a game in Yankee Stadium and meeting the famous Connie Mack. "That was a tremendous experience for me," she recalled. She ended the barnstorming season with a 9–5 mark on the mound and a .172 average at the plate.

Agnes "Aggie" L. Allen

Kalamazoo signed the pitching prospect. Noted for a fastball, "Aggie" also threw a roundhouse curveball, change and a drop. However, she had trouble with control and walked 126 batters in 100 innings and struggled to a 6.21 ERA and 3–10 record. During the middle of the season, she was loaned to Battle Creek for five games, which she doesn't recall now.

She had just as much trouble on the mound for the Lassies the next season — her record was 1–7 — so she was put in the outfield. Allen improved her control the following season and her ERA dropped to 3.70 and her record improved to 10–9.

Allen decided to turn her baseball cap in for a mortar board at Western Michigan University. After teaching for three years, she went to work as a physical therapist at the Mayo Clinic and has been there ever since. She now lives in Sioux Falls, South Dakota.

PITCHING										BATTING			FIELDING			
W–L	PCT	ERA	G	IP	H	R	ER	BB	SO	BA	AB	H	PO	A	E	FA
14–26	.350	4.87	60	324	290	235	178	196	134	.169	267	45	100	144	24	.914

Alspaugh, Melba

Wichita, Kansas. Died: Feb. 15, 1983. Outfield. Fort Wayne Daisies, 1948; Rockford Peaches, 1948–49; Muskegon Lassies, 1949.

Melba Alspaugh was a reserve outfielder for three teams in two seasons in the league.

BATTING												FIELDING				
G	BA	AB	H	2B	3B	HR	SB	BB	SO	R	RBI	PO	A	E	DP	FA
112	.199	297	59	1	0	0	40	29	46	41	19	104	10	5	2	.958

Alvarez, Isabel

Born: Oct. 31, 1933, Havana, Cuba. 5'3", 140, Pitcher, Outfield, TL, BL. Chicago Colleens, 1949–50; Fort Wayne Daisies, 1951; Battle Creek Belles, 1951–52; Kalamazoo Lassies, 1953; Grand Rapids Chicks, 1954.

Isabel Alvarez was one of the Cuban imports after the league held spring training in Cuba in 1947. She joined the barnstorming teams in 1949 and 1950. She was 6–6 as a hurler on the road with the Chicago Colleens in 1950. She also hit .256 on the season. Then when she joined the league itself, she relieved in 13 games in 1951 with Fort Wayne and Battle Creek before being put in the outfield the remainder of her career. Her hitting and fielding were below par. She now calls Fort Wayne her home.

PITCHING									
W–L	PCT	ERA	G	IP	H	R	ER	BB	SO
2–0	1.000	3.71	13	34	41	29	14	26	7

BATTING											FIELDING				
G	BA	2B	3B	HR	SO	BB	SO	R	RBI		PO	A	E	DP	FA
105	.195	7	1	0	3	14	19	15	18		53	12	8	0	.883

Anderson (Perkin), Janet

Bethune, Saskatchewan, Canada. Outfield, Pitcher. Kenosha Comets, 1946.

Janet Anderson was a pitcher-outfielder for one season with Kenosha. She had no luck on the mound and was 0–6. After baseball, she worked for Allied Van Lines. She also took up bowling. She now lives in Regina, Saskatchewan.

PITCHING

W–L	PCT	G	IP	H	R	BB	SO
0–6	.000	10	36	45	49	30	8

BATTING												FIELDING			
G	BA	AB	H	2B	3B	HR	SB	BB	SO	R	RBI		PO	A	E	FA
36	.173	75	13	0	2	0	2	10	12	5	2		22	18	3	.930

Anderson (Sheriffs), Vivian "Andy"

Born: April 21, 1921, Milwaukee, Wisconsin. 5'2", 140, 3rd Base, BR. Milwaukee Chicks, 1944.

An injury cut short the playing career of Vivian Anderson during her rookie season.

The Milwaukee native started playing softball at the age of 13 in a league which required its players to be 16. "I cheated on my age a little," she explained. She married Daniel Anderson, her assistant coach, in 1942, at the age of 21 and continued to play the game she loved so much. Scouts from the All-American League saw her play and sent her an invitation to spring training in LaSalle, Illinois.

Anderson tried out as a third baseman and was accepted into the league with her hometown Milwaukee Chicks. She was the only player from her hometown on the team. Her rookie season was going along fine until one road game. "The ball, the base and the runner all came together at one time," she recalled. The result was two broken fingers — her index and middle fingers — on her throwing hand. One doctor advised amputation! Another said he could fix them, but they would be crooked the rest of her life. She chose the latter.

She played in the Chicago National League for the next few years. She divorced her husband after the war and worked as a secretary. Then in 1960 she went to work as a dispatcher for Allied Van Lines. She continued to be active in sports, such as bowling and basketball. She still works part time for a moving company and lives in Wauwatose, Wisconsin.

BATTING												FIELDING				
G	BA	AB	H	2B	3B	HR	SB	BB	SO	R	RBI		PO	A	E	DP	FA
11	.147	34	5	0	0	0	1	6	1	3	1		22	22	7	1	.863

Applegren, Amy Irene "Lefty"

Born: Nov. 16, 1926, Peoria, Illinois. 5'4", 125, Pitcher, 1st Base, TL, BL. Rockford Peaches, 1944–46; Muskegon Lassies, 1947–49; Rockford Peaches, 1949–53.

One of the few pitchers in the league to pitch all three styles in the league's history, Amy Applegren threw two no-hitters during her decade in the league.

After playing baseball with the boys in grade school, Amy joined a girls softball team at age 11. She was playing for the Caterpillar Dieselettes when an AAGPBL scout noticed her in the national tournament in Detroit. She received an invitation to spring training the next year in LaSalle, Illinois.

Using underhand fastball pitching, she was 16–15 in her first season and 13–11 the next. In 1946, the league converted over to sidearm pitching and Applegren wasn't as effective, but coaches worked with her. Then on July 31, she tossed a no-hitter at Grand Rapids.

She went from an 8–18 mark in 1946 to 16–10 the following season with Muskegon. Then the league switched over to overhand pitching in 1948 and moved the mound back further, giving her problems. "As the mound moved back, I wasn't as effective because I wasn't big and strong," she said.

After losing seasons three years in a row, she gave up pitching and moved to first base. She admitted she wasn't a power hitter and had only one homer in her career, which came in her last season. She saw the demise of the league coming, so she went to play for the Chicago Queens, a professional softball team. "A lot of the girls I played with were gone and I wasn't happy playing anymore," she explained.

She ended up playing in the Chicago National League for four years before going to work for several companies until 1969. Her father became ill, so she went back to Peoria to help the family. She retired in 1985 and now lives with her mother. Once an avid bowler, she now enjoys a round of golf.

Amy Irene "Lefty" Applegren

PITCHING											BATTING			FIELDING			
W–L	PCT	ERA	G	IP	H	R	ER	BB	SO		BA	AB	H	PO	A	E	FA
86–98	.467	2.52	206	1451	905	586	407	880	501		.231	1363	315	2435	535	90	.971

Arbour (Parrott), Beatrice "Bea"

Born: Dec. 2, 1920, Somerset, Massachusetts. 5'6", 128, Shortstop, BR. Racine Belles, 1947.

Beatrice Arbour was sweet 16 when she joined the league. She batted only once for Racine. She married after baseball and raised three boys and a girl. She drove a school bus for 19 years. Now she travels a lot and enjoys gardening in her hometown of Somerset, Massachusetts.

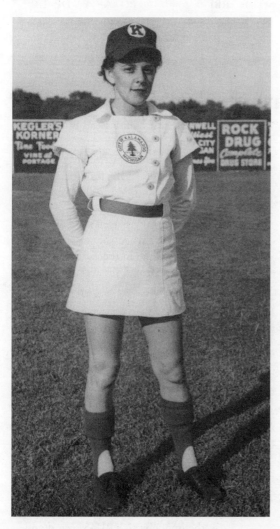

Ange "Lil Bonnie" Armato

BATTING

G	BA	AB	H
1	.000	1	0

Armato, Ange "Lil Bonnie"

Born: Oct. 27, 1929, Rockford, Illinois. 5'2", 123, 2nd Base, BR, TR. Peoria Redwings, 1949; Kalamazoo Lassies, 1953.

Injury and illness prevented Ange Armato from playing more than one season in the league.

Growing up in Rockford, Armato witnessed the Rockford Peaches firsthand and wanted to be a player in the league from the time she was 14. "I tormented Bill Allington to play on the team," she explained. She watched every game! Allington talked her into going to a baseball school in Chicago at age 16.

Armato finally got an invitation to go to spring training in 1947, but didn't make the cut. Then she went to spring training again in 1949 in Peoria and signed a contract with the Redwings to play. Unfortunately, on the last day of spring training, she broke her foot. "I was so disappointed. I thought my baseball career was over," she said.

She went to work in Chicago as an artist in advertising. One day a few years later, she ran into the manager of the baseball camp who now managed Kalamazoo. He invited her to play with the Lassies. She jumped at the opportunity. She played second base, but wasn't made a starter, because the manager wanted to save her rookie status until the next year. Players who played in less than 50 games would continue to be considered a rookie. Armato was tagged with the nickname "Lil Bonnie" when a newspaper reporter thought she looked a lot like former player Bonnie Baker. Then she developed allergy problems which prevented her from returning the next season.

Armato returned to Chicago and continued to work in advertising until retiring in 1992 to Rockford. Right after retiring, she traveled to Cooperstown to be in the movie *A League of Their Own*. "That was one of the most exciting times of my life," she said of the experience.

BATTING													FIELDING				
G	BA	AB	H	2B	3B	HR	SB	BB	SO	R	RBI		PO	A	E	DP	FA
27	.077	26	2	0	0	0	1	8	6	5	2		25	21	7	1	.868

Armstrong, Charlotte T. "Skipper"

Born: June 17, 1924, Dallas, Texas. 5'7", 145, Pitcher, TR, BR. South Bend Blue Sox, 1943–44.

Charlotte T. "Skipper" Armstrong

Charlotte Armstrong was one of the top starters in the league for two years before jumping to the rival Chicago National League.

Armstrong played sandlot baseball with the boys when she was a little girl. "They stuck me in the outfield, so I had to learn to throw," she recalled. She started playing softball in grammar school. After she finished grade school, she played for a commercial team whose public address announcer stuck her with the nickname "Skipper." Then she advanced to the Phoenix Queens, a professional softball team. A scout for the All-American League spotted her and asked her parents if they would let her play in the new league. They refused because the league was new. He persisted the following season until her parents let her join.

In her first season with South Bend, she was one of the best pitchers in the league with a 21–15 record and a minuscule 1.51 ERA. At one point during the next season, all the pitchers were injured or sick for a doubleheader, so the manager called on her to pitch both games. She responded with two extra-inning shutouts — a total of 32 innings without giving up a run! Robert Ripley was so impressed with the feat that he wrote about it in his "Ripley's Believe It or Not" column. The record also made the *Guinness Book of World Records.* She topped that performance with a seven-inning no-hitter on Aug. 21 against Grand Rapids. The manager almost used her too much, as she ended up leading the league in games started, hits allowed and runs allowed.

She was offered a lucrative contract to play for the Chicago Cardinals the next year, so she jumped to the other league. She returned to the Phoenix Queens in 1947 and was the leading pitcher in the World Championships three times and an All-Star six times.

After softball, she operated a gift shop for 13 years before becoming a full-time artist, which she still is today in Phoenix. She has been inducted into the Arizona Softball Hall of Fame.

PITCHING											BATTING			FIELDING			
W–L	PCT	ERA	G	IP	H	R	ER	BB	SO		BA	AB	H	PO	A	E	FA
39–37	.513	1.76	85	676	511	236	132	154	159		.149	249	37	27	239	15	.947

Arnold, Lenna "Sis"

**Born: Oct. 29, 1920, Fort Wayne, Indiana.
5'7", 135, Pitcher, TR, BR.
Fort Wayne Daisies, 1946.**

Lenna Arnold was an undistinguished pitcher for a season with the Fort Wayne Daisies in 1946. She still lives in Fort Wayne today.

PITCHING

W–L	PCT	G	IP	H	R	BB	SO
2–4	.333	6	40	37	32	23	1

BATTING

BA	AB	H
.214	14	3

Arnold, Louise "Lou"

**Born: May 11, 1923, Pawtucket, Rhode Island.
5'3", 125, Pitcher, TR, BR. South Bend Blue
Sox, 1948–52.**

Louise Arnold tossed a one-hitter during her five years in the league and helped the South Bend Blue Sox to two championships.

Arnold began playing softball at age 15

Louise "Lou" Arnold

in Rhode Island at Newport Naval Base. A few years later she was given a tryout in Opa-locka, Florida. The league was switching to overhand pitching in 1948 and the manager liked Arnold's arm. She went 4–4 in 1948 with a 4.06 ERA.

After being used sparingly in 1949 and 1950, "Lou" helped the team win the pennant in 1951 with a 10–2 mark, which tied her for the best winning percentage (.833) in the league. During the 1951 championship playoffs, she pitched and won one of the games. "That was a big thrill," she said.

The following season she was hit hard and ended with a 4–8 record with a 3.43 ERA. "I loved every minute of it. The fans were great," she reflected.

After her baseball days, she went to work for Bendix for 40 years and retired in 1983. Arnold lives in South Bend and is now restricted to a wheelchair because of paralysis in her foot.

PITCHING										BATTING			FIELDING			
W–L	PCT	ERA	G	IP	H	R	ER	BB	SO	BA	AB	H	PO	A	E	FA
23–16	.590	3.02	72	366	325	183	123	117	75	.124	105	13	17	110	14	.890

Arnold (Witzel), Norene "Blondie"

Born: Nov. 21, 1927, Oregon, Illinois. Died: Jan. 27, 1987, TR, BR. Springfield Sallies, 1949; Muskegon Lassies, 1949.

Norene Arnold spent a season in the league with the traveling Springfield Sallies and Muskegon Lassies. No statistics were kept by the Sallies in 1949 and she likely played less than 10 games with the Lassies.

Norene "Blondie" Arnold

Baker (George), Mary Geraldine "Bonnie"

Born: July 10, 1918, Regina, Saskatchewan, Canada. 5'5", 133, Catcher, Utility Infielder, BR, TR. South Bend Blue Sox, 1943–50; Kalamazoo Lassies, 1950, 52.

Twice an All-Star, Mary Baker became a rare player-manager in the league for part of one season.

She began playing softball in a city league at age 12. When she was 17, she married Maurie Baker. A few years later, her Canadian team went barnstorming in the United States and she really liked Chicago. A Scottish public address announcer kept calling her "Bonnie" and the nickname stuck with her the rest of her playing days.

When she got a call from a league scout in 1943 to play, she jumped at the opportunity.

She also became a scout for the new league and brought a few other Canadians with her to the AAGPBL.

The excellent fielding catcher had a good bat to boot as she hit .250 in her first season, including the only homer of her career. She said it was a line drive that hit second base and rolled all the way to the fence. Baker was named to the All-Star team as catcher for her performance. She received the same honor in 1946 after hitting .286 and stealing 94 bases on the season. Her sister, Gene George, joined the league as a catcher in 1948 for one season. In 1949, Baker helped South Bend win the pennant as a utility infielder.

The following season she accepted the managerial job at Kalamazoo, therefore becoming the first female manager in the league. The league took advantage of the situation and used her as a public relations tool. She appeared in magazines and on the television show *What's My Line*. The last person finally guessed what she did for a living.

One season of being a manager was enough for Baker. "There were a lot of professional jealousy in the league," she explained. She skipped the 1951 season to deliver a baby girl, Maureen. She came back in 1952 and the Lassies put her at second base where she became the league's best fielder at the position with a .955 average.

Mary Geraldine "Bonnie" Baker

Bonnie saw the end of the league coming, so she returned to Canada to work in the restaurant her husband owned. She worked as a sportscaster for awhile, but didn't like it. Then she managed a curling rink for 19 years before retiring in 1986. Now she watches sports and occasionally gambles on the outcomes.

				BATTING										FIELDING			
G	BA	AB	H	2B	3B	HR	SB	BB	SO	R	RBI		PO	A	E	DP	FA
930	.235	3308	776	44	20	1	506	404	210	465	244		3591	1146	236	213	.953

Phyllis Baker

Baker (Wise), Phyllis

Born: June 3, 1937, Marshall, Michigan. 5'8", 155, Pitcher, TR, BR. Battle Creek Belles, 1952; Muskegon Lassies, 1953; South Bend Blue Sox, 1954; Fort Wayne Daisies, 1954.

Manager Bill Allington considered Phyllis Baker the best rookie pitching prospect in 1953.

Baker began playing sandlot baseball as a youngster. "We had a vacant lot next door to my house," she explained. One day the public address announcer for the Battle Creek Belles saw her playing and told her she was good enough to play in the league. She went to a Belles tryout and was signed in 1952. The teenager was still in high school and spent the season throwing a lot of batting practice, she recalled.

In 1953 the franchise moved to Muskegon and she struggled to a 7–12 mark on the year. One of her victories was very memorable to Baker. She pitched into the 11th inning and then won the game with a hit. Baker also had a one-hitter against Fort Wayne. At the end of the season, the team folded. "They put our names in a hat and split us up," she explained. She went to South Bend.

South Bend didn't have a good team in 1954 and she finished with a 5–11 record. At the end of the season, the Blue Sox folded and she was sent to Fort Wayne for the championship playoffs. "I got a couple of relief jobs," she explained her role in the playoffs.

After the league folded, she went back to high school to graduate. Then she went to work for State Farm Insurance. In 1961, she married Clifton Wise, a softball coach and former baseball player. He retired from Kellogg in 1993 and both are retired now, living in her hometown of Marshall, Michigan.

PITCHING										BATTING			FIELDING			
W–L	PCT	ERA	G	IP	H	R	ER	BB	SO	BA	AB	H	PO	A	E	FA
12–23	.342	3.86	50	317	306	173	136	166	66	.150	127	19	20	121	8	.946

Ballingall, Chris

Born: May 17, 1932, Ann Arbor, Michigan. 5'6", 145, 1st Base, Outfield, Catcher, BL, TR. Muskegon Belles, 1953; Kalamazoo Lassies, 1954.

Chris Ballingall filled in at several positions during her two seasons in the league. She belted out 17 homers in 1954 and was one of the "Home Run Twins" with teammate Carol Habben. She also led the league in strikeouts (56). She now lives in Mattawan, Michigan.

			BATTING											FIELDING				
G	BA	AB	H	2B	3B	HR	SB	BB	SO	R	RBI		G	PO	A	E	DP	FA
162	.218	473	103	9	1	18	4	83	108	68	53		167	454	25	26	13	.949

Barbaze, Barbara

Born: Toronto, Ontario, Canada. Outfield. Springfield Sallies, 1948.

Barbara Barbaze was a light-hitting outfielder for the expansion Springfield Sallies in 1948.

			BATTING										FIELDING				
G	BA	AB	H	2B	3B	HR	SB	BB	SO	R	RBI		PO	A	E	DP	FA
80	193	223	43	2	0	0	23	24	29	19	16		104	5	11	1	.908

Barker, Lois Anna "Tommie"

Born: April 7, 1923, Dover, N.J. 5'3", 130, Outfield, 3rd Base, BR, TR. Fort Wayne Daisies, 1950; Grand Rapids Chicks, 1950.

The oldest rookie in 1950 at age 27, Lois Anna Barker spent a season with Grand Rapids and had to quit due to her father's illness.

"Tommie"—a nickname she was given because she was supposed to have been a boy—recalled catching batting practice for a local men's team when she was 8 years old. Her first organized softball came in 1947 with the Chester Farmerettes. She played all the positions except catcher and once had an unassisted triple play while playing shortstop.

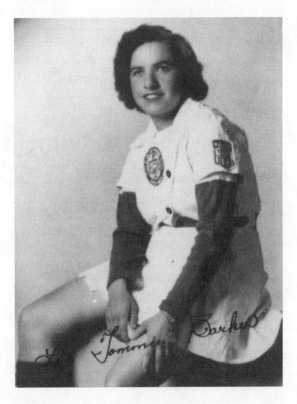

Lois Anna "Tommie" Barker

After attending a league tryout in Irvington, New Jersey, she signed and went to rookie camp in South Bend. During her only season in the league, she was used primarily in the outfield and at third base. In one game, she lost the ball in the lights and was hit in the head. "I thought I was going on the next train out," she said about the embarrassing moment.

After 40 years as a supervisor in an aerospace company, she retired in 1990. Now she lives in Chester, New Jersey, and loves to watch baseball and travel.

BATTING											FIELDING					
G	BA	H	2B	3B	HR	SB	BB	SO	R	RBI	G	PO	A	E	DP	FA
32	.125	8	0	0	0	0	6	15	4	3	31	16	1	1	0	.944

Barnes (McCoy), Joyce

Born: October 18, 1925, Hutchinson, Kansas. 5'8", 125, Pitcher, TR, BR. Kenosha Comets, 1943.

Barnett, Charlene "Barney"

Elgin, Illinois. Died: Date Unknown. 2nd Base, BR. Grand Rapids Chicks, 1947; Chicago Colleens, 1948; Rockford Peaches, 1949–50.

Charlene Barnett played four seasons in the league, including two with the championship Rockford Peaches. After baseball, she became a flight attendant.

BATTING												FIELDING				
G	BA	AB	H	2B	3B	HR	SB	BB	SO	R	RBI	PO	A	E	DP	FA
355	.175	1216	213	16	7	1	89	144	128	120	85	725	657	84	104	.943

Barney, Edith "Little Red"

Born: Feb. 3, 1923, Bridgeport, Connecticut. 5'6", 136, Catcher, BR, TR. Grand Rapids Chicks, 1948.

Were it not for All-Star Ruth Lessing at catcher, Edith Barney might have received more playing time during her only season in the league.

She began playing softball at age 13 around her hometown of Bridgeport, Connecticut. She was spotted by the league and was sent to Opa-locka, Florida, for spring training in 1948. She was assigned to Grand Rapids and played backup to Ruth Lessing.

In October 1948, Barney landed a job as a technician with Raybestos-Manhattan and left baseball. She worked there for 36 years and retired in 1985. Now she lives in Venice, Florida, where she bowls, golfs and runs.

BATTING			
G	BA	AB	H
4	.000	4	0

Barr, Doris "Dodie"

Born: Aug. 26, 1921, Starbuck, Manitoba, Canada. 5'6", 145, Pitcher, Outfield, TL, BL. South Bend Blue Sox, 1944–46; Racine Belles, 1945–47; Springfield Sallies, 1948; Muskegon Lassies, 1949; Kalamazoo Lassies, 1950; Peoria Redwings, 1950.

One of the original players of the league, Doris Barr was one of the few pitchers who made the transition from underhand pitching to overhand pitching, albeit not with much success.

Barr had control problems her first season in the league with South Bend, as she gave up the most walks (155) and threw the most wild pitches (34) in the league. She still pulled off a winning season, though, with a 15–13 mark. After an off year in 1944, "Dodie" had her career-best season in 1945 when she went 20–8 with Racine, although she again led the league in walks (168) and wild pitches (38). On July 1, she threw a no-hitter against Fort Wayne. The following season she was 6–9, but helped the Belles win a pennant and championship.

Before the league switched completely to sidearm and overhand pitching in 1947, Barr had a 49–41 record. Like other pitchers, she had trouble making the conversion from underhand pitching. She failed to have a winning season after 1947 and was 1–11 in 1950, her last year in the league.

PITCHING										BATTING			FIELDING			
W–L	PCT	ERA	G	IP	H	R	ER	BB	SO	BA	AB	H	PO	A	E	FA
79–96	.451	2.80	218	1474	1021	660	458	959	572	.201	677	136	171	348	38	.932

Barringer, Patricia

Born: Sept. 14, 1924, New Carlisle, Ohio. 5'7", 145, 2nd Base, BR, TR. Muskegon Lassies, 1947.

Patricia Barringer was in the league for a season before she became a chaperone with the Chicago Colleens and the Battle Creek Belles. After baseball, she was an auditor and tax accountant. She now lives in Port Charlotte, Florida.

BATTING			
G	BA	AB	H
1	.000	1	0

Batikis, Annastasia "Stash"

Born: May 15, 1927, Racine, Wisconsin. 4'11", 125, Outfield, BL, TL. Racine Belles, 1945.

Annastasia Batikis was used sparingly during her only season in the AAGPBL.

"Stash" started playing ball in high school. A boy she knew gave her a right-hand mitt to use, so she became a lefty on the field. She writes and eats right handed, though. While attending high school, she watched the Racine Belles play. Then in 1945 when she was 18, she and around 100 other girls went to a tryout. She and another girl were picked to go to spring training at Wrigley Field. "I was in awe of all the players and being able to play with the Racine team," she said.

Batikis' first game came when the regular center fielder was late arriving. She recalled one game in Kenosha when it was foggy and the outfielders were not visible from home plate. Sophie Kurys, the best basestealer of the league, taught her how to hook slide.

After her only year in the league, she went on to college for a degree in physical education, which she taught for 35 years. "Sometimes I still can't believe I was part of all this," she commented. She still lives in Racine.

BATTING

G	BA	AB	H	R	RBI
5	.000	11	0	0	0

Battaglia, Fern

Born: Jan. 6, 1931, Chicago, Illinois. 5'4", 120, 2nd Base, 3rd Base. Chicago Colleens/Springfield Sallies, 1950; Battle Creek Belles, 1951.

While on the player development teams in 1950, Fern Battaglia hit .204 with a home run in 67 games. She then played half a season before going home due to her mother's illness. She later worked for the Illinois Board of Education. She now lives in Bensonville, Illinois.

BATTING												FIELDING				
G	BA	AB	H	2B	3B	HR	SB	BB	SO	R	RBI	PO	A	E	DP	FA
19	.167	60	10	1	0	0	4	6	8	5	4	38	21	5	5	.922

Baumgartner, Mary "Wimp"

Born: Sept. 13, 1930, Fort Wayne, Indiana. 5'5", 145, Catcher, BR, TR. Chicago Colleens, 1949; Peoria Redwings, 1949; Kalamazoo Lassies, 1950; South Bend Blue Sox, 1950–54.

Now president of the AAGPBL Players Association, Wimp Baumgartner was an All-Star catcher in the league for six seasons.

The Fort Wayne native was exposed to softball early in life as a batgirl for the Zollner Pistons, whose factory was across the street from where she lived. When she was a sophomore in high school, Fort Wayne manager Bill Wamscott asked her to try out for the team. The shy teenager decided she wasn't ready and waited until after she graduated from high school to give the league a try. After a tryout with the Blue Sox in the spring of 1949, Baumgartner was sent to Chicago for another look-see. The outfielder was moved to catcher. "They said I wasn't fast enough for the outfield," she explained. "I liked it back there."

The league assigned her to one of the league's two traveling teams for more work. The teams publicized the league and helped acquire new players. She was paid $25 a week and $3 a day for meals. "That was a lot for food back in those days," she said.

In late July the catcher for the Peoria Redwings was injured and "Wimp," who got the nickname from her oldest sister at age 3, got her call up. She played regularly the rest of the season.

During the winter she was traded to Muskegon. She attended spring training with the Lassies at Cape Girardeau, Missouri, but was dealt at the end of camp to South Bend. Wimp spent the first month of the season as a back-up receiver to Shirley Stovroff before being loaned to Kalamazoo for a little over a month.

South Bend became a powerhouse team in the 1951 season with Wimp still backing up Stovroff. Baumgartner hit .205 on the year in helping the Sox to the pennant and championship.

South Bend continued its winning ways the following season with Baumgartner still in reserve until late in the season. She was thrust into a starting role when Stovroff and five other players were suspended from the team. The remaining team members became known as the "Dutiful Dozen" as they had to go into the playoffs with just 12 players. In the playoffs against Fort Wayne, Wimp hit a game-winning home run with her parents in the crowd. It was one of her most exciting moments in the league. Despite its dwindled numbers, South Bend won the playoffs with Baumgarter as the regular receiver.

In 1953, Baumgarter led the league in put outs for a catcher. During the season, she broke a thumb but continued to play. "I was afraid someone would take my position." At the end of the season she saw the writing on the wall — the league was coming to an end. "They could hardly make the payroll," she said. She decided to go to college and get a degree in physical education, something she had wanted to do all her life.

Nineteen fifty-four was the last season for the league and just as Wimp was reaching her playing peak she was selected to the All-Star team. The game was played in Fort Wayne in front of her family. Wimp hurt her elbow near the end of the season and was out for the rest of the year.

The Hoosier finished up her degree and went on to become a physical education teacher for 28 years. She retired in 1985 and now lives in Fremont, Indiana. In October 1992, she took over as president of the Players Association. She was honored by the Fort Wayne Women's Bureau as a recipient of their annual Naney Rehm award for outstanding Indiana sportswomen in 1992.

BATTING												FIELDING				
G	BA	AB	R	H	2B	3B	HR	SB	SO	R	RBI	PO	A	E	DP	FA
280	.177	678	67	120	16	1	4	24	132	67	49	890	179	59	16	.948

Bayse (Schuller), Betty

Bisbee, Arizona. Died: 1992. Outfield. Chicago Colleens/Springfield Sallies, 1950.

Betty Bayse played on the barnstorming teams in 1950 and never advanced to the league.

BATTING									
G	BA	AB	H	2B	3B	HR	SB	R	RBI
49	.220	200	44	2	2	0	14	20	30

Beare, Kathryn "Katie"

Born: Nov. 7, 1917, Syracuse, New York. **Died:** January 27, 1997. 5'7", 170, Catcher, BR, TR. Fort Wayne Daisies, 1946.

Kathryn Beare was a backup catcher for Fort Wayne for a season. After baseball, she played softball for many years in Syracuse, New York, where she still lives today.

BATTING												FIELDING				
G	BA	AB	H	2B	3B	HR	SB	BB	SO	R	RBI	PO	A	E	DP	FA
24	.111	45	5	0	0	0	0	6	3	1	0	61	10	4	2	.947

Beck, Lottie

Jackson, Michigan. Fort Wayne Daisies, 1946.

Becker, Donna "Beck"

Born: Aug. 6, 1932, Kenosha, Wisconsin. 5'7", 145, Pitcher, TR, BR. Kalamazoo Lassies, 1951.

Donna Becker spent a season with Kalamazoo and relieved in three games. She began playing softball at age 14. After baseball, she remained single and became an elementary teacher. Her baseball philosophy is: "If you are good to baseball, it will be good to you." It was to her. She still lives in Kenosha.

PITCHING	
G	IP
3	3

Bell, Virginia "Ginger"

Born: July 30, 1927, Muskegon, Michigan. **Died:** April 19, 1994. 5'3", 128, Pitcher, Outfield, TR, BR. Springfield Sallies, 1948.

Virginia Bell pitched eight innings for Springfield in 1948. She was a WAC in the Army in Japan before joining the league. She lived in Many, Louisiana, before her death.

PITCHING										BATTING		
W–L	PCT	ERA	G	IP	H	R	ER	BB	SO	BA	AB	H
0–0	.000	7.88	1	8	6	10	7	88	58	.500	4	2

Bellman, Lois "Punky"

Berwyn, Illinois. 2nd Base. Chicago Colleens/Springfield Sallies 1949.

Bennett, Catherine

Born: Sept. 4, 1920, Craven, Saskatchewan, Canada. 5'5", 120, Pitcher, TR, BR. Kenosha Comets, 1943. South Bend Blue Sox, 1943–44.

Catherine Bennett was one of the original players in the league. In her first year, she recorded ten losses in a row, which became a league record. She bounced back the following season with a 14–9 record.

PITCHING										BATTING			FIELDING			
W–L	PCT	ERA	G	IP	H	R	ER	BB	SO	BA	AB	H	PO	A	E	FA
22–22	.500	2.84	65	418	364	221	132	113	122	.135	155	21	22	72	30	.758

Berger (Brown), Barbara Ann "Bergie"

Born: Dec. 6, 1930, Maywood, Illinois. 5'2", 115, Catcher, BR, TR. Chicago Colleens, 1949; Racine Belles, 1950.

Barbara Berger played very little in two seasons in the league before leaving for college and a career in teaching.

Berger played softball with her sister in grade school. After trying out in a gym in Chicago, the league assigned her to the traveling Chicago Colleens in 1949. "That was a treat to travel all over the United States," she recalled. The following season she was assigned to Racine, where she was used sparingly as a backup receiver. Meanwhile, her sister, Norma, was on one of the traveling teams.

"Bergie" gave up baseball to attend college. She obtained a bachelor's and master's degree

Barbara Ann "Bergie" Berger (Brown)

from the University of Illinois. Then she taught at her alma mater for 19 years. She married George Brown in 1969. Now retired and living in Murray, Kentucky, she golfs and cycles.

BATTING												FIELDING				
G	BA	AB	H	2B	3B	HR	SB	BB	SO	R	RBI	PO	A	E	DP	FA
11	.176	17	3	0	0	0	1	1	3	2	1	18	2	5	0	.800

Joan "Bergie" Berger

Berger (Knebl), Joan "Bergie"

Born: Oct. 9, 1933, Passaic, New Jersey. 5'4", 132, 3rd Base, 2nd Base, Shortstop, Outfield, TR, BR. Rockford Peaches, 1951–54.

An All-Star second baseman, Joan Berger played several positions well during her four years in the league.

When Berger was in eighth grade, her father formed a girl's softball team, the Garfield Flashettes. She tried out for the All-American League when she was a sophomore in high school, but she was too young to join the league. She went to a tryout the next year and her father said she had better wait another year. After she graduated from high school, she was ready and the league gladly assigned her to Rockford as an outfielder.

In her first season, "Bergie" was used sparingly by the Peaches in order to maintain her rookie status. In 1952, she was put at second base where she shined and was selected for the All-Star team. She finished the season with a .251 batting average.

During one game in 1952 she recalled blocking second base to put a tag on veteran player Alma Ziegler, who took offense to the maneuver. "Ziegler got mad at me. She said, 'Next time I will come in sliding with my spikes up!' I replied, 'I got the ball, the bag is mine,'" Berger explained.

The following season Berger filled in at shortstop for a departed player. In 1954, she was moved to third base. She hit a career high .280 in the last season of the league. Rockford made the playoffs for the third year in a row but failed to win the championship.

After the league folded, Bergie joined several other players on Bill Allington's All-American team, a barnstorming remnant of the league. She played for four seasons with the team, which traveled all over the United States. She remembered traveling as far as 500 miles overnight to get to the next game.

Berger married Andrew Knebl in 1959 and settled down to raise a family. She delivered three boys: Andrew Jr., Kevin and Robert. Now she has five granddaughters. She worked for Ferrero USA, a candy factory, for eight years and retired in 1994. She now lives in Lodi, New Jersey.

PITCHING		BATTING												FIELDING				
G	IP	G	BA	H	2B	3B	HR	SB	SO	BB	SO	R	RBI	PO	A	E	DP	FA
1	1	345	.250	298	27	12	4	78	75	119	75	173	98	374	542	96	60	.905

Berger, Margaret

Born: Dec. 24, 1921, Homestead, Florida. 5'3", 129, Pitcher, TR, BR. South Bend Blue Sox, 1943–44.

One of the original players in the league, Margaret Berger tossed four one-hitters during her two years in the league. She tied for the most appearances (47) on the mound in 1943. She now lives in Prescott, Arizona.

PITCHING										BATTING			FIELDING			
W–L	PCT	ERA	G	IP	H	R	ER	BB	SO	BA	AB	H	PO	A	E	FA
46–30	.605	1.75	88	621	395	187	120	134	203	.153	222	34	44	158	25	.890

Berger (Taylor), Norma "Bergie"

Born: Dec. 22, 1932, Maywood, Illinois. 5'3", 140, Pitcher, TR, BR. Springfield Sallies, 1950.

Norma Berger followed in the footsteps of her older sister in joining the league. She spent a season with one of the two traveling teams in 1950 before heading off to college to satisfy her father.

Berger and her sister, Barbara, played baseball and basketball together during their childhood. After her sister joined the league in 1949, she followed a year later with the touring team. Norma and her sister were much like the sisters in the movie *A League of Their Own,* but the battery never competed against each other in the league.

After the season was over, her father talked her into attending college, but that lasted less than a year. She now regrets having given up her baseball career. "I wish I could do it over again," she commented.

Berger married Bobby Taylor in 1955 and the couple fostered two children: Bonnie and Vickie. Her husband retired in 1994, but she continues to work as a bank supervisor. They now live in Villa Park, Illinois.

Norma "Bergie" Berger

PITCHING			BATTING		
W–L	PCT	G	BA	AB	H
8–8	.500	18	.118	51	6

Bergmann, Erma M. "Bergie"

Born: June 18, 1924, St. Louis, Missouri. 5'7", 155, Pitcher, Outfield, TR, BR. Muskegon Lassies, 1946–47; Springfield Sallies, 1948; Racine Belles, 1949–50; Battle Creek Belles, 1951.

Erma Bergmann was a mediocre hurler, but once in her six-season career she threw a no-hitter.

She began playing softball at age 14. After eight years of amateur softball, she joined the league and was assigned to the Muskegon Lassies. In her first season she was 15–16 on the mound and played the outfield. The biggest thrill of her rookie season came when she hit a home run in the top of ninth and then shut down the opposition in the bottom of the inning for a victory with her parents in attendance. It was the only home run of her career.

The following season she was used strictly as a pitcher. On May 22 she tossed a no-hitter against Grand Rapids. She ended up the season with an 11–10 record, her only winning season, and helped the Lassies to the pennant.

For the next couple of years she played with some losing teams and her record reflected it. Then in 1951 she went 7–18 and led league in losses (18), runs (119) and earned runs (87). It would be her last season.

After baseball, she served as a police officer in St. Louis for 25 years. She still resides there today in retirement.

Erma M. "Bergie" Bergmann

PITCHING									BATTING			FIELDING			
W–L	PCT	ERA	G	H	R	ER	BB	SO	BA	PO	E	PO	A	E	FA
64–91	.413	3.28	182	1046	627	381	462	338	.201	68	52	68	389	52	.898

Beschorner (Baskovich), Mary Lou "Bush"

Born: Sept. 18, 1929, Sandwich, Illinois. 5'9", 145, Outfield, BR. Grand Rapids Chicks, 1949; Peoria Redwings, 1950.

Mary Lou Beschorner played two seasons and left the league for a brighter future — marriage.

Beschorner's brother-in-law, who raised her from age 9, played catch with her when she was young. As a teenager, she played organized softball with the Dekalb Hybrids. She heard about league tryouts in Chicago and went with eight other girls. She and Norene Arnold were selected for the league.

Spring training in 1949 was in West Baden, Indiana, and "Bush" recalled walking to French Lick for entertainment. The Chicks used her mainly as a pinch hitter the first season. She was still considered a rookie when she was talked to Peoria. The manager of Peoria traded for her after she hit two triples in a game against his team.

After the 1950 season, she married Robert Michealson in January 1951 and decided not to go back to the league. "My husband said I could go back, but the league was beginning to fold, so I quit," she explained.

She had a son, Kirk, through her first marriage. Her husband died when her son was 3 years old. She remarried in 1972, to John Baskovich. She is very proud of her son, who graduated from the Naval Academy and went on to be a commander in the Navy. A bookkeeper for 32 years, she retired in 1992. She went from baseball to golf and once had a four handicap, but arthritis benched her. She now resides in Plano, Illinois.

Mary Lou "Bush" Beschorner

BATTING												FIELDING				
G	BA	AB	H	2B	3B	HR	SB	BB	SO	R	RBI	PO	A	E	DP	FA
85	.156	218	34	5	1	0	4	12	41	12	14	77	4	4	0	.953

Bevis, Muriel

Born: October 7, 1928, Corona, New York. Pitcher, Outfield, TL, BL. Kenosha Comets, 1950.

PITCHING

W–L	PCT	ERA	G	IP	H	R	ER	BB	SO
1–2	.333	6.83	7	29	30	27	22	25	5

BATTING												FIELDING					
G	BA	AB	H	2B	3B	HR	SB	BB	SO	R	RBI	G	PO	A	E	DP	FA
56	.212	165	35	4	2	1	4	5	38	13	13	46	43	3	6	2	.885

Bird (Phillips), Nelda

Born: Feb. 11, 1927, Hawthorne, California. 5'1", 115, Pitcher, Outfield, TL, BR. South Bend Blue Sox, 1945.

Nelda Bird had many problems on the mound in her only season in the league. She allowed the most earned runs (87) and tied the league record for the most balks in one season with six.

Bird grew up with three brothers, so she found herself playing ball with them. Then at age 10 she began playing organized softball. The following year she took up semipro softball. She was a top all-around athlete in high school.

In 1945 she received a telegram from the All-American League, inviting her to spring training at Wrigley Field. Before she came, a player from the Los Angeles Angels worked with her on playing baseball.

The southpaw was a steady performer during her only season in the league. Her most cherished performance was a doubleheader shutout in Kenosha. "I was ready on that day and threw nothing but strikes," she said.

However, during another game she couldn't hit home plate. "I walked seven batters in a row," she explained. The manager had left her out on the mound too long in that game.

After the season ended, she married Jesse Phillips. She became pregnant and delivered her only son, Michael. In 1947, she went to the National League in Chicago to pitch, because the All-American League no longer used underhand pitchers. She pitched the first no-hitter of the season. She played for a season in Chicago before hanging up her spikes for good. Now retired, she attends league reunions from her home in Yorba Linda, California.

PITCHING										BATTING			FIELDING			
W–L	PCT	ERA	G	IP	H	R	ER	BB	SO	BA	AB	H	PO	A	E	FA
13–17	.433	2.70	31	223	135	117	67	160	128	.162	117	19	13	55	13	.850

Bittner, Jaynne B.

Born: March 17, 1926, Lebanon, Pennsylvania. 5'9", 140, Pitcher, TL, BL. South Bend Blue Sox, 1947; Muskegon Lassies, 1948; Grand Rapids Chicks, 1949–52; Fort Wayne Daisies, 1952–53; Grand Rapids Chicks, 1954.

Like a fine wine, Jaynne Bittner got better with time and aged into an excellent pitcher during her nine seasons in the league.

Bittner was a top all-around athlete in high school. She won the tennis championship three years in a row, held the table tennis crown for two years and was the leading scorer on the basketball team. In fact, she was picked for the league because of her basketball prowess. She went to a league tryout in Allentown, Penn., and was shipped to Cuba for spring training.

She had no baseball position, but the league was desperate for overhand pitchers, so she seemed like a good candidate for the mound. It took a few years to take her raw talent and mold it into a winning formula. She led the league in wild pitches (13) in 1949 and the following year she issued the most balks (5).

In 1951 Bittner came of age on the mound and was 15–8 with a 2.95 ERA. When she was traded the following year in mid-season from Grand Rapids to Fort Wayne, one of her first starts (which she won) was against her old team. "That was a fine game. I even got some hits," she recalled. Two years later she also had a fine season with Fort Wayne — compiling a 16–7 record and a 2.45 ERA — to help the Daisies win the pennant.

She will never forget her last game in uniform in 1954. She was playing for Grand Rapids in the Shaughnessy playoffs against her old team, the Daisies. Fort Wayne lost a player due to injury and obtained Ruth Richards, the best catcher in the league, for the playoffs. Manager Woody English felt Fort Wayne had brought in a ringer and decided to pull his team off the field and go home. The Chicks forfeited the game and series. "The thing that makes me angry is that I didn't take my uniform," Bittner reflected.

After the league folded in 1954, she stuck around the Detroit area and drove a school bus. She also coached a softball team for 20 years, which she said was very "satisfying." In 1980 she was the first woman inducted into the Pennsylvania Sports Hall of Fame.

Bittner retired in 1991 and began reminiscing about the league with her old teammates. She was one of the women who appeared in the movie *A League of Their Own*. She now resides in Canton, Michigan.

PITCHING										BATTING			FIELDING			
W–L	PCT	ERA	G	IP	H	R	ER	BB	SO	BA	AB	H	PO	A	E	FA
66–69	.489	3.38	177	1126	973	599	423	647	392	.132	392	52	62	315	22	.945

Blair, Maybelle

Born: Jan. 16, 1927, Inglewood, California. 5'6", 150, Pitcher, BR, TR. Peoria Redwings, 1948.

Maybelle Blair appeared in only one game with Peoria in 1948. She played with the Chicago Cardinals before joining the league.

	BATTING		
G	BA	AB	H
1	.000	1	0

Blaski, Alice

Wallingford, Conn. Died: Date Unknown. Outfield, BR, TR. Fort Wayne Daisies, 1953–54.

Alice Blaski roamed the outfield part time for the pennant-winning Fort Wayne Daisies in 1953 and 1954. She had some pop in her bat as she hit five homers during limited action.

				BATTING										FIELDING			
G	BA	AB	H	2B	3B	HR	SB	BB	SO	R	RBI		PO	A	E	DP	FA
92	.225	306	69	5	4	5	23	58	34	68	31		115	10	6	0	.954

Bleiler (Thomas), Audrey

Born: Jan. 12, 1933, Philadelphia, Pennsylvania. Died: June 20, 1975. 5'7", 125, 3rd Base, Shortstop, BR, TR. South Bend Blue Sox, 1950–52.

A weak-hitting infielder, Audrey Bleiler was a member of the Blue Sox when they won the pennant and championship in 1951. She left the Sox and was married on July 4, 1951. She went on to have four children — Thomas, Charles, Audrey and Marie — and three grandchildren.

BATTING

G	BA	AB	H	2B	3B	HR	SB	BB	SO	R	RBI
103	.180	261	47	4	3	0	9	33	42	31	30

FIELDING

PO	A	E	DP	FA
94	213	32	7	.906

Audrey Bleiler

Blumetta, Catherine "Kay" "Swish"

Born: May 1, 1923, North Plainfield, New Jersey. 5'8", 150, Pitcher, Outfield, 1st Base, TR, BR. Minneapolis Millerettes, 1944; Milwaukee Chicks, 1944; Grand Rapids Chicks, 1944; Peoria Redwings, 1946–47; Fort Wayne Daisies, 1947–50; Kalamazoo Lassies, 1951–54.

Catherine Blumetta had one of the longest careers in league history. "Kay" began her career as a first baseman and outfielder with Milwaukee, the team that won the pennant and championship in 1944. She began pitching sidearm in 1946 when the league turned more toward baseball. Her best season as a pitcher came in 1948 when she was 14–13 with Fort Wayne. "The 11 years of playing in the All-American League were the best years of my life," she said about her playing days. She now lives where she was raised in North Plainfield, N.J.

PITCHING										BATTING			FIELDING			
W–L	PCT	ERA	G	IP	H	R	ER	BB	SO	BA	AB	H	PO	A	E	FA
84–105	.444	2.51	224	1613	1183	659	445	679	673	.138	740	102	239	418	42	.940

Borg (Alpin), Lorraine "Borge"

Born: July 18, 1923, Minneapolis, Minnesota. 5'9", 145, Catcher, BR, TR. Minneapolis Millerettes, 1944.

Lorraine Borg played less than a season and quit the league because she was homesick.

Borg remembered being a batgirl at age 9 before she began playing softball in a park league. At 13 she started playing organized softball and by 15 she was in the top league. She switched from playing outfield to going behind the plate.

One Sunday in the spring of 1944, she attended a league try-out in Minneapolis with about 200 other girls. A few girls made the cut, including her. "They would have taken others, but they had short hair. Some didn't have a good reputation," she explained.

Lorraine "Borge" Borg

Borg enjoyed spring training in Peru, Illinois, and meeting women from all over the country. She enjoyed the league at first, but didn't like the road trips. "I didn't like being away from home," she admitted. After the second road trip, she left the team along with Loraine Torrison and never returned. Fortunately, her softball league didn't exclude her because she had turned professional, so she immediately went back to playing locally. She played and managed a few more years.

In 1946 she married Eric Erickson and they fostered two children, Gregory and Robin, before Eric perished in a truck accident. She remarried, to Lou Aplin, in 1954 and the couple had three children: Thomas, Richard and Walter. Lou passed away in 1989. She is now retired in Baxter, Minnesota, and travels a lot. She has nine grandchildren.

BATTING												FIELDING				
G	BA	AB	H	2B	3B	HR	SB	BB	SO	R	RBI	PO	A	E	DP	FA
23	.133	83	11	0	0	0	2	7	5	7	2	157	12	10	1	.944

Born, Ruth

Born: Aug. 8, 1925, Bay City, Michigan. 5'3", 125, Pitcher, TR, BR. South Bend Blue Sox, 1943.

Ruth Born was a member of the original South Bend Blue Sox and played the inaugural season.

As soon as she was big enough to swing a bat, Born began playing sandlot softball. At age 12 she started playing at school and in park leagues. Then at 13 she joined a Moose Lodge team.

She spotted an advertisement about the new league and wrote the league office. She was given a try-out in South Bend after the season had begun and was accepted on the team.

Born pitched in 11 games during the season, but wasn't comfortable in the new league. "I was in over my head," she explained.

Ruth Born

She quit after her first year and went to college. She received a bachelor's degree from Valparaiso University and a master's degree from Loyola University. Then she went to work for the federal government in child welfare for 23 years. She retired in 1990 and now lives in a condo in Valparaiso where she enjoys golfing.

PITCHING										BATTING			FIELDING			
W–L	PCT	ERA	G	IP	H	R	ER	BB	SO	BA	AB	H	PO	A	E	FA
4–5	.444	3.59	11	67	61	47	27	47	6	.111	18	2	5	15	2	.909

Boyce (Phoebe), Ethel

Born: June 27, 1917, Vancouver, British Columbia, Canada. Died: August 24, 1996. 5'8", 130, Outfield, 1st Base, Catcher, BR, TR. Kenosha Comets, 1946.

Ethel Boyce spent a season with Kenosha in 1946.

BATTING			
G	BA	AB	H
5	.000	3	0

Briggs, Rita "Maude"

Ayers, Massachusetts. Died: Sept. 6, 1994. 5'3", 120, Catcher, Outfield, BL, TR. Rockford Peaches, 1947–48; Chicago Colleens, 1948; South Bend Blue Sox, 1949; Racine Belles, 1949; Peoria Redwings, 1949–51; Battle Creek Belles, 1952; Fort Wayne Daisies, 1953–54.

Once an All-Star, Rita Briggs was a catcher-outfielder for seven teams during her eight-year career. Her best year came in 1951 when she had career highs in batting average (.275), runs scored (57) and RBI (44). She helped the Daisies to pennants in 1953 and 1954. She was named to the All-Star team in 1953.

BATTING												FIELDING				
G	BA	AB	H	2B	3B	HR	SB	BB	SO	R	RBI	PO	A	E	DP	FA
757	.206	2465	507	42	10	6	186	318	145	274	227	2112	496	108	57	.960

Rita "Maude" Briggs (on right)

Briggs, Wilma "Willie" "Briggsie"

Born: Nov. 6, 1930, East Greenwich, Rhode Island. 5'4", 138, Outfield, 1st Base, BL, TR. Fort Wayne Daisies, 1948–53; South Bend Blue Sox, 1954.

Outfielder Wilma Briggs was one of the league's career leaders in home runs, yet was never selected to an All-Star team.

After milking the cows, Briggs played baseball in her backyard when she was 8 years old. She advanced to a church league and then joined her father in a baseball league when she became a teenager. She also played on the boy's baseball team in high school.

Wilma "Willie" Briggs

Briggs became interested in the league after reading about it. She missed a tryout in nearby New Jersey because she was graduating from high school on the same day, so her parents drove her from Rhode Island to Fort Wayne to try out for the league. She won a regular spot in the outfield in her first year and hit .228.

A good eye at the plate, Briggs drew the most walks (79) in the league in 1950. The following season she committed only two errors to become the best outfielder in the league with a .987 fielding average. Her .275 average placed her 13th among league hitters on the season. She now credits Max Carey in teaching her how to hit.

In 1952, she helped Fort Wayne to its first-ever pennant with her fielding and hitting. The next year she had a power surge and hit nine homers to lead the league and again help her team win the pennant.

In its last year, the league switched to a major league–sized ball; as a result, hitters knocked the cover off some of them. "I had only three or four home runs when the ball came out," she recalled. She finished the season with 25 dingers, second best in the league. One of her homers was a grand slam and it came with her parents in the stands. Her 43 career home runs was third best lifetime in the league. Because she was on a team with a number of star players, she probably got overlooked for the All-Star team.

After the league, she took up softball for the first time and played for awhile. She obtained a bachelor's degree and went on to teach at a public school for 23 years before retiring in 1992. Now she lives in East Greenwich, Rhode Island, and enjoys golf. "I've done a number of speaking engagements," she added. "Being part of the AAGPBL was the greatest experience of my life."

BATTING

G	BA	AB	H	2B	3B	HR	SB	BB	SO	R	RBI
691	.258	2456	633	64	24	43	128	380	214	375	301

FIELDING

PO	A	E	DP	FA
1092	65	44	17	.963

Brody, Leola Mae

Infielder. Racine Belles, 1943.

Brown, Patricia "Pat"

Born: April 23, 1931, Boston, Massachusetts. 5'5", 135, Pitcher, BR, TR. Chicago Colleens, 1950; Battle Creek Belles, 1951.

Like many, Pat Brown struggled to get a chance to play in the league. Then she only got to pitch one game in the regular league during her two seasons with the All-Americans.

A sandlot baseball player who didn't play softball until high school, she was reading the Boston newspaper one day and decided to write P.K. Wrigley about the league. She was invited to a tryout involving hundreds of women. After not being considered, she wrote the league again and received another look the following season. This time she impressed the scouts with her arm. "Finding women who could pitch was a problem for the league," she explained. She was signed as a pitcher.

She was assigned to the Kenosha Comets. The manager felt she was too wild and needed more seasoning, so she was assigned to the traveling Chicago Colleens in 1950. Brown's record with the Colleens was 9–9. In 1951, the Battle Creek Belles took the promising pitcher, but she didn't get much of a chance to show her abilities.

Patricia "Pat" Brown

She attended Suffolk University in Boston in the off-season. When the college wouldn't release her early to play and the league wouldn't allow her to report late, she decided to quit and continue her studies. She went on to obtain four degrees and be listed in *Who's Who*. After 40 years at Suffolk, she retired in 1992 and lives in her hometown of Boston. When the movie *A League of Their Own* came out in 1992, some players swore actress Rosie O'Donnell looked just like Brown.

PITCHING

G	IP
1	2

Delores "Dolly" Brumfield

Brumfield (White), Delores "Dolly"

Born: May 26, 1932, Prichard, Alabama. 5'6", 125, 1st Base, 2nd Base, 3rd Base, Outfield, BR, TR. South Bend Blue Sox, 1947; Kenosha Comets, 1948–51; Fort Wayne Daisies, 1952–53.

One of the youngest players to join the league at age 14, Delores Brumfield was a dependable, versatile fielder who helped Fort Wayne win two pennants during her seven-year career in the league.

Brumfield played sandlot ball before trying out for the league in 1946 at age 13. After failing to make the league, she joined a women's softball team at Brookley Field, Alabama. She received an invitation the following year to attend spring training in Cuba. Her parents didn't want her to go, but agreed after a player, Marge Holgerson, agreed to chaperone their daughter to Cuba. She obtained her nickname "Dolly" in Havana and it stuck with her the rest of her career.

When her first season began, she turned 15 and the players on the Blue Sox made her stand in front of the crowd while they sang, "I'm a Big Girl Now." Manager Chet Grant worked with the young player and when he went to Kenosha the following season, he selected her from the player pool. "I attribute a lot of my success in the league to Chet," she claimed.

By 1949, Dolly was coming into her own as a player, hitting above .200. She shined at first base and was the position's best fielder in 1950 (.988 average).

In 1952 she struggled at Fort Wayne until the manager put her at first base for a doubleheader. She went six-for-eight with a homer, which convinced Jimmie Foxx to put her at first for good. Near the end of the season, she slid into home and broke her left ankle. That made her miss the rest of the season and the playoffs.

Brumfield had her career year behind the plate in 1953, hitting .332 with two homers in leading the Daisies again to the pennant. A bad case of anemia during the season drained her and convinced her she should go on with her life, specially since she would graduate from college the following spring. "Playing in the league allowed me to pay for my college education," she explained.

Dolly obtained a master's degree and doctorate from the University of Southern Alabama. She took up teaching at Henderson State University and retired in 1994 after 40 years. Now married, she lives in Arkadelphia, Arkansas.

BATTING												FIELDING					
G	BA	AB	H	2B	3B	HR	SB	BB	SO	R	RBI	G	PO	A	E	DP	FA
533	.231	1767	408	61	17	4	107	247	176	215	160	498	3841	453	95	193	.978

Bryson, Marion

California. Pitcher. Peoria Redwings, 1946.

PITCHING										BATTING			FIELDING			
W–L	PCT	ERA	G	IP	H	R	ER	BB	SO	BA	AB	H	PO	A	E	FA
0–8	.000	5.32	14	71	74	60	42	36	11	.111	18	2	3	38	7	.854

Buckley, Jean "Buckets"

Born: Dec. 4, 1931, Boston, Massachusetts. 5'9", 145, Outfield, BR, TR. Kenosha Comets, 1950–51; Rockford Peaches, 1952.

Jean Buckley added some power to the line-up during her three seasons in the league.

She began playing softball at age 12 in a Catholic youth organization in Boston. Then she joined the Quinsey Raiderettes. Mary Pratt, a former player in the league, took her and several others to a tryout in a gym in Everett, Massachusetts. "I had never thrown a baseball in my life," she admitted. She and two others from the team were picked for further tryouts in South Bend. She never expected to make it, but she did and went to spring training in West Baden, Indiana.

"Buckets" learned to hit on her own as the manager didn't provide any help. She hit .207 with two homers in her first season. After two seasons with Kenosha, she was sent to Rockford. She recalled one game in which manager Bill Allington fined her $50. "I ran down to first base, got thrown out and said 'Oh, shit!'," she explained.

She quit after the 1952 season and moved to California. She attended San Francisco State and graduated with a degree in 1954. She taught school for the next 29 years and retired in 1995. Now she lives in Antioch, California, and goes to league reunions.

BATTING												FIELDING				
G	BA	AB	H	2B	3B	HR	SB	BB	SO	R	RBI	PO	A	E	DP	FA
255	.200	827	165	20	6	7	33	66	149	77	88	338	35	41	9	.901

Bureker, Geraldine

Born: Dec. 18, 1924, Portland, Oregon. 5'2", 125, Outfield, BR, TR. Racine Belles, 1948.

Geraldine Bureker was a member of the Tonseth Flowers, a team that won the Oregon State Championship in 1945. She played in the Chicago softball leagues before signing with the All-American League, where she spent a season as an outfielder.

			BATTING										FIELDING				
G	BA	AB	H	2B	3B	HR	SB	BB	SO	R	RBI		PO	A	E	DP	FA
28	.140	53	8	0	0	0	2	9	9	5	2		8	1	0	1	1.000

Shirley "Hustle" Burkovich

Burkovich, Shirley "Hustle"

Born: Feb. 4, 1933, Swissvale, Pennsylvania. 5'8", 150 Utility fielder, Pitcher, BR, TR. Muskegon Lassies, 1949; Chicago Colleens/Springfield Sallies, 1949–50; Fort Wayne Daisies, 1950; Rockford Peaches, 1951.

Shirley Burovich was "super sub" and filled in wherever she was needed during her three seasons in the league.

The suburbanite of Pittsburgh started playing sandlot ball at a tender age, but she never played softball. When she grew up she saw an advertisement in the paper for All-American League tryouts. "I wasn't going to go, but my brother talked me into it," she recalled. Months later she received an invitation to spring training. She was only 15, so she needed permission from her parents and her school to go to West Baden Springs, Indiana.

In her first at-bat in the league she recalled flying out to deep center. The young player filled in at every position, except catcher. During the 1949 and 1950 season, she played a utility role on both of the barnstorming teams and hit .286.

After the 1951 season, she saw the end coming for the league, so she bailed out and went to work for Pacific Bell. "It was the three most wonderful years of my life. We were so happy just to play," she explained. She worked for the phone company for 30 years and retired in 1983.

When *A League of Their Own* was filmed in Cooperstown, Burkovich was there. "I have a different view of movies now. It took ten days to do ten minutes. They earn their money," she commented. She now lives in Cathedral City, California.

BATTING									PITCHING	
G	BA	AB	H	2B	3B	BB	SO	RBI	G	IP
17	.071	28	2	0	0	2	7	0	3	2

Burmeister (Dean), Eileen "Burmy"

Born: Nov. 30, 1924, Thiensville, Wisconsin. Died: March 23, 1990. 5'5", 140, Utility fielder, BL, TL. Rockford Peaches, 1943–44.

Eileen Burmeister was one of the original players in the league and played two seasons.

BATTING												FIELDING				
G	BA	AB	H	2B	3B	HR	SB	BB	SO	R	RBI	PO	A	E	DP	FA
167	.198	571	113	10	11	0	27	62	46	57	60	212	229	52	8	.895

Butcher (Marsh), Mary "Butch"

Born: Oct. 12, 1927, Berne, Indiana. 5'7", 170, Pitcher, BR, TR. Kenosha Comets, 1945; Grand Rapids Chicks, 1946.

Mary Butcher was an up-and-coming pitcher in the league when she joined up at age 17, but she married and went on to other things.

The Hoosier grew up near Berne, Indiana, and began pitching softball at 13. After graduating from Jefferson High School, she was recruited by the AAGPBL. She remembered being approached by a league scout after a softball game in Fort Wayne. "He asked me if I wanted to play pro ball. I just laughed," she said.

The scout was serious and gave her money to go to Chicago and try out in front of league president Max Carey. She was good enough for the league and was assigned to Kenosha, getting paid $90 a week, which she said was "big bucks" in those days.

"Butch" only pitched batting practice her first year in the league. In 1945, the pitchers still threw underhand. "The ball was smaller than a softball and larger than a baseball," she explained.

The following season she continued pitching batting practice, but played in one game. Then she married Bill Marsh and quit the league. She ended up playing softball in Geneva, Indiana, some years later. Then she moved to Nevada in the 1960s. At age 40 she played softball for the Sprout Ritz in Carson City much to the surprise of her three children.

She retired from Carson Tahoe Hospital in 1994, where she had been a medical records clerk. Now the retiree, who has three grandchildren, takes up bowling three times a week.

PITCHING	
W–L	G
0–0	1

Calacurcio (Thomas), Aldine

Shortstop. Rockford Peaches, 1947.

Aldine Calacurcio, who wore number 9, saw limited action with Rockford in 1947.

Callaghan (Candaele), Helen "Cally"

Born: March 13, 1923, Vancouver, British Columbia, Canada. Died: Dec. 8, 1992. 5'1", 115, Outfield, BL, TL. Minneapolis Millerettes, 1944; Fort Wayne Daisies, 1945–46, 48; Kenosha Comets, 1949.

The younger Callaghan sister, Helen was the better hitter and once led the league in batting average. Helen also has the distinction of being the only woman in the league to foster a major league player — Casey Candaele.

Callaghan played sandlot ball in her youth because girls weren't allowed to play softball at her Catholic school. As a teenager, she joined the Vancouver Western Mutuals with her sister. The team ended up at the World Series Softball Tournament in Detroit in 1943, which is where they were recruited by the league. She reported to spring training in 1944, but her sister stayed behind because she was working for the government. Midway through the season, Margaret joined her on the same team. The Minneapolis franchise folded and both girls were sent to Fort Wayne the following season.

With the Daisies, both girls realized their full potential in 1945. "Cally," as teammates called her, tied for the batting crown (.299) with Mary Crews, while leading the league in hits (122), total bases (336) and doubles (17). She shared the home run (3) title with Faye Dancer.

In 1946, when the league went to sidearm pitching, Callaghan's batting average dipped, but she made up for some of the deficit by stealing a career high 114 bases. After the season, she married Robert Candaele and sat out the 1947 season to deliver her first son, Ricky. She saw limited action on her return in 1948 and played in just 54 games.

The league decided to break up the pair for the 1949 season, so Cally went to Kenosha. Whenever the two met, Margaret was playing at third base and would come in on her sister. "I wouldn't let her get on base. She was a good drag bunter, but I knew how to play her," Margaret explained.

Callaghan quit after the 1949 season to concentrate on raising a family of five boys. She also divorced and remarried, to Ron St. Aubin. Her son Casey went on to become a professional ball player with the Montreal Expos and Houston Astros. Her son Kelly wrote the documentary *A League of Their Own*, which was later turned into a full-length motion picture of the same name.

While Callaghan passed on in 1992, her memory remains in the British Columbia Softball Hall of Fame and the National Baseball Hall of Fame.

BATTING												FIELDING				
G	BA	AB	H	2B	3B	HR	SB	BB	SO	R	RBI	PO	A	E	DP	FA
495	.256	1756	449	44	20	7	419	271	220	299	117	823	43	55	9	.940

Helen Callaghan Candaele (left), Audrey Haines (middle), Marge Callaghan (right).

Callaghan (Maxwell), Margaret

Born: Dec. 23, 1921, Vancouver, British Columbia, Canada. 5'3", 112, 3rd Base, 2nd Base, BR, TR. Minneapolis Millerettes, 1944; Fort Wayne Daisies, 1945–48; South Bend Blue Sox, 1949; Peoria Redwings, 1950–51; Battle Creek Belles, 1951.

The older Callaghan sister, Margaret was a good defensive outfielder over her eight seasons and led the league in fielding a couple of seasons.

Callaghan played sandlot ball until she joined the Vancouver Western Mutuals. The team ended up at the World Series Softball Tournament in Detroit in 1943, which is where she and her sister were recruited by the league. During the series, she hit an 11th inning four-bagger to win the game, which she rates as one of her biggest thrills.

While Helen reported to spring training the following year, Margaret couldn't go because of her military work commitments. She finally obtained special permission in midseason and joined her sister on the Millerettes. "I played the first night I got there. That was a shock," she recalled.

Margaret had the best fielding average among third basemen in 1944 and 1945. Then she had the most putouts (236) in 1946. Margaret hit behind her sister in the order. "Helen would steal second, and I would bunt her to third," she explained. Margaret also had some speed and stole a career high 80 bases in 1946. She hit one of the longest homers over the fence in South Bend in 1947.

In 1949, the league broke up the duo and sent Margaret to South Bend, while Helen went to Kenosha. The two played against each other for the first time in their lives.

After the 1951 season, Margaret wed Merv Maxwell instead of continuing her playing career. She had two children: Guy and Dale. She continued to play softball until she was 42. Then she coached the Mount Pleasant Legion to the Canadian championship in 1965.

She has been inducted in the British Columbia and Southhill Softball halls of fame. She retired in 1987 and lives in her hometown of Vancouver.

BATTING												FIELDING				
G	BA	AB	H	2B	3B	HR	SB	BB	SO	R	RBI	PO	A	E	DP	FA
672	.196	2058	403	18	9	3	283	371	219	280	143	1218	1473	224	130	.923

Callow, Eleanor "Squirt"

Winnipeg, Manitoba, Canada. Died: Date Unknown. Pitcher, Outfield, TR, BB.
Peoria Redwings, 1947; Chicago Colleens, 1948; Rockford Peaches, 1948–54.

A three time All-Star, Eleanor Callow was the Babe Ruth of the AAGPBL with more home runs and triples than any other player in league history. She was one of the best lifetime hitters in the league and set several season and career marks.

Beginning in 1948, Callow led the league in triples for four straight years and ended up with 60 in her career. She started off slow in the home run category with none her rookie year, but by the end of her eight year career, she had hit more dingers (55) than any player in the history of the league. Callow led the league just once in RBI (1951), yet she ended up second on the all time chart with 407. Her clutch hitting helped the Peaches win a pennant in 1950 and two championships.

Nineteen fifty-one was her best year in the league. She hit a career high .326 and led the league in triples (10), homers (4) and RBI (84).

Callow also was a solid fielder and led the league in fielding with a .969 average in 1952.

PITCHING										
W–L	PCT	ERA	G	IP	H	R	ER	BB	SO	
0–2	.000	5.42	4	15	16	12	9	18	3	

BATTING												FIELDING				
G	BA	AB	H	2B	3B	HR	SB	BB	SO	R	RBI	PO	A	E	DP	FA
778	.273	2765	756	88	60	55	214	147	192	391	407	1316	87	60	19	.960

Campbell, Georgia

Syracuse, New York. Fort Wayne Daisies, 1947.

Campbell, Jean

Syracuse, New York. Fort Wayne Daisies, 1946.

Carey, Mary "Pepper"

Born: Sept. 8, 1925, Detroit, Michigan. Died: 1977. 5'3", Utility Player, BR.
Kenosha Comets, 1946; Peoria Redwings, 1947–51; Kalamazoo Lassies, 1952–53;
Muskegon Belles, 1953; Rockford Peaches, 1953; South Bend Blue Sox, 1954.

Mary Carey was a dependable fielder during her nine seasons and filled in where she was needed. She also was the co-manager of Peoria in 1950. She grew up with one brother and five sisters in Detroit and also played basketball in her youth.

BATTING													FIELDING				
G	BA	AB	H	2B	3B	HR	SB	BB	SO	R	RBI		PO	A	E	DP	FA
596	.186	2807	523	41	9	2	198	263	255	281	169		1065	1761	307	169	.902

Carlson, Phyllis

Muskegon Lassies, 1949.

Carver, Virginia

Born: 1933, New Brighton, Pennsylvania. Pitcher, Outfield. South Bend Blue Sox, 1953; Fort Wayne Daisies, 1954.

Virginia Carver was a pitcher-outfielder for two seasons, including one with the pennant-winning Daisies in 1954.

PITCHING										
W–L	PCT	ERA	G	IP	H	R	ER	BB	SO	
5–7	.417	8.78	17	80	102	91	78	70	12	

BATTING													FIELDING				
G	BA	AB	H	2B	3B	HR	SB	BB	SO	R	RBI		PO	A	E	DP	FA
32	.173	75	13	0	0	0	1	5	3	7	7		15	0	1	0	.938

Carveth (Dunn), Betty

Edmonton, Alberta, Canada. Pitcher. Rockford Peaches, 1945; Fort Wayne Daisies, 1945.

Betty Carveth pitched one season in the league and ended it with a 4–11 ledger.

PITCHING										BATTING			FIELDING			
W–L	PCT	ERA	G	IP	H	R	ER	BB	SO	BA	AB	H	PO	A	E	FA
4–11	.267	2.28	21	138	116	57	35	47	24	.149	47	7	6	63	9	.885

Castillo (Kinney), Ysora "Chico"

Born: May 16, 1932, Havana, Cuba. 5'1", 117, 2nd Base, 3rd Base, BR, TR. Chicago Colleens, 1949–50; Kalamazoo Lassies, 1950–51; Kenosha Comets, 1951.

Ysora Castillo was one of the Cuban players who came to the United States after the league visited there for spring training in 1947 and exhibition in 1948. She played on the player development teams for two seasons before advancing to the league. After baseball, she worked in electronics for 40 years and became a hospital volunteer. She now lives in Hialeah, Florida.

BATTING												FIELDING				
G	BA	AB	H	2B	3B	HR	SB	BB	SO	R	RBI	PO	A	E	DP	FA
250	.128	399	51	7	2	0	8	102	70	38	23	243	402	50	35	.928

Chester, Bea

Brooklyn, New York. 3rd Base, BR, TR. South Bend Blue Sox, 1943; Rockford Peaches, 1944.

One of the original players of the league, Bea Chester played sparingly for two teams in two seasons.

BATTING												FIELDING				
G	BA	AB	H	2B	3B	HR	SB	BB	SO	R	RBI	PO	A	E	DP	FA
29	.200	100	20	2	2	0	7	13	16	10	9	25	31	17	1	.767

Chiano, Clara "Gabby"

Born: Sept. 19, 1921, Pennsylvania. 5', 108, Utility Infielder. Racine Belles, 1944.

The diminutive Clara Chiano lived in Dorchester, Massachusetts, before joining the league in 1944 for one season.

Childress, Thelma

Richmond, Virginia. Grand Rapids Chicks, 1946.

Christ, Dorothy

Sept. 19, 1925, LaPorte, Indiana. South Bend Blue Sox, 1948.

Dorothy Christ played in one game for South Bend in 1948. She now lives in Mishawaka, Indiana.

BATTING

G	BA	AB	H
1	.000	0	0

Cindric, Ann "Cindy"

Born: Sept. 5, 1922, Muse, Pennsylvania. 5'6", 135, Pitcher. Muskegon Lassies, 1948; Springfield Sallies, 1949–50.

Ann Cindric played very little with Muskegon before being assigned to the traveling teams for further development in her three seasons in the league.

PITCHING			BATTING		
W–L	PCT	G	BA	AB	H
3–2	.600	5	.231	13	3

(1950 Statistics)

Cione, Jean "Cy"

Born: June 23, 1928, Rockford, Illinois. 5'8", 143, Pitcher, Outfield, 1st Base, TL, BL. Rockford Peaches, 1945; Peoria Redwings, 1946; Rockford Peaches, 1947; Kenosha Comets, 1947–51; Battle Creek Belles, 1952; Muskegon Belles, 1953; Rockford Peaches, 1954.

An All-Star in 1952, Jean Cione was one of the best overhand southpaw pitchers in the league and threw two no-hitters (in the same month) during her ten-year career.

Cione recalled playing catch with the girl next door when she was 5. Then she began playing sandlot ball. At age 12, she began playing her first organized softball with the park district. "My mother said my glove was part of my anatomy," Cione said.

At 15, the teenager started playing for J.L. Clark Manufacturing, an industrial softball league. She had to work four hours on Saturdays to qualify to play on the team. She played first base and pitched. When the league held tryouts in the city in 1945, she attended and was sent to spring training in Chicago. The league assigned her to her hometown team where she was a utility player. She learned to play the game from manager Bill Allington, who worked with his rookies on a daily basis. "He taught us everything. If it hadn't been for him, I would have never made it in the league," she explained. The Peaches won the pennant and the championship in 1945. It would be the only time she was on a championship team.

After a season in Peoria, "Cy" came back to Rockford. The Peaches tried her out as a pitcher and found out she was a strong hurler as well. She was 19–14 her first season on the mound. When she wasn't pitching, she was used at first base because she was a valuable fielder and hitter.

The league made her pack her bags again in 1947 and she was sent to Kenosha, where she played for the next four seasons.

Nineteen fifty turned out to be her best on the mound. She recorded two no-hitters in August and ended up 18–10. Her first no-no was a 12-inning affair against Grand Rapids. On August 29, she blanked Rockford in a seven-inning game.

After the 1950 season, her pitching performance tailed off and she was used more in the field. She had her best year behind the plate in 1952 when she hit career highs in average (.275) and doubles (17). Cione hurt her arm in 1953 and thereafter couldn't go more than five innings. She developed a knucklecurve, which became her best pitch. "I threw it with the same motion as the curveball. When it got up to the plate, it fell off," she remembered.

After the league folded in 1954, Cione continued her education. She finished a bachelor's degree at Eastern Michigan University, a master's at the University of Illinois and some post graduate work at the University of Michigan. She taught elementary school for 10 years before going back to Eastern Michigan to teach for 30 more years. She retired in 1992. Now she frequently golfs, travels and goes to league reunions. She has been inducted into the Eastern Michigan Athletic Hall of Fame and the Italian Hall of Fame in Rockford. She now lives in Birchwood, Wisconsin.

PITCHING

W–L	PCT	ERA	G	IP	H	R	ER	BB	SO
75–65	.536	2.31	169	1195	852	461	307	460	411

BATTING													FIELDING				
G	BA	AB	H	2B	3B	HR	SB	BB	SO	R	RBI		PO	A	E	DP	FA
758	.224	2447	548	67	27	8	86	232	299	240	247		4163	593	148	153	.970

Clapp, Louise

Harrod, Ohio. Pitcher. Grand Rapids Chicks, 1954; South Bend Blue Sox, 1954.

PITCHING

G	IP
3	5

Clark, Corrine

Born: Sept. 28, 1923, Yorkville, Illinois. Utility Player, TR, BR. Peoria Redwings, 1947.

Clark now lives in Alburquerque, New Mexico.

Coben, Muriel

Saskatoon, Saskatchewan, Canada. Died: Date Unknown. Pitcher, TR, BR. South Bend Blue Sox, 1943; Rockford Peaches, 1943.

One of the original members of the league, Muriel Coben turned in one of the worst pitching performances in 1943, allowing the most earned runs (102).

		PITCHING									BATTING			FIELDING			
W–L	PCT	ERA	G	IP	H	R	ER	BB	SO		BA	AB	H	PO	A	E	FA
4–16	.200	4.71	37	193	218	150	102	55	43		.143	70	10	21	46	10	.932

Colacito (Appugliese), Lucille "Lou"

Born: Dec. 27, 1921, Florence, Colorado. 5'3", 120, Catcher, BR, TR. Kenosha Comets, 1944–45.

Lucille Colacito played two seasons in the league with Kenosha. She and her husband had a son after baseball and they now have two grandchildren. She played softball after baseball and was named to the Denver Softball Hall of Fame.

				BATTING									FIELDING				
G	BA	AB	H	2B	3B	HR	SB	BB	SO	R	RBI		PO	A	E	DP	FA
153	.164	445	73	9	0	2	42	38	50	37	28		560	65	22	9	.966

Cook, Clara "Babe" R.

Born: June 19, 1921, Pine City, New York. Died: July 23, 1996. 5'2", 130, Pitcher, TL, BL. Rockford Peaches, 1943; Kenosha Comets, 1943–44; Milwaukee Chicks, 1944.

Clara Cook didn't have much success on the mound. In 1943, she gave up more runs (177) than any other pitcher. She spent two seasons in the league with three different teams.

		PITCHING									BATTING			FIELDING			
W–L	PCT	ERA	G	IP	H	R	ER	BB	SO		BA	AB	H	PO	A	E	FA
8–19	.196	4.25	39	248	255	201	117	68	33		.157	102	16	15	45	5	.923

Cook, Donna "Cookie"

Born: May 24, 1928, Muskegon, Michigan. 5'2", 121, Pitcher, Outfield, TL, BR. Muskegon Lassies, 1946–48; Chicago Colleens, 1948; Fort Wayne Daisies, 1948–49; Grand Rapids Chicks, 1950; Battle Creek Belles, 1951–52; Kalamazoo Lassies, 1952; South Bend Blue Sox, 1952–53; Muskegon Belles, 1953; Rockford Peaches, 1954.

Donna Cook was a journeywoman in the league, playing for nine teams in nine years. Her younger sister, Doris, later joined the league.

Donna played five years of competitive softball in Muskegon before she joined the league and was assigned to her hometown team. "I was kinda glad when I first started that I was assigned here," she said. She played outfield in her rookie year and hit .156. The following season, after being switched to pitcher, she turned in a sparkling 14–8 record to help the Lassies win the pennant. During one stretch, she won four games in one week and hit two home runs in one game (the only ones of her career).

"Cookie" played on three different teams in 1948, which took a toll on her performance as she went 4–9 on the mound and hit .123. She made an excellent comeback the next season for Fort Wayne with a 9–9 record, but she hurt her knee toward the end of the season, which affected the rest of her playing career. Her pitching performance dropped off considerably after 1949. Her best season behind the plate came in 1952 when she hit a career-high .246 for Battle Creek.

After baseball she had three operations on the knee she hurt in 1949. She now lives in Muskegon, Michigan.

PITCHING

W–L	PCT	ERA	G	IP	H	R	ER	BB	SO
28–39	.418	3.38	108	596	451	315	224	419	246

BATTING												FIELDING			
G	BA	AB	H	2B	3B	HR	SB	BB	SO	R	RBI	PO	A	E	FA
439	.190	1294	246	20	7	2	46	95	85	99	76	599	160	45	.944

Cook, Doris "Little Cookie"

Born: June 23, 1931, Muskegon, Michigan. 5'1", 130, Pitcher, Outfield, BR, TR. Springfield Sallies, 1949–50; Kalamazoo Lassies, 1951–53; South Bend Blue Sox, 1953.

Doris Cook followed in the footsteps of her sister, Donna, who joined the AAGPBL in 1946.

At age 14, Cook joined a city softball league. She was scouted by the league because of her sister and was assigned to barnstorming Springfield Sallies in 1949. "Cookie" remembered winning her first game as a pitcher on the tour, which started in Chicago and ended up in Canada. "We played in Yankee Stadium and Griffin Stadium in Washington," she recalled. She traded autographed balls with Tommy Henrich of the Yankees.

She was elevated to the league in 1951 as pitcher and outfielder. "I was more of a defensive player than an offensive one," she admitted. In one game she had 11 putouts in left field. Cook saw limited action during her three years in the league, playing about half the time.

After baseball, Cook worked in banking for more than 20 years and retired in August 1994. She was elected to the Muskegon Sports Hall of Fame with her sister in 1993. She now lives in her hometown of Muskegon.

BATTING

G	BA	AB	H	2B	3B	HR	SB	BB	SO	R	RBI
109	.128	250	32	1	0	0	1	29	33	19	14

	PITCHING										FIELDING				
W–L	PCT	ERA	G	IP	H	R	ER	BB	SO		PO	A	E	DP	FA
0–1	.000	5.74	8	22	19	16	14	19	5		147	7	7	0	.957

Cook, Dorothy

St. Catherine, Ontario, Canada. Fort Wayne Daisies, 1946; Rockford Peaches, 1946

BATTING

G	BA	AB	H	2B	3B	HR	SB	BB	SO	R	RBI
14	.000	24	0	0	0	0	1	5	5	0	2

Cooper, Bonnie

Tremont, Illinois. Battle Creek Belles, 1952.

Bonnie Cooper played in less than ten games in 1952 with Battle Creek. She now lives in her hometown of Tremont, Illinois.

Cordes (Elliott), Gloria "Cordie"

Born: Sept. 21, 1931, Staten Island, New York. 5'8", 138, Pitcher, 1st Base, TR, BR. Kalamazoo Lassies, 1950; Racine Belles, 1950; Battle Creek Belles, 1951; Kalamazoo Lassies, 1951–54.

Although never credited with a no-hitter because the game ended in a 0–0 tie, two time All-Star Gloria Cordes once pitched 34 consecutive scoreless innings and went a whole season without ever being relieved. She also was a 1952 All-Star team selection.

Cordes was age 11 when she began playing baseball with her five brothers. It was "nothing organized" because there were no teams for young girls. When the AAGPBL touring teams stopped for an exhibition game in Yankee Stadium in 1949, she tried out for the league. She was invited to another tryout in South Bend the following year. She attended and was selected by Kalamazoo as a pitcher.

"Cordie" pitched in nine games for the Lassies and was 0–5 on a team made up mainly of rookies from the traveling team. Later traded to Racine, she finished out her first season with a 5–10 mark and 3.63 ERA. Racine moved to Battle Creek and she threw in eight contests before being traded back to Kalamazoo. Her ERA improved slightly during the 1952 season, but her record dropped to 3–15. "We couldn't win for losing," she explained.

When the 1953 season opened, Cordes felt more confident about her game. She won three of the team's first four victories and her manager congratulated her for already achieving her win mark from the season before. The right-hander depended on a good fastball and curveball, but she also had a knuckler that baffled batters who tried to analyze her pitches. Cordes went the whole season without being relieved in a single game. She compiled a 16–8 mark with the second best ERA (1.44) in the league. She was named to the All-Star team.

Gloria "Cordie" Cordes

The following season she continued with an excellent ERA (1.98) but she didn't get as much support from her team and ended up with a 13–11 record. She hurled a no-hitter against Grand Rapids on July 17, 1953, but the game ended in a tie. Her low ERA did gain her a selection to the All-Star team.

In the last year of the league, Cordie's control dropped off and her ERA jumped to 4.59, yet she ended up with a better record, 12–7. More importantly she helped her team make the AAGPBL playoffs.

After baseball, she played in the New Jersey softball leagues for several seasons. Then she coached Little League girls softball for 20 seasons. She married Edward Elliott in 1959 and they had one son, Edward Jr., who died in a car wreck at age 20.

One of her uniforms was hung in the National Baseball Hall of Fame after the women were inducted in 1988. She now lives in her hometown of Staten Island, New York.

PITCHING										BATTING			FIELDING			
W–L	PCT	ERA	G	IP	H	R	ER	BB	SO	BA	AB	H	PO	A	E	FA
49–51	.490	2.82	128	874	750	422	274	361	369	.130	323	42	47	289	22	.939

Cornett, Betty Jane "Curly"

Born: Nov. 24, 1932, Pittsburgh, Pennsylvania. 5'5", 125, 3rd Base, Pitcher. Rockford Peaches, 1950; Springfield Sallies, 1950; Kalamazoo Lassies, 1951; Battle Creek Belles, 1952.

Betty "Curly" Cornett saw limited action in two seasons in the league.

Cornett was on her way to rookie camp in Indiana when she picked up her nickname. "We had a layover in Cleveland and my hair went 'poof' on the way because of the wet weather," she explained. She remembered that rookie camp had been inside a gym and she broke a lightbulb with a hit.

After rookie camp, Rockford decided she wasn't ready for the league and sent her to the Springfield Sallies for their barnstorming tour. At one game in New Castle, Pennsylvania, her family came to see her play, which was a big thrill for her. She spent the whole season with the

Sallies and hit a respectable .205 in 66 games. "We had two Cubans with us. One didn't know English, so we taught her how to swear in English," Curly mused.

In 1951 she came to the league and played for Kalamazoo before being dealt to Battle Creek. The Belles turned her into a pitcher for a couple of games with poor results, as she posted an 11.26 ERA. Her best position was third base, but she didn't perform well at the plate — witnessed by a .132 average — and she committed 18 errors. The Belles didn't offer her a contract the following season.

Cornett still wanted to play, so she waited five years to get her amateur status back. Then she played softball in Ohio, West Virginia and Pennsylvania until 1970. She also worked for H.J. Heinz in Pittsburgh and retired there in 1987 with a disability for crest-syndrome arthritis.

Betty Jane "Curly" Cornett

BATTING

G	BA	AB	H	2B	3B	HR	SB	BB	SO	R	RBI
47	.132	114	15	2	0	0	7	18	30	10	6

PITCHING | FIELDING

W–L	PCT	ERA	G	IP	H	R	ER	BB	SO		G	PO	A	E	DP	FA
0–1	.000	11.26	2	8	12	15	10	12	4		39	32	78	18	2	.859

Corrigan, Rita

Pitcher. Racine Belles, 1943.

Rita Corrigan was added to Racine's roster during the 1943 season, but she pitched in less than ten games.

Courtney, Patricia

Born: Oct. 8, 1931, Everett, Massachusetts. 5'5", 125, 3rd Base, BR, TR. Grand Rapids Chicks, 1950; Chicago Colleens/Springfield Sallies, 1950.

Pat Courtney spent one season with the league, but had little success.

She began playing softball at age 13 and came to the league when she was 18.

BATTING

G	BA	AB	H	2B	3B	HR	SB	BB	SO	R
10	.059	17	1	0	0	0	0	3	8	3

Cramer, Peggy

Born: June 22, 1937, Buchanan, Michigan. 5'4", 125, Catcher, BR, TR. South Bend Blue Sox, 1954.

Peggy Cramer was just 16 when she joined the league in its last season. She played in less than ten games. After the league folded, she went on to become a teacher for 28 years. She now lives in Columbiaville, Michigan.

Crawley, Pauline "Hedy"

Born: Sept. 11, 1924, Phoenix, Arizona. 5'4", 145, Outfield, BR, TR. Peoria Redwings, 1946; Battle Creek Belles, 1951.

Pauline Crawley played two seasons in the league over a six-year span due to a knee injury.

Crawley began playing softball at age 11 in a league in Phoenix where she grew up. She gained her nickname as a teenager because she kiddingly said she looked like movie star Hedy Lamarr, although she really didn't. Her softball team went to the national tournament several times. Her friend Joanne Winter had joined the league in 1943 and arranged for her to try out with Max Carey. She was accepted and assigned to Peoria.

About halfway through her first season, she twisted her knee and had to have surgery. She even paid for it herself. "I had injured it in Phoenix and I didn't think it was their fault," she explained. The league didn't send her a contract the next season, so she joined the National League in Chicago for four seasons. In 1951 she worked for United Airlines before deciding to go back to the league without a contract. This time she was assigned to Battle Creek and played the whole season.

After the season ended, she decided she had had enough of professional ball and went to California State University to get a bachelor's degree. She became an executive secretary at United Airlines for

Pauline "Hedy" Crawley

32 years. Then she worked four years with Northrup Aircraft before retiring for good. She had four surgeries on the knee before she had it replaced in 1993 by the same doctor who replaced President Gerald Ford's knee. She now lives in California, golfs and goes to league reunions. She's also part of the Golden Diamond Girls, a group of former players who attend card shows and sign autographs.

					BATTING								FIELDING				
G	BA	AB	H	2B	3B	HR	SB	BB	SO	R	RBI		PO	A	E	DP	FA
125	.160	418	67	2	2	0	21	33	44	40	25		166	17	9	3	.953

Crigler, Idona

California. 3rd Base, BR, TR. South Bend Blue Sox, 1947.

Idona Crigler played a season for South Bend in 1947.

					BATTING									FIELDING				
G	BA	AB	H	2B	3B	HR	SB	BB	SO	R	RBI		G	PO	A	E	DP	FA
20	.138	65	9	0	0	0	0	5	7	2	0		20	32	47	7	3	.919

Crites, Shirley "Squirrely"

Born: Aug. 21, 1934, Cape Giradeau, Missouri. Died: Dec. 28, 1990. 3rd Base, BR, TR. Fort Wayne Daisies, 1953.

Shirley Crites was a member of the pennant-winning 1953 Fort Wayne Daisies.

					BATTING								FIELDING				
G	BA	AB	H	2B	3B	HR	SB	BB	SO	R	RBI		PO	A	E	DP	FA
47	.129	132	17	3	1	0	7	15	17	15	11		41	92	11	5	.924

D'Angelo, Josephine "Jo Jo"

Born: Nov. 23, 1924, Chicago, Illinois. 5', 135, Outfield, BR, TR. South Bend Blue Sox, 1943–44.

Josephine D'Angelo, one of the original players in the league, holds the league record for fewest strikeouts in a season.

As a child, she snuck out with the boys to play sandlot baseball. Then at 13 she joined the De Young Florals on the southside of Chicago where she grew up. They gave her a uniform. The following year she played for Raab Taylors and received $1 a night for playing. "They drew very good crowds—3,000 to 4,000," she said.

She continued to advance up the softball ladder and when tryouts for the All-American League were held at Wrigley Field, she was there. She made the grade and was assigned to South Bend. The money the steel worker received allowed her to make a down payment

Josephine "Jo Jo" D'Angelo (front row, middle)

toward college. "Jo Jo" once made the headlines after hitting a homer to win a game for the Blue Sox.

After two seasons in the league, she was offered more money by the Chicago Bluebirds and jumped at the opportunity, as did some other players in the league. She continued her college education and after obtaining a bachelor's degree from DePaul University, Jo Jo became a physical education teacher. She later received a master's degree from Chicago State University and taught for 34 years, retiring in 1980.

She took up golf, but knee replacement surgery in 1992 made her less mobile. She still lives in Chicago.

				BATTING										FIELDING				
G	BA	AB	H	2B	3B	HR	SB	BB	SO	R	RBI		PO	A	E	DP	FA
144	.200	499	100	9	2	2	62	67	11	73	47		204	27	11	8	.955

Dabbs, Sarah Mavis

Born: March 10, 1922, Largo, Florida. 5'5", 130, Outfield, BR, TR. Fort Wayne Daisies, 1947.

Sarah Dabbs was an outfielder with Fort Wayne in 1947. She played softball for ten years in Florida before joining the league. She was with the R.H. Hall team that won the state championship in 1941.

BATTING

G	BA	AB	H	2B	3B	HR	SB	BB	SO	R	RBI
12	.091	22	2	0	0	0	1	2	1	0	1

Daetweiler, Louella "Daets"

Born: April 30, 1918, Lynwood, California. 5'3", 160, Catcher, BR, TR. Rockford Peaches, 1944.

Louella Daetweiler was a backup receiver with Rockford in 1944. After baseball, she coached and officiated for 39 years at Compton Community College in California. She now lives in Long Beach, California.

BATTING												FIELDING				
G	BA	AB	H	2B	3B	HR	SB	BB	SO	R	RBI	PO	A	E	DP	FA
33	.079	76	6	0	0	0	4	6	3	4	8	38	7	12	0	.789

Dailey, Mary

Lexington, Massachusetts. Died: Date Unknown. Outfield, Pitcher. Peoria Redwings, 1950–51; South Bend Blue Sox, 1950–51; Battle Creek Belles, 1951.

Mary Dailey was a light-hitting outfielder for two seasons in the league. She also was tried out at pitcher, but she didn't show much promise.

BATTING

G	BA	AB	H	2B	3B	HR	SB	BB	SO	R	RBI
114	.162	314	51	4	1	0	10	34	48	24	16

PITCHING										FIELDING				
W–L	PCT	ERA	G	IP	H	R	ER	BB	SO	PO	A	E	DP	FA
1–0	1.000	6.02	3	15	18	12	10	10	5	163	6	9	2	.950

Damaschke, Dorothy "DD"

Born: August 26, 1917, Racine, Wisconsin. 5'3", 135. TR, BR. Racine Redwings, 1945.

BATTING

G	AB	H
1	2	0

Dancer, Faye "Fanny"

**Born: April 24, 1925, Santa Monica, California.
5'6", 145, Outfield, 1st Base, Pitcher, BR, TR.
Minneapolis Millerettes, 1944; Fort Wayne
Daisies, 1945–47; Peoria Redwings, 1947–50.**

Faye "Fanny" Dancer

Faye Dancer, portrayed by Madonna in the movie *A League of Their Own*, was one of the most colorful characters and best players of the league. An injury ended her seven-year stint in the league.

Dancer began playing softball in the sixth grade. "I ate, slept and dreamed about playing ball," she recalled. She advanced to the amateur softball leagues and played for Jim Thorpe's Thunderbirds. She remembered getting paid $2.50 a game. She and five other girls from California were recruited by Bill Allington for the league in 1944. She was given a salary of $75 a week, which was much more than some of the other girls.

In her rookie year she showed how valuable a player she was despite her antics. During the season, she hit two grand-slam homers — her only two homers of the year — and posted a .274 average to help Minneapolis win the pennant. The following season with Fort Wayne she hit three home runs to lead the league. Dancer was a powerful hitter, but the outfielders would simply back up more in the fields that had no fences.

As the years rolled by, Dancer became famous for her practical jokes, especially on the chaperones. She would rub Limburger cheese on the bed light and when the light was turned on it would emit the foulest of odors. Or she might take an Oreo cookie and replace the white filling with toothpaste. "I got fined once for throwing a chaperone off the bus. She was trying to take a beer off of me," she explained.

She also became a heavy beer drinker and more than once came to a game with a few beers under her belt. She even admits now of coming to a playoff game after drinking too many beers. She joined other players in driving out of town for some beer drinking and dancing.

Dancer was loved by the fans for her fun-loving attitude. She would swipe the eyes out of horses on carousels or dolls and present them to the fans. "We got along real good," she said.

During the 1950 season she ruptured a spinal disc, which ended her season and career. She didn't play softball again until about five years later. Dancer went to work for the Howard Hughes aircraft plant and began a long career in electronics. She now works at Henry Electronics at the age of 70. She gave up drinking and smoking on her own. "You have to make a promise to yourself," she explained.

Dancer became a board member on the AAGPBL Player's Association, which brought about the recognition of the league and the reunions. She's also a member of the Golden Diamond Girls, a group of former players who travel to card shows to sign autographs. She lives in her hometown of Santa Monica.

"I was known for the crazy things that I did rather than my ball playing," she reminisced. "If I had put as much effort in my ball playing, I might have been a great player."

BATTING

G	BA	AB	H	2B	3B	HR	SB	BB	SO	R	RBI
591	.236	2072	488	53	14	16	352	261	223	323	193

PITCHING

W–L	PCT	ERA	G	IP	H	R	ER	BB	SO
11–11	.500	2.28	25	174	133	82	44	70	43

FIELDING

PO	A	E	DP	FA
1061	83	48	25	.960

Danhauser (Brown), Margaret L. "Marnie"

Born: June 9, 1921, Racine, Wisconsin. Died: Date Unknown. 1st Base, BR, TR. Racine Belles, 1943–49.

One of the original members of the league, Margaret Danhauser was an excellent fielding first baseman on three championship Racine teams.

Danhauser attended Racine Catholic schools when she was a child and was a member of the state champions in 1936 and 1937. She was selected for the league and assigned to her hometown Belles.

Number 15 was the best first baseman in 1945 with only 15 errors and a fielding average of .987. She also tied a league record that year with three sacrifices in one game. Her best season behind the plate came in 1946 when she hit .196 with a career high 35 RBI. Racine won pennants in 1943, 1946 and 1948 with her at first base.

After baseball, she got married and worked for Western Printing and Lithographing Company.

BATTING

G	BA	AB	H	2B	3B	HR	SB	BB	SO	R	RBI
728	.144	2257	325	16	10	3	94	166	189	167	176

FIELDING

PO	A	E	DP	FA
7409	243	142	179	.982

Danz, Shirley

Born: Aug. 16, 1926, Oak Park, Illinois. 5'4", 130, Shortstop, 2nd Base, Outfield, BR, TR. Chicago Colleens, 1949; Racine Belles, 1950.

Shirley Danz played two years in the league then went on to become a professional women's bowler.

At age 13, Danz first started playing amateur softball in Forest Park, Illinois. Then she jumped to the pros and played with the Chicago Cardinals, receiving $85 a week. She was noticed by the league and was assigned to the traveling Chicago Colleens in 1949. She recalled one game in Tyler, Texas, that had a huge turnout. They treated the Texans to a 14–inning game. "At first it was fun, but it got tedious," she said about the barnstorming trip.

The following season she was assigned to Racine and played in the outfield. Her season ended abruptly when she hurt her shoulder after tripping over first base.

A few years later when the women's professional bowling tour began, Danz joined on. She bowled on the tour until 1969. Although she never won a tournament, she became a bowling instructor and made more money doing that. She also worked at Motorola for 21 years, retiring in 1985.

In 1994 she suffered a heart attack. She had bypass surgery in 1995 and is recovering now in Hendersonville, North Carolina. She likes to golf and garden.

					BATTING								FIELDING				
G	BA	AB	H	2B	3B	HR	SB	BB	SO	R	RBI		PO	A	E	DP	FA
23	.145	55	8	0	0	0	1	4	18	4	1		18	0	4	0	.818

Dapkus (Wolf), Eleanor "Slugger"

Born: Dec. 5, 1923, Chicago, Illinois. 5'6", 160, Outfielder, Pitcher, BR, TR. Racine Belles, 1943–50.

Eleanor Dapkus, one of the original players of the league, was a power hitter who led the league in several categories during her career.

Dapkus grew up with six brothers and played sandlot baseball with them. When she reached her teens, she joined a park's department softball league. At age 19, a scout from the Chicago Cubs spotted her for the women's league and signed her up. She came to Wrigley for the final tryout. "I wasn't sure I'd make it," she admitted. She was taken by the Racine Belles.

During her first year in the league, the outfielder was named to the All-Star team. She sustained a knee injury and tore ligaments from sliding. Then she hurt the other knee. The women wore skirts above the knee and the only protection they had when sliding was a pad under their panties, which didn't protect their legs at all. Many picked up strawberries and injuries from sliding.

"Slugger" earned her nickname in her rookie year when she led the league with 10 home runs. The total is reminiscent of the "dead-ball" era of baseball, but that wasn't the reason for the low amount of home runs. "There weren't too many fences. You had to hit one over the fielders," explained Dapkus.

In 1944 the outfielder led the league in extra-base hits (19) and doubles (10). Then in 1946 she tied two other players for the league lead in triples (9).

When the league turned to overhand pitching in 1948, she was called on to take the mound. In her first appearance she pitched a 22-inning game but lost a heartbreaker, 2–1. "I didn't have an arm for a couple of weeks after that," she recalled.

Dapkus liked pitching more than roaming the outfield. She ended up pitching for four years and led the league in games started (39) in 1948, which was her best season on the mound with a 24–9 record. She ended up with the second most career RBI.

After her playing days, she got married and raised a family of two sons, Frank and Richard. She became a legal secretary for 25 years. In 1991 she had knee replacement surgery to repair the damage caused during her playing days. She now lives in Lansing, Illinois.

BATTING

G	BA	AB	H	2B	3B	HR	SB	BB	SO	R	RBI
775	.229	2549	583	50	36	30	154	276	252	275	317

PITCHING											FIELDING				
W–L	PCT	ERA	G	IP	H	R	ER	BB	SO		PO	A	E	DP	FA
53–34	.609	1.97	102	664	431	208	145	268	397		641	203	34	16	.961

Davis, Gladys "Terry"

Born: Sept. 1, 1919, Toronto, Ontario, Canada. 5'5", 130, Shortstop, Outfield, 2nd Base, BR, TR. Rockford Peaches, 1943–44; Milwaukee Chicks, 1944; Muskegon Lassies, 1946–47.

Gladys Davis was the league's first batting champion and was selected to its first All-Star team.

Davis was married and had a child before joining the league. In her first season, she hit .331, which was 16 points higher than anyone else. She also hit 20 triples and four homers.

The following season she slumped a little after a move to Milwaukee. However, she still hit .246 and helped lead the Chicks to a pennant and championship.

She missed the 1945 season and when she returned in the middle of the 1946 season, the league assigned her to Muskegon. Her batting average dipped to .202. Nineteen forty-seven turned out to be her last season and she returned to her family and interior decorating business in Toronto.

BATTING													FIELDING				
G	BA	AB	H	2B	3B	HR	SB	BB	SO	R	RBI		PO	A	E	DP	FA
240	.272	819	223	19	11	5	137	113	55	142	123		353	492	115	29	.880

DeCambra, Alice G. "Moose"

Born: Aug. 18, 1921, Somerset, Massachusetts. Died: June 19, 1988. 5'3", 126, Shortstop, 2nd Base, Pitcher, BR, TR. Fort Wayne Daisies, 1946–47; Peoria Redwings, 1947–50; Kalamazoo Lassies, 1950.

Alice "Moose" DeCambra was a versatile player in her five seasons in the league.

Coming from a family of ten children, DeCambra was indoctrinated in all sports, but she excelled in baseball. She played for the St. Patrick's Rhode Island All-Stars before joining the league. Her younger sister, Lillian, also tried out for the league, but didn't make it.

Number 4 pitched during her first two years in the league and then was used strictly as an infielder. Her best season was her last, when she hit for a career-high .244 average. After baseball, she worked for Firestone.

Alice G. "Moose" DeCambra

BATTING

G	BA	AB	H	2B	3B	HR	SB	BB	SO	R	RBI
490	.198	1578	313	29	6	0	107	138	76	152	105

PITCHING

W–L	PCT	ERA	G	IP	H	R	ER	BB	SO
11–8	.579	3.38	31	165	154	81	62	36	26

FIELDING

PO	A	E	FA
940	825	111	.941

DeCambra, Lillian

Born: Nov. 21, 1925, Somerset, Massachusetts. 5'2", 102, Infielder, BR, TR. Fort Wayne Daisies, 1947.

Lillian DeCambra signed with Fort Wayne but never played a regular season game. She joined her sister, Alice, at spring training in Havana, Cuba, in 1947. She played in exhibition games before the start of the season.

Deegan, Mildred "Millie"

Born: Dec. 11, 1919, Brooklyn, New York. 5'7", 155, Pitcher, Outfield, 2nd Base, TR, BR. Rockford Peaches, 1943–47; Kenosha Comets, 1947–48; Springfield Sallies, 1948; Fort Wayne Daisies, 1949–51; Peoria Redwings, 1951; Rockford Peaches, 1952.

Mildred Deegan started out as a pitcher but ended up as a second baseman during her decade in the league.

"Millie" was the best fielding second baseman in her sophomore season with Rockford, committing just 12 errors for a .969 average, the third best single season fielding average in league history. The following season she helped the Peaches win a pennant and championship with her .208 batting average and 57 runs scored.

When the league went to the sidearm delivery in 1946, pitching was added to her chores and she responded with a 10–5 record for the Peaches. After losing seasons the next two years, Fort Wayne decided to use her only as a pitcher and she came through with a 16–11 record. Number 31 tied Lois Florreich for the most complete games (26) during the season.

Deegan improved to 16–9 the next season despite walking the most batters (134) in the league. Her pitching went downhill after that and she quit the league in 1952. In the off-season, she was a commercial photographer.

PITCHING

W–L	PCT	ERA	G	IP	H	R	ER	BB	SO
66–59	.528	2.26	146	1081	755	444	271	514	412

BATTING

BA	AB	H	2B	3B	HR	SB	BB	SO	R	RBI
.200	1560	312	48	24	5	100	160	100	175	152

FIELDING

PO	A	E	DP	FA
708	759	103	45	.925

Deemer, Audrey

Steubenville, Ohio. Utility Fielder. Chicago Colleens/Springfield Sallies, 1950.

Audrey Deemer was with the player development teams in 1950.

BATTING

G	BA	AB	H	2B	3B	HR	SB	BB	SO	R	RBI
25	.129	85	9	0	1	0	6	11	16	14	8

Degner, Betty

Amboy, Illinois. Pitcher, BR, TR. Muskegon Lassies, 1949; Chicago Colleens/ Springfield Sallies, 1949.

BATTING

G	BA	AB	H
2	.200	5	1

Delmonico (Surkowski), Lena

Born: Oct. 26, 1925, Moose Jaw, Saskatchewan, Canada. 5'5", 128, Outfield, BR, TR. South Bend Blue Sox, 1944–46; Rockford Peaches, 1946–48; Fort Wayne, 1948.

A Canadian who became an American citizen, Lena Delmonico was a good fielding outfielder and a solid hitter during her five seasons with the league.

Delmonico was playing softball in Canada when a scout from the league saw her and offered her a contract without a tryout. "He was convinced because I was a good ball player," she remembered.

She came to the league in its second season and became a starting outfielder for South Bend. During the season, she once hit two homers against Kenosha in the same game. Both came off Lee Harney and she considers that her greatest game. The following season her sister, Ann, joined her on the team for a year.

In 1946, the league assigned her to Rockford, where she continued to start in centerfield. The following season she

Lena Delmonico

married Alphonso Delmonico and went through some marital problems, which limited her play on the field.

Delmonico moved to California in 1957 and became a U.S. citizen in 1970—something she's very proud of. "When I played, I loved America," she explained. "When we went to Miami that was paradise." She also changed her name to Lee. The Californian raised three children: Barry, Randy and Teri Lee.

BATTING												FIELDING				
G	BA	AB	H	2B	3B	HR	SB	BB	SO	R	RBI	PO	A	E	DP	FA
288	.200	940	195	19	11	5	74	85	89	95	85	418	38	21	7	.956

Dennert (Hill), Pauline

Born: April 8, 1926, Hart, Michigan. 5'4", 145, Outfield, BR, TR. Muskegon Lassies, 1947.

BATTING			
G	BA	AB	H
3	.000	4	0

Denoble, Jerre

Outfield, BR, TR. Peoria Redwings, 1947.

Jerre Denoble was a light-hitting outfielder for Peoria for one season.

BATTING											FIELDING				
G	BA	AB	H	2B	3B	HR	SB	SO	R	RBI	PO	A	E	DP	FA
21	.107	28	3	1	0	0	4	11	3	0	12	0	1	0	.923

Denton, Mona

Denver, Colorado. Pitcher, TR, BR. South Bend Blue Sox, 1946; Kenosha Comets, 1947.

Mona Denton enjoyed little success in the league as she compiled one of the worst career pitching marks (1–11) in two seasons. However, neither team she played with gave her much run support.

PITCHING											BATTING			FIELDING			
W–L	PCT	ERA	G	IP	H	R	ER	BB	SO		AB	H	BA	PO	A	E	FA
1–11	.083	3.54	26	125	123	90	44	39	22		56	11	.196	10	46	5	.918

Descombes (Lesko), Jean "Lefty"

Born: March 28, 1935, Springfield, Ohio. 5'5", 130, Pitcher, TL, BL. Grand Rapids Chicks, 1953–54.

Despite a high earned run average, Jean Descombes had a winning record over her two years in the league.

"Lefty" also contributed at the plate with her .179 average. After the league folded in 1954, "Lefty" joined Bill Allington's All-American Baseball Team for two years. She also went on to become a professional golfer. After pro sports, she taught and coached at the high school level for ten years. She got married and had three children: Matthew, Michael and Gregory. Now living in Bellevue, Washington, she is a real estate agent.

PITCHING										BATTING			FIELDING			
W–L	PCT	ERA	G	IP	H	R	ER	BB	SO	BA	AB	H	PO	A	E	FA
10–9	.526	5.31	29	134	140	94	79	94	68	.179	39	7	8	32	8	.884

DeShone (Rockwell), Nancy

Born: March 22, 1932, Osceola, Indiana. 5'3", 120, Outfield, BL, TL. South Bend Blue Sox, 1948; Fort Wayne Daisies, 1948.

Nancy DeShone joined the league in 1948 and was being groomed as a pitcher, but she decided school was more important.

She began playing baseball before she attended school. "I played baseball with the boys," she explained. In her teens she played for Miles, a fast-pitch softball factory team. The aggressive base stealer recalled one game in which a second baseman took exception to her stealing. "I was going into second and she was going to cleat me. I put my right foot up and spiked her, and slid in safely with my left foot," she recalled.

The strong hitter helped lead Miles to a South Bend championship. Noticed by the South Bend Blue Sox, she was drafted in 1948. DeShone didn't see much action — playing in one game — because she was being primed as a pitcher. The teen got $50 a week for sitting on the pine.

Nancy DeShone

"At an away game, one of the players from the other team came up to me and said, 'When did the Blue Sox start carrying their bat girl?'" The 16-year-old DeShone told the player in no uncertain terms that she was a player. Later in the season, the league sent her to the Fort Wayne Daisies.

After one season in the league, she decided to go back to high school and earn her diploma. When she married Rocky Rockwell in 1950, her baseball days ended. She remained interested in baseball and coached women's softball and Little League over the years.

DeShone was the chairperson for the 50th reunion of the All-American Girls Professional Baseball League in August 1993 in South Bend, where she once played. She coordinated events for more than 200 former players at the five-day event. DeShone is now in sales with a local glass company. Her husband died in 1992. She has four daughters: Debbie, Sherry, Jacki, and Conni.

BATTING

G	BA	AB	H
1	.000	2	0

Dokish, Wanita "Lee"

Born: April 6, 1936, Van Meter, Pennsylvania. 5'5", 125, 3rd Base, Outfield, BB, TR. Rockford Peaches, 1954.

Wanita Dokish entered the league near its end and didn't get much of a chance to play.

At 6 years of age, she recalled playing baseball, but it wasn't until she was 14 that she played organized softball in high school. She saw an article in a magazine about the league and went to Battle Creek for a tryout.

She recalled her first at-bat in the league: "I got a single to right field." She was used sparingly during the league's final season. "They said they weren't coming back," she remembered team officials saying.

"Lee" continued to play softball up until she encountered leg problems in 1974. She worked at Westinghouse and now makes cabinets. She went to the 1988 reunion at the National Baseball Hall of Fame. She lives in Belle Vernon, Pennsylvania.

Wanita "Lee" Dokish

BATTING

G	BA	AB	H	2B	3B	HR	SB	BB	SO	R	RBI
27	.113	44	5	0	0	0	0	10	14	5	2

FIELDING

PO	A	E	DP	FA
50	28	11	6	.876

Donahue, Terry

Born: Aug. 22, 1925, Melaval, Saskatchewan, Canada. 5'2", 125, Utility Fielder, BR, TR. Peoria Redwings, 1946–49.

Terry Donahue was one of 23 players from Saskatchewan to play in the league. The versatile player was used at many different positions during her four-year career.

Donahue grew up on a farm and her brother taught her how to play the game. She played softball in school and for the Moose Jaw Royals. She was scouted in 1945 and invited to spring training the next year in Pascagoula, Mississippi. She was assigned to Racine after spring training.

One of her most memorable games was the night her team's catcher broke her finger. Since Donahue was the utility player, the manager came to her and asked her if she had ever caught before. She told him she hadn't, but the manager replied, "Then you're going in." She caught the 19-inning game and was the catcher for the rest of the season.

In 1950 she joined the rival National League in Chicago. Then she went on to become a bookkeeper and interior designer. She retired in 1990 and now lives in Chicago.

"We played for the love of the game," she said.

Terry Donahue

BATTING													FIELDING					
G	BA	AB	H	2B	3B	HR	SB	BB	SO	R	RBI		G	PO	A	E	DP	FA
287	.127	722	92	3	2	0	44	123	7	7	0		258	734	261	56	30	.947

Downs, Dorothea "Dottie"

South Bend, Indiana. Died: Date Unknown. 1st Base, TR, BR. South Bend Blue Sox, 1945.

Doyle (Childress), Cartha "Duckie"

Born: Oct. 12, 1929, Knoxville, Tennessee. 5'5", 130, 2nd Base, BR, TR. Rockford Peaches, 1947.

While most players cherished the years they played in the league as the best time of their lives, Cartha Doyle didn't have such great experiences and was unimpressed with the league. Now, though, she's honored to be a member of the league.

"Duckie," as she was nick-named, began playing softball in her teens and was convinced to try out in Miami by AAGPBL player Doris Sams and her father. She made the league and was sent to spring training in Cuba.

The 17 year old played for the Peaches and at the end of the season married Albert Childress. She decided not to go back to the league the following season. "I didn't think it was so special. I didn't want to go back," she commented.

Instead, she played softball in her hometown until 1967. Then she coached and umpired until 1982. Meanwhile, she gave birth to one daughter, Janet, and helped her husband run a business. She developed arthritis in both knees and has since had knee replacement surgery. Her husband passed away in 1975 and she retired in 1982. She was inducted into the Knoxville Hall of Fame in 1990. She now lives in Maryville, Tennessee.

Cartha "Duckie" Doyle

BATTING												FIELDING				
G	BA	AB	H	2B	3B	HR	SB	BB	SO	R	RBI	PO	A	E	DP	FA
59	.169	166	28	4	0	0	2	5	24	5	7	74	97	9	7	.950

Drinkwater (Simmons), Maxine "Max"

Born: May 19, 1936, Camden, Maine. 5'5", 136, 1st Base, 2nd Base, BR, TR. South Bend Blue Sox, 1954

Maxine Drinkwater played the final season in the league as an infielder for South Bend. She still is active in sports and enjoys golf. Today she lives in East Newport, Maine.

BATTING												FIELDING				
G	BA	AB	H	2B	3B	HR	SB	BB	SO	R	RBI	PO	A	E	DP	FA
45	.147	95	14	0	0	0	1	12	22	8	4	233	27	16	14	.942

Dunn, Gertrude "Gerty"

Born: Sept. 30, 1933, Sharon Hill, Pennsylvania. 5'2", 125, Shortstop, BR, TR. Battle Creek Belles, 1951; South Bend Blue Sox, 1951–54.

Gertrude "Gerty" Dunn

Gertrude Dunn played on two championship teams during her four years in the league.

She first played organized softball at age 14 in the Philadelphia suburbs after being encouraged by her father. The AAGPBL held tryouts in Allentown and she was one of the best prospects, so South Bend signed the junior in high school.

During the 1951 season, she was used sparingly and then loaned to Battle Creek, which needed some rookies to complete its roster. "Every team had to have a rookie," explained Dunn. She returned to South Bend near the end of the season but wasn't able to play in the playoffs because she had to return to school.

The day after Dunn graduated from high school, she flew to South Bend and was put in the lineup to stay. In her first at bat, the rookie was so nervous her knees were shaking. She yelled out to the pitcher. "Throw it right here!" The pitcher did just that and she spanked it to center field for a hit.

"Gerty," as players liked to call her, played well and contributed to the team repeating as champions — this time with just 12 players, as six had left the team near the end of the season. In the off-season she played field hockey with the national team. It was a sport she had started before baseball.

Dunn remembered one play of significance during her time with the league. A grounder was hit to Jean Faut, who was playing third. She backed up Faut on the play and when the ball came through Faut's legs, Dunn picked up the ball and tossed it to first to catch the runner.

After the league folded in 1954, Dunn played with a barnstorming remnant of the league for two years. She continued to play on the national field hockey team, too. Then in 1955 she became involved with the national lacrosse team. In all she played 13 years of national field hockey and 7 years on the national lacrosse team. She was inducted into the National Field Hockey Hall of Fame.

Dunn graduated from Weschester University in 1960 and then taught for several years. She became self-employed in 1968 and has been an entrepreneur ever since. In 1980, the six-handicap golfer won the Delaware state golf title. She lives in Chaddsford, Pennsylvania.

BATTING													FIELDING				
G	BA	AB	H	2B	3B	HR	SB	BB	SO	R	RBI		PO	A	E	DP	FA
344	.261	1,226	320	49	5	6	70	138	46	154	105		557	1,028	140	77	.919

Dusanko (Sabo), Julianna "Julie"

Born: Feb. 22, 1922, Leross, Saskatchewan, Canada. 5'5", 122, 3rd Base, BR, TR. Minneapolis Millerettes, 1944; Racine Belles, 1944.

"Julie" Dusanko married two months before she started playing for the league and lasted one season. She had one son, who passed away in 1991. Now retired, she lives in Arizona.

BATTING													FIELDING				
G	BA	AB	H	2B	3B	HR	SB	BB	SO	R	RBI		PO	A	E	DP	FA
76	.167	246	41	3	2	0	29	21	26	21	16		123	150	38	10	.878

Dwojak, Loretta

Born: Dec. 19, 1925, Chicago, Illinois. 5'5", 135, Outfield, 3rd Base, BR, TR. Minneapolis Millerettes, 1944; South Bend Blue Sox, 1944.

Loretta Dwojak played with two teams during her only season in the league.

BATTING													FIELDING				
G	BA	AB	H	2B	3B	HR	SB	BB	SO	R	RBI		PO	A	E	DP	FA
63	.201	174	35	4	2	0	18	18	17	19	19		52	24	7	0	.916

Earp, Mildred

Born: Oct. 7, 1925, West Fork, Arkansas. 5'6", 135, Pitcher, TR, BR. Grand Rapids Chicks, 1946–50.

Selected once to the All-Star team, Mildred Earp recorded the second best single season ERA and the second best career ERA during her five-year career.

Earp began playing softball in the fourth grade. She first heard of the league when it came through a town 50 miles away and played an exhibition game. She decided to get on a bus for Chicago to try out for the league. She was sent to Racine for a look-see and made the league as a sidearm pitcher. Since she didn't know anything about baseball, she sat on the bench her first season and got paid to learn.

In 1947, Earp got her chance to pitch—she threw a curve, drop and a blazing fastball to mow down batters. She had excellent control and walked just 32 batters in 35 games. By the end of the year her record was 20–8 with a 0.68 ERA, lowest on the season and second lowest ever. She helped Grand Rapids win their first championship and was a shoe-in for the All-Star team as a rookie.

The next season was more of a thrill for her as she recorded a no-hitter against the Chicago Colleens and led the Chicks to their first-ever pennant.

In 1949, she was 14–10 and threw an 18-inning contest against Anna May Hutchison and Racine. She now doesn't remember who won the game.

The following season became her last after her arm weakened. She underwent therapy over the winter, but the arm never responded and her career was over. She ended up with a 1.35 ERA, the best career ERA at the time.

She moved to California and worked in manufacturing until she retired in 1995. Now she lives in her hometown of West Fork, Arkansas, and plays golf.

PITCHING											BATTING			FIELDING			
W–L	PCT	ERA	G	IP	H	R	ER	BB	SO		BA	AB	H	PO	A	E	FA
54–38	.587	1.35	108	860	576	195	129	175	534		.137	278	38	41	187	9	.962

Eisen, Thelma "Tiby"

Born: May 11, 1922, Los Angeles, California. 5'4", 130, Outfield, Pitcher, BR, TR. Milwaukee Chicks, 1944; Grand Rapids Chicks, 1945; Peoria Redwings, 1946; Fort Wayne Daisies, 1947–52.

Once an All-Star, Thelma Eisen was one of the league's career hitting leaders in her nine-season career. She was a member of the 1944 champion Milwaukee Chicks and the 1952 pennant winning Fort Wayne Daisies.

The Californian began playing organized softball when she was 13 and played throughout high school. If women's pro football had ever gotten off the ground, she would have been a player in the league. She played fullback for a team that toured Mexico, but the league never started. Instead, AAGPBL scout Bill Allington spotted her and got her to join the All-American League in 1944.

Max Carey, her first manager, taught her how to play the game. Eisen had speed, so Carey taught her how to steal. He also taught her to concentrate on hitting the ball to the spot she wanted. She did it one game and knocked in two runs.

One of her most memorable experiences was the league's trip to Cuba for spring training in 1948. She then joined one of the touring teams that traveled through Central America.

Eisen ended up being the second best base stealer in league history with 674 thefts. She also was third in career runs scored (591) and at-bats (3,706).

After baseball, she worked 17 years at GTE before retiring. She now lives in Pacific Palisades, California.

BATTING												FIELDING				
G	BA	AB	H	2B	3B	HR	SB	BB	SO	R	RBI	PO	A	E	DP	FA
966	.224	3706	830	85	23	11	674	372	164	591	241	1857	124	93	38	.955

Emerson, June "Venus"

Born: June 4, 1924, Moose Jaw, Saskatchewan, Canada. Died: Oct. 1, 1990. 5'5", 135, Outfield, BR, TR. Springfield Sallies, 1948; Peoria Redwings, 1949.

June Emerson, a reporter for the *Toronto Star* before the league, was a weak-hitting outfielder for two seasons in the league. After baseball, she was the director of Hyde Park YMCA in Chicago. She also worked 37 years for an airline.

BATTING												FIELDING				
G	BA	AB	H	2B	3B	HR	SB	BB	SO	R	RBI	PO	A	E	DP	FA
68	.164	159	26	2	0	0	7	31	16	11	5	40	5	4	0	.918

Emry, Betty

Born: Jan. 20, 1923, Manistique, Michigan. Died: April 18, 1995. 5'4", 130, Pitcher, Shortstop, TR, BR. Racine Belles, 1945–46.

Betty Emry played two years in the league first as a shortstop and then as a pitcher. She helped Racine win a pennant in 1946 with her seven victories. A knee injury hampered her performance, though. She played with the Kellers in Detroit before coming to the league.

PITCHING										
W–L	PCT	ERA	G	IP	H	R	ER	BB	SO	
7–4	.636	2.15	15	91	65	39	22	24	16	

BATTING												FIELDING				
G	BA	AB	H	2B	3B	HR	SB	BB	SO	R	RBI	PO	A	E	DP	FA
134	.147	365	54	1	0	0	11	43	42	24	34	151	173	27	4	.923

English, Madeline "Maddy"

Born: Feb. 22, 1925, Everett, Massachusetts. 5'4", 130, 3rd Base, BR, TR. Racine Belles, 1943–50.

A three time All-Star, Madeline English was an excellent third baseman known more for her fielding than hitting, although she did hit six career homers.

English was 10 years old when she started playing softball. She also played baseball with her brother when his team was short on players. "They put me out in right field, so I wouldn't get hurt," she said. She emulated her brother, who was 2 years older than her.

When she was about to graduate in 1943, she was spotted by scout

Madeline "Maddy" English

Ralph Wheeler and given a tryout at Wrigley Field. She made the cut and was assigned to Racine.

She helped Racine win three pennants and two championships during her eight-year stint with the team. She was an adept base stealer and swiped seven bases on May 21, 1947, to tie a league record. Her best season behind the plate came in 1946 when she hit .214. "1946 was our best year," she said, reflecting on the teams she played on. When the franchise moved to Battle Creek, she decided to quit. "To me, the league was over," she said. She enjoyed playing in Racine and wouldn't have thought of playing elsewhere.

During her playing days she attended Boston University and obtained a bachelor's degree soon after she left the league. Then she went on to get a master's degree and teach for 10 years. She then became a guidance counselor for 17 years before retiring in 1984 when her mother became ill and needed her help. She now attends league reunions.

BATTING												FIELDING				
G	BA	AB	H	2B	3B	HR	SB	BB	SO	R	RBI	PO	A	E	DP	FA
832	.171	2817	482	26	27	6	397	356	315	333	197	1439	2255	430	106	.896

Erickson (Sauer), Louise "Lou"

Born: June 2, 1929, Arcadia, Wisconsin. 5'9", 162, Pitcher, TR, BR. Racine Belles, 1948; Rockford Peaches, 1949–50.

Selected to All-Star teams in 1949 and 1950, Louise Erickson's 36 wins drove Rockford to championships during both seasons.

Erickson's father, uncles and five brothers taught her baseball when she was a child. She was allowed to shag balls for a neighboring town team, which drew the attention of the manager, who put her in contact with the league. She was given a tryout and immediately signed on as a pitcher for the 1948 season, which was already underway. Her first major league win came on September 1. She entered the game as a relief pitcher in the first inning, behind 5–0. She held the other team at bay, while the Belles roared back to give her the win, 12–7. She was used in relief two more times in her rookie season.

Louise "Lou" Erickson

The following season Erickson responded to more mound time with a 17–6 record, including seven shutouts. She had a fastball, curve and changeup, and "Lou" could change speeds on the curve. But she said the key to her pitches was that she had control of them.

Her performance in 1950 was nearly a reflection of the year before, and the Peaches won the pennant and championship with her help. She was 16–10 and hit .239 on the season. Her best game in the league was a two-hitter, but she once threw a one-hitter in exhibition.

Erickson decided to retire after three seasons because "we won just about everything." However, she had other motives. "I hated those all-night bus trips," she admitted. She also married Burt Sauer in November 1950. The couple produced two children: Nancy and Jim. Lou went to work in her husband's bowling alley and became a housewife. She also coached girl's softball. She now lives in Arcadia, Wisconsin.

PITCHING										BATTING			FIELDING			
W–L	PCT	ERA	G	IP	H	R	ER	BB	SO	BA	AB	H	PO	A	E	FA
34–16	.680	2.13	55	448	343	133	106	122	130	.210	167	35	27	129	9	.946

Fabac (Bretting), Elizabeth "Betty"

Born: April 6, 1922, Detroit, Michigan. 5'3", 115, 2nd Base, BR, TR. Kenosha Comets, 1945–48.

Elizabeth Fabac was an excellent second baseman for the Kenosha Comets and once led the league in fielding at her position.

Fabac was playing with a softball league in Detroit when a scout asked her to come to the All-American League. "I wasn't sure of going at first," she said of the experience. She went and enjoyed playing at military bases when the league was in spring training at Opa-locka, Florida, in 1945.

In her first season with Kenosha, she hit .199 and fielded her position well. The following season she broke her ankle when a girl jumped on it trying to break up a double-play attempt. She was out for the season, but the team let her stay for a morale booster. She came back from the injury and played two more seasons. In her last season in 1947, she led the league in fielding with a .963 average, which included 19 errors. She also swiped a career high 43 bases that year.

Elizabeth "Betty" Fabac

She gave up baseball to wed Naval Academy graduate Ralph Bretting in 1949. They raised two children: George and Patricia. Fabac took up golf and became quite good at the sport, winning six local club and county tournaments in a row during one stretch.

Her husband suffered a stroke in 1990 and she now cares for him on a full-time basis. She had a hip replaced in 1992, which slowed her golf game. She now lives in Palm Desert, California.

				BATTING										FIELDING			
G	BA	AB	H	2B	3B	HR	SB	BB	SO	R	RBI		PO	A	E	DP	FA
321	.179	1102	197	7	5	1	124	144	114	141	47		548	581	60	43	.950

Lillian "Lil" Faralla

Faralla, Lillian "Lil"

Born: July 29, 1924, Brooklyn, New York. 5'6", 160, Pitcher, Second Base, Outfield, TR, BR. Peoria Redwings, 1946; Fort Wayne Daisies, 1947; South Bend Blue Sox, 1948–49; Grand Rapids Chicks, 1950; Kalamazoo Lassies, 1950; South Bend Blue Sox, 1951.

Lillian Faralla threw two no-hitters and played for one championship team during her rollercoaster six year career.

Faralla moved to California at an early age and started playing softball at age 12. When the war came, softball was suspended because of the blackouts. She joined the Coast Guard and became a boatswain's mate. After the war, she received a telegram from the league. "I've got no idea why they sent me a telegram," Faralla recalled.

She took a train to Chicago and the league assigned her to Peoria without a tryout. "They let me watch the first game of a doubleheader, signed me and then let me play the second game. In my first at bat I got hit in the nose," she said. The nose wasn't broken, but she still has a seam across her nose where the ball hit.

She began her career as an infielder before Fort Wayne tried her out as a pitcher. The first two seasons on the mound were a humbling experience for her as she went 3–12 for the Daisies in 1947 and 10–20 for the Blue Sox the following year. Number 18 once pitched in a 19-inning contest that ended in a tie.

Then in 1949 Faralla found her rhythm, throwing two no-hitters during the season. She nearly had a perfect game in a seven-inning affair that was spoiled by an error in the last inning. The other was a nine-inning game. "That's when I asked for a raise and got it," she remembered.

After an off year with two teams, she returned to South Bend to help them win the pennant and championship with her 15–4 mark. One of her victories came during the playoffs.

Faralla could foresee the demise of the league so she decided to end her career on a high note. She served as a deputy sheriff for the Los Angeles County Sheriff's Department for 23 years and retired in 1976. She now lives in Coronado, California.

PITCHING										BATTING			FIELDING				
W–L	PCT	ERA	G	IP	H	R	ER	BB	SO	BA	AB	H	PO	A	E	DP	FA
55–56	.495	2.00	146	979	706	330	217	398	240	.206	617	127	144	378	25	4	.964

Farrow (Rapp), Elizabeth

Born: Aug. 10, 1926, Peoria, Illinois. 5'7", 130, Pitcher, TR, BR. Minneapolis Millerettes, 1944; Rockford Peaches, 1944.

Elizabeth Farrow had one of the poorest season performances on record with her 1–12 mark in 1944 for two teams. She still lives in Peoria.

PITCHING										FIELDING			
W–L	PCT	ERA	G	IP	H	R	ER	BB	SO	PO	A	E	FA
1–12	.077	5.64	19	99	72	93	62	85	16	12	33	6	.882

BATTING										
BA	AB	H	2B	3B	HR	SB	BB	SO	R	RBI
.167	36	6	1	0	0	0	2	3	1	1

Faut (Eastman), Jean

Born: Nov. 17, 1925, Greenville, Pennsylvania. 5'4", 137, Pitcher, 3rd Base, Outfield, TR, BR. South Bend Blue Sox, 1946–53.

Twice the Player of the Year, Jean Faut is regarded by many as the best overhand pitcher in the league's history. She set many season and career records during her eight-year career.

Unlike many of the women she played with, Faut never played softball when she was growing up in East Greenville, Pennsylvania. Her interest in hardball stemmed from living two blocks from a semi-pro team and practicing with them. "They taught me all the pitches," she admitted. The team even let her pitch in some exhibition games. She also met her first husband, Karl Winsch.

A scout spotted the young pitcher and asked her to come to spring training in Pascagoula, Mississippi, in 1946. There were some 500 players at the camp, and Faut was one of the first selections by the South Bend Blue Sox, a team that had finished next to last place in the league the year before.

Jean Faut

The Blue Sox started their new acquisition at third base because of her strong arm. She didn't pitch because the league was still using the underhand motion. Near the end of the season, the league began allowing sidearm delivery and Faut was called on to pitch. She wasn't used to the delivery, but that didn't hinder her performance. The following season she compiled a 8–3 record. She once pitched a marathon 22-inning contest.

In 1948, the ball was reduced to 10½ inches and pitching was now all overhand. Faut couldn't ask for a better situation. She had an arsenal of pitches and could now unleash them on the players. "I knew what I was going to throw. They would try to guess, but the pitcher's in charge. The batter has to watch for the ball," she explained.

She didn't get off to a great start in 1948 due to the delivery of her first son in March. She started 34 games and compiled a 16–11 record. Her record improved to 24–8 the next season and her ERA dropped to 1.10.

Faut was a fierce competitor. Once when a weak-hitting batter got a hit off of her, she slammed her mitt to the ground and uttered: "She's hitting .050 and gets a hit off me!"

By 1951 she was mowing down batters with her control and trickery on the mound. This led to a masterful performance on July 21. She retired 27 Rockford Peaches in a row for a perfect game. On the season she was 15–7 with a 1.33 ERA. She helped lead the Blue Sox to their first Shaughnessy Series victory. To top off her year, the league named her Player of the Year.

In 1952, she put up even better numbers, 20–2 with a minuscule 0.93 ERA. But the year was not without the controversy of her being married to the manager. Dissension set in and some players wouldn't speak to her or her husband. Then near the end of the season, six players walked out over a controversy, leaving the team with a dozen players. They were called the "Dutiful Dozen." Faut still led the team to the playoffs with her marvelous pitching and clean-up hitting. In the final game of the series, she almost singlehandedly beat the Peaches. She hit two triples and also stopped Rockford on the mound. "I was hitting good that night," she said.

The following season she continued her mastery over league batters. Then on September 3 she pitched her second perfect game. She was again picked as the Player of the Year. The team finished next to last place, however.

Because of all the hassle with the other players, Faut decided to quit the league after the 1953 season. She opted to watch her husband manage from the bleachers. "I would sit in the stands and cry," she regretfully recalled. She really wanted to be out in the field. She got tired of sitting in the stands and took up bowling.

Faut became an excellent bowler and became one of the charter members of the women's pro tour. She rolled with the pros until 1988 and once recorded a 299 game, one pin short of perfection. She still bowls occasionally with the senior women's tour. She also spent five years at Notre Dame doing research on mosquitoes.

She ended the league with the second most career wins (140) and best career ERA (1.23). She also set the single season record for best winning percentage (.909, 20–2) and led the league in ERA, wins and strikeouts for three seasons.

Faut divorced Winsch and remarried. Her second husband died in 1993. She has two sons, Larry and Kevin Winsch, and four grandchildren. She now lives in Rock Hill, South Carolina.

PITCHING

W–L	PCT	ERA	G	IP	H	R	ER	BB	SO
140–64	.686	1.23	235	1780	1093	403	243	589	913

FIELDING

PO	A	E	DP	FA
467	1392	143	34	.929

BATTING

AB	H	2B	3B	HR	SB	BB	SO	R	RBI
1610	391	52	8	3	112	233	100	180	203

Fenton, Peggy

Born: Oct. 12, 1927, Forest Park, Illinois. 5'6", 128. BL, TL. Muskegon Lassies, 1948; South Bend Blue Sox, 1948.

Peggy Fenton signed with the league in 1948. She now lives in Palos Hills, Illinois.

Ferguson (Key), Dorothy "Dottie"

Born: Feb. 17, 1923, Winnipeg, Manitoba, Canada. 5'6", 125, 2nd Base, 3rd Base, Outfield, Pitcher, BR, TR. Rockford Peaches, 1945–54; Peoria Redwings, 1946.

Dorothy Ferguson was one of the career leaders in the total games she played during her decade in the league. She was a dependable fielder and hitter and played on four championship Rockford teams. She married Don Key in 1949 and the couple fostered two children, Douglas and Donna. She became an American citizen in 1955. She now lives in Rockford, Illinois.

BATTING

G	BA	AB	H	2B	3B	HR	SB	BB	SO	R	RBI
950	.201	3216	645	49	14	2	461	396	281	520	199

PITCHING

W–L	PCT	ERA	G	IP	H	R	ER	BB	SO
0–2	.000	10.00	4	12	11	14	10	14	3

FIELDING

PO	A	E	DP	FA
1596	334	100	45	.951

Ferguson, Fern

Pitcher, TR, BR. Racine Belles, 1945

Fern Ferguson pitched in one game for Racine in 1945.

PITCHING											BATTING			
W–L	PCT	ERA	G	IP	H	R	ER	BB	SO		BA	G	AB	H
0–0	.000	4.90	1	11	12	10	6	9	0		.250	3	4	1

Figlo, Josephine

Born: April 9, 1923, Milltown, New Jersey. 5'3", 140, Outfield, BR, TR. Racine Belles, 1944; Milwaukee Chicks, 1944.

Josephine Figlo was a weak-hitting outfielder for a season with two teams in the league.

BATTING												FIELDING				
G	BA	AB	H	2B	3B	HR	SB	BB	SO	R	RBI	PO	A	E	DP	FA
15	.059	34	2	1	0	0	4	4	13	7	3	11	0	4	0	.733

Filarski (Steffes), Helen "Fil"

Born: May 11, 1924, Detroit, Michigan. 5'2", 125, 3rd Base, 2nd Base, Outfield, BR, TR. Rockford Peaches, 1945–46; Peoria Redwings, 1947; Kenosha Comets, 1947; South Bend Blue Sox, 1948–50.

Helen Filarski was the best defensive third baseman in 1946 when she committed 32 errors for a .931 fielding average. Her best season at the plate came in her last year as she hit .209. She was a member of the 1945 championship Rockford Peaches in her first season. After baseball, she got married and raised six children. She had 16 grandchildren at last count and lives in Harper Woods, Michigan.

BATTING												FIELDING				
G	BA	AB	H	2B	3B	HR	SB	BB	SO	R	RBI	PO	A	E	DP	FA
534	.189	1683	318	25	15	1	115	248	137	189	141	866	1224	300	99	.875

Fischer, Alva Jo "Tex"

Born: Aug. 23, 1926, San Antonio, Texas. Died: Aug. 13, 1973. 5'9", 135, Pitcher, Shortstop, TR, BR. Rockford Peaches, 1945; Muskegon Lassies, 1947–49.

An average pitcher, Alva Jo "Tex" Fisher was a member of the pennant-winning Muskegon and Rockford Peaches. Fischer began playing organized softball at age 11. When she first came to the league, she was used primarily as a pitcher, but she evolved into a good shortstop as well. As a hitter, she was one of the best in the league in 1946 with a .309 average. She was the best fielding shortstops in 1949 with a .972 average and only 23 errors. Her best season on the mound came in 1949 when she was 10–7.

After baseball she was a physical education teacher in San Antonio, Texas.

PITCHING									
W–L	PCT	ERA	G	IP	H	R	ER	BB	SO
34–37	.479	2.40	91	608	419	239	162	296	228

BATTING											FIELDING				
BA	AB	H	2B	3B	HR	SB	BB	SO	R	RBI	PO	A	E	DP	FA
.223	1228	274	24	6	0	65	107	89	91	131	604	982	135	48	.922

Fisher (Stevens), Lorraine

Born: July 5, 1928, Detroit, Michigan. 5'6", 120, Pitcher, Outfield, TR, BR. Rockford Peaches, 1947; Grand Rapids Chicks, 1948–49.

Lorraine Fisher was a winning pitcher for two teams in three years. Her 16–11 record in 1948 helped Grand Rapids win the pennant. She now lives in Jackson, Michigan.

PITCHING

W–L	PCT	ERA	G	IP	H	R	ER	BB	SO
33–26	.559	2.52	70	460	231	187	129	250	127

BATTING												FIELDING				
G	BA	AB	H	2B	3B	HR	SB	BB	SO	R	RBI	PO	A	E	DP	FA
131	.138	327	45	2	1	0	7	28	30	29	18	94	93	14	2	.930

Fitzgerald, Meryle

Rapid City, South Dakota. Pitcher. Fort Wayne Daisies, 1946

PITCHING

G
2

Flaherty, Mary

Ozone Park, New York. Racine Belles, 1948.

Florreich, Lois "Flash"

Born: April 29, 1927, Webster Grove, Missouri. Died: Sept. 11, 1991. 5'5", 140, Pitcher, Outfield, 3rd Base, TR, BR. South Bend Blue Sox, 1943–45; Kenosha Comets, 1945–46; Rockford Peaches, 1947–50.

One of the original players of the league, Lois Florreich was the 1949 pitching champion and a three time All-Star. She holds the league's best single season ERA.

Florreich was one of the youngest players in the league when it began. "Flash," who

Lois "Flash" Florreich

earned the nickname for stealing bases, started out as an outfielder but was moved to third base when she went to Kenosha in 1945. In 1946, sidearm pitching came about in the league and she was put on the mound where she had two losing seasons in a row before she found her touch.

In 1948 she compiled a 22–10 record in leading Rockford to the championship. She was named to the All-Star team.

Florreich continued her domination the next year with a 22–7 record and lowest ERA (0.67) for the pitching crown and a spot on the All-Star squad. She also threw the most innings (269) and had the best winning percentage (.759) in 1949.

In her last year in the league, she again led the Peaches to the championship with a 20–8 record and the league lead in strikeouts (171). She was named to her third consecutive All-Star team.

After baseball, she owned and operated the Sonic Wire Company until 1968. Then she moved to northern Idaho to run a mobile home park. She retired and moved to Mexico, where she enjoyed fishing until her death in 1991.

PITCHING

W–L	PCT	ERA	G	IP	H	R	ER	BB	SO
86–60	.589	1.40	165	1304	708	343	203	449	774

BATTING

BA	AB	H	2B	3B	HR	SB	BB	SO	R	RBI
.204	1774	362	31	27	6	251	170	238	242	139

FIELDING

PO	A	E	DP	FA
547	919	152	36	.906

Folder (Powell), Rose

Born: May 12, 1926, Auburn, Illinois. 5'6", 140, Pitcher, Outfield, TR, BR. Kenosha Comets, 1944.

Rose Folder spent one season in the AAGPBL with the pennant-winning Kenosha Comets.

A pastor taught her everything about baseball when she was a teenager at a Lutheran school. Then she played for a fast-pitch softball town team.

In 1943, Folder made spark plugs in a factory in Chicago during the day and played softball for the Tungsten Sparks at night. A scout for the league spotted her with the team and invited her to a tryout the following season.

Folder got a tryout in Peru, Illinois, and was taken as a relief pitcher and pitch hitter. "We learned to play baseball from former major leaguers and were turned from tomboys to ladies by the charm school classes," she recalled.

During the season, she played in less than ten games. In the playoffs against Racine she dove for a ball in left field and sprained an ankle. "They went on to the playoffs and I went home," she said. She married a sailor, but the marriage didn't last. She married again in 1946 and raised six children: Barbara, Rita, Roger, David, Susan and Mary Ellen. She now has ten

grandchildren and one great grandchild. She ran a day care business in Carnation, Washington, for 25 years.

She traveled to the National Baseball Hall of Fame in 1994 to see her name. "That was the biggest thrill of my life," she said.

PITCHING

W–L	PCT	ERA	G	IP	H	R	ER	BB	SO
2–7	.222	5.67	14	73	75	67	46	49	15

BATTING

BA	AB	H
.261	207	54

FIELDING

PO	A	E	FA
2	31	3	.917

Rose Folder

Foss, Anita

Born: Aug. 5, 1921, Providence, Rhode Island. 5'2", 118, Pitcher, Utility, TR, BR. Springfield Sallies, 1948; Grand Rapids Chicks, 1948; Muskegon Lassies, 1948–49; Rockford Peaches, 1949.

Anita Foss played two lackluster seasons in the league as an infielder and pitcher.

Foss began playing baseball at any early age with her four brothers in Rhode Island. When she was in high school, she played many sports and became the captain of the varsity softball team. After high school, she married and her husband went off to war. He was killed in action.

She tried to heal the wounds of death by playing softball. She went to a tryout in New Jersey that was held inside an armory because of rain. After making the league, she was sent to Opa-locka, Florida, for spring training with Springfield. "That was the right kind of medicine to get away," she commented.

Before she played a game with the Sallies, she was sent to Muskegon, who used her at second base. Then at the end of the season, Foss went to Grand Rapids. She hit .122 for the season.

The following year, Rockford attempted to turn her into a pitcher. She threw a couple of games there before coming back to Muskegon. She pitched in three games but had no decisions.

Her career ended and she went back home. A few years later she visited California. She liked it so much, she decided to move there and has been there ever since. She went to work for Douglas Aircraft and became the first woman supervisor in her department. She retired in 1969 after 17 years with the company.

Recently, she was named Woman of the Year by the Santa Monica YMCA. "It's the highlight of my life," she said. She now golfs frequently and is on the rules committee.

PITCHING

G	IP
3	6

BATTING												FIELDING				
G	BA	AB	H	2B	3B	HR	SB	BB	SO	R	RBI	PO	A	E	DP	FA
28	.117	51	6	1	0	0	5	14	11	5	5	35	26	7	2	.897

Foss (Weaver), Betty

Born: May 10, 1929, Metropolis, Illinois. 5'10", 180, 1st Base, Outfield, Pitcher, BB, TR. Fort Wayne Daisies, 1950–54.

Player of the Year in 1952, Betty Foss set many single-season and career records and was named to two All-Star teams.

As the oldest of the three Weaver sisters, she set an example for her younger sisters on the softball fields. All three played for Magnavox before joining Fort Wayne in 1950. Betty, who was already married, made an immediate impact on the team with her hitting. She led the league with a .346 average. Her fielding still needed some refining, though, as she committed 47 errors the first season.

Foss' fielding improved the next season and her bat was even hotter as she led the league in doubles (34) and average (.368). Surprisingly, she was still overlooked for the All-Star team because sports writers voted more for the veterans of the league.

In 1952 she led her team to its first-ever pennant. Foss led the league in runs (81), hits (137), doubles (26), triples (17) and RBI (74). She was second in batting to her sister, Joanne. Her accomplishments were rewarded with an All-Star selection and Player of the Year, the league's highest honor.

She led the league in several categories in 1953: runs (99), hits (144) and stolen bases (80). Her average —.321— was one of the best in the league. Fort Wayne won another pennant.

Betty Foss

The Daisies made it a three-peat in 1954 again with Foss' help. She was one of the best hitters in the league with a .352 average.

Her career .342 batting average is second only to her sister Joanne. Betty holds the single-season league records for hits, doubles and triples. She also holds the all-time record for doubles (117).

After the league folded, she joined Bill Allington's All-American Baseball Team and toured the country. When her traveling days were over, she went to work for Wangs Pumps in Fort Wayne.

She retired in 1995 and moved back to her hometown of Metropolis, Illinois.

BATTING

G	BA	AB	H	2B	3B	HR	SB	BB	SO	R	RBI
498	.342	1898	649	117	30	32	294	199	176	401	312

PITCHING

W–L	PCT	ERA	G	IP	H	R	ER	BB	SO
0–1	.000	54.05	2	1	2	7	6	5	1

FIELDING

PO	A	E	DP	FA
3638	330	151	194	.963

Francis, Betty "BF"

Born: July 7, 1931, Maquoketa, Iowa. 5'4", 140, Outfield, BR, TR. Chicago Colleens, 1949; Muskegon Lassies, 1949; Kalamazoo Lassies, 1950–53; South Bend Blue Sox, 1954.

Francis played five years in the league and displayed some power with nine home runs.

The Iowa native moved to Chicago before her playing days and was a track and field star. She first played for the Chicago Colleens rookie touring team in 1949 before being called up to the Muskegon team, which moved to Kalamazoo the next season.

In 1954, she was traded to South Bend for the last season of the league.

After baseball, she worked as a machine operator for 28 years in a canning company in the Windy City, while still playing professional softball. Retired, she still calls Chicago her home. In all, she played 14 years of amateur ball and 17 years of professional ball.

Betty "BF" Francis

BATTING

G	BA	AB	H	2B	3B	HR	SB	BB	SO	R	RBI
429	.251	1318	331	38	3	9	42	185	76	157	125

FIELDING

PO	A	E	DP	FA
438	55	38	7	.929

Frank (Dummerth), Edna "Frankie"

Born: June 15, 1924, St. Louis, Missouri. 5'5", 128, Catcher, BR, TR. Minneapolis Millerettes, 1944; Racine Belles, 1944.

Edna Frank played only part of one season. When she was traded to Racine, she never reported and went back home.

She joined the Navy and spent two years in the service. Then she went to work for Southwestern Bell Telephone and played amateur softball. In 1950 she married a man she had met at the ballpark. They had eight children: Dennis, Diane, Donna, Denise, Danny, Dale, Danette and Darlene. She now has 24 grandchildren, probably more than any other former player. Her husband died in 1995. She now lives in St. Louis.

BATTING												FIELDING				
G	BA	AB	H	2B	3B	HR	SB	BB	SO	R	RBI	PO	A	E	DP	FA
16	.109	46	5	0	0	0	1	1	4	1	2	53	10	6	2	.913

Franks, Hermina

Born: Sept. 7, 1914, Ocanta, Wisconsin. 5'4", 120. Kenosha Comets, 1946

BATTING			
G	BA	AB	H
1	.000	1	0

Fritz, Betty Jane

Oshkosh, Wisconsin. Died: Date Unknown. 5'5", 130, Outfield, BR, TR. Rockford Peaches, 1943.

One of the original players of the league, Betty Fritz was good-hitting outfielder for Rockford for one season.

BATTING												FIELDING				
G	BA	AB	H	2B	3B	HR	SB	BB	SO	R	RBI	PO	A	E	DP	FA
98	.210	348	73	4	1	0	29	9	16	38	43	152	17	9	4	.949

Froning (O'Meara), Mary

Born: Aug. 26, 1934, Minster, Ohio. 5'3", 118, Outfielder, Pitcher, TR, BR. South Bend Blue Sox, 1951–54.

Mary Froning played on two championship teams in her four years in the league.

Froning recalled playing softball in the 5th grade. The following year she joined a Catholic youth organization team managed by a priest. The teenager was scouted by Karl Snider of the Blue Sox and signed to the team in 1951.

The 1951 team was loaded with talent, so she spent a lot of time on the bench. The team won the pennant and playoffs that year. The following season Froning finally got her chance to play regularly after six players left the team in a dispute with manager Karl Winsch. She was one of only 12 players who helped the team capture its second consecutive playoff championship.

The Blue Sox broke up in 1953. "They traded a bunch of players," she explained. She became a regular the last two seasons before the league folded in 1954. Then she joined Bill Allington's All-American Girls Baseball Team, a barnstorming continuation team from the league.

In 1956, she became a stewardess with American Airlines along with her twin sister, Martha. She married Tom O'Meara in 1958 and raised four children: Kathy, Susan, John and Patricia. She now lives in Madison, Wisconsin.

Mary Froning

PITCHING

W–L	PCT	ERA	G	IP	H	R	ER	BB	SO
1–2	.333	5.55	6	13	10	14	8	16	4

BATTING · FIELDING

G	BA	AB	H	2B	3B	HR	SB	BB	SO	R	RBI	PO	A	E	DP	FA
209	.212	651	136	18	0	3	58	62	73	95	56	239	34	22	3	.925

Gacioch, Rose "Rosie"

Born: Aug. 31, 1915, Wheeling, West Virginia. 5'6", 160, Pitcher, Outfielder, 1st Base, 2nd Base, 3rd Base, TR, BR. South Bend Blue Sox, 1944; Rockford Peaches, 1945–54; Grand Rapids Chicks, 1950.

Twice an All-Star, Rose Gacioch was one of the best overhand pitchers in the All-American League for 11 seasons.

Gacioch's professional experience began in 1934 when she played a season with the All-Star Ranger Girls, a barnstorming team based in Chicago. By the time she came to the All-American League, she was 28, which led her teammates to call her "grandma." In her first season with South Bend, she was the best fielding outfielder, committing just two errors.

The following season she went to Rockford, and her team won the pennant and championship. When sidearm pitching started in 1946, she was tried out at pitcher and showed some promise, but she was needed more in the field. She could hit with the best of them, averaging .262 and tying two others for the most triples (9) on the season.

In 1948 the Peaches turned her into a full-time pitcher and she responded with a 14–5 record. She also helped her team win the championship. She was 9–2 the next year and the Peaches again won the championship. "Rosie" wasn't as sharp in 1950 and struggled to a 7–9 mark, but her team again won the pennant and championship.

Her best year on the mound came in 1951. She went 20–7 and was selected to the All-Star team. The next season she tied Jean Faut for the most wins (20), and she pitched the most innings (259). Again, she was picked as an All-Star.

In 1953 she threw her best game ever — a no-hitter against South Bend in a 5–1, seven-inning victory. In 1954, though, she led the league in losses (15) and runs allowed (113).

PITCHING

W–L	PCT	ERA	G	IP	H	R	ER	BB	SO
94–62	.603	2.48	174	1337	1118	545	368	412	326

BATTING | FIELDING

G	BA	AB	H	2B	3B	HR	SB	BB	SO	R	RBI	PO	A	E	DP	FA
925	.238	2955	703	69	34	18	167	200	162	270	352	1092	725	85	35	.955

Galdonik, Barbara

Born: Oct. 26, 1934, Kenosha, Wisconsin. 5'5", 130, 3rd Base. Battle Creek Belles, 1950–51.

Barbara Galdonik played in less than ten games with the league with Battle Creek over two seasons.

Gallegos, Luisa

Havana, Cuba. Pitcher. Peoria Redwings, 1948; South Bend Blue Sox, 1948.

Luisa Gallegos was a Cuban import who played one season in the league. The league held spring training in Cuba in 1947 and played exhibition games there in 1948.

PITCHING | BATTING

W–L	PCT	ERA	G	IP	H	R	ER	BB	SO	BA	AB	H
2–6	.250	5.79	16	73	46	55	47	76	37	.083	36	3

Ganote (Weise), Gertrude "Lefty"

Born: Feb. 17, 1920, Louisville, Kentucky. 5'4", 130, 1st Base, Pitcher, TL, BL. Kenosha Comets, 1944; South Bend Blue Sox, 1945.

Gertrude Ganote was an excellent fielder and the top defensive first baseman in 1944. She had some trouble making contact at the plate in her rookie season, as she led the league in strikeouts (60). She was sometimes used on the mound and appeared there in 22 games. She got married and was a cashier after baseball. She now lives in her hometown of Louisville, Kentucky.

PITCHING

W–L	PCT	ERA	G	IP	H	R	ER	BB	SO
6–8	.429	3.69	22	144	123	76	59	80	20

BATTING												FIELDING				
G	BA	AB	H	2B	3B	HR	SB	BB	SO	R	RBI	PO	A	E	DP	FA
178	.160	625	100	8	10	0	33	66	92	61	30	1421	23	25	27	.983

Garman (Hosted), Ann

Born: March 11, 1933, Avilla, Indiana. 5'6", 140, 1st Base. South Bend Blue Sox, 1953.

Ann Garman played in one season and became a teacher and a housewife after baseball. She has three children and seven grandchildren. She now lives in Wawaka, Indiana.

BATTING												FIELDING				
G	BA	AB	H	2B	3B	HR	SB	BB	SO	R	RBI	PO	A	E	DP	FA
21	.154	65	10	0	0	0	1	13	13	5	7	195	17	7	6	.967

Gascon, Eileen "Ginger"

Born: Dec. 1, 1931, Chicago, Illinois. 5'2", 115, 3rd Base, Outfield, BR, TR. Springfield Sallies, 1949; Grand Rapids Chicks, 1951; Battle Creek Belles, 1951; Peoria Redwings, 1951.

Eileen Gascon saw little action with three teams during the 1951 season. In 1972 she received a Presidential Sports Award for jogging. She taught for 33 years and has a pilot's license. She now lives in Elk Grove, Illinois.

BATTING												FIELDING				
G	BA	AB	H	2B	3B	HR	SB	BB	SO	R	RBI	PO	A	E	DP	FA
27	.184	87	16	2	0	0	7	16	22	12	4	51	2	2	0	.964

Gates, Barbara

Downers Grove, Illinois. Pitcher. Grand Rapids Chicks, 1953; South Bend Blue Sox, 1953; Fort Wayne Daisies, 1954.

Barbara Gates pitched the last two seasons of the league with three different teams, including the pennant-winning Fort Wayne Daisies. She ended up with a high ERA and a losing record.

PITCHING										BATTING			FIELDING			
W–L	PCT	ERA	G	IP	H	R	ER	BB	SO	BA	AB	H	PO	A	E	FA
1–4	.200	7.42	19	57	53	62	47	69	20	.105	19	2	6	15	1	.952

Geissinger (Harding), Jean Louise "Dutch" "Squeaky"

Born: June 25, 1934, Huntingdon, Pennsylvania. 5'6", 120, 2nd Base, Shortstop, Outfield, Relief Pitcher, BR, TR. Fort Wayne Daisies, 1951–54; Grand Rapids Chicks, 1952.

Twice an All-Star, Jean Geissinger was an excellent defensive player and a clutch hitter who led the league in RBI for two years, while helping the Daisies win two pennants.

Geissinger started playing baseball when she was a "little shaver," as her family had more boys in it than girls. When she moved to West Chester, Pennsylvania, she started playing organized sports such as field hockey, softball, track and basketball. Following her junior year in high school, her sister made contact with Max Carey during spring training and got her a tryout in Washington, D.C. Carey liked what he saw and assigned her to Fort Wayne.

"Dutch" mostly sat on the bench until veteran Dottie Schroeder sprained an ankle. She appeared in a few games, but she didn't become a starter until Evie Wawryshyn retired after the 1951 season. Geissinger was sent to Grand Rapids the next season because the Chicks needed a rookie. There she picked up the nickname "Squeaky" for her high-pitched voice. Then she was returned to the Daisies to play out the rest of her career.

No longer a rookie, Geissinger started swinging the bat like the rest of her teammates and the Daisies were unstoppable during the regular season, winning two pennants in a row. "We had a lot of free swingers," she said.

Jean Louise "Dutch" "Squeaky" Geissinger

She led the league in RBI in 1953 (81) and 1954 (91), which led to two All-Star team selections. She also finished second in hitting in 1954 with a .377 average.

After the league folded, she continued to tour and barnstorm the country with Bill Allington's All-Americans for three seasons. When the team faced a men's team, the two teams would switch batteries—that's how she met Blaine Harding. The two fell in love and finally married in 1959. She ran clinics and umpired for 15 years after she quit the league. They fostered three athletic daughters: Ann, Karla and Jana. Now they are retired and have three grandchildren.

BATTING

G	BA	AB	H	2B	3B	HR	SB	BB	SO	R	RBI
.328	.306	1184	362	55	17	41	60	96	165	177	235

PITCHING

G	IP
5	10

FIELDING

PO	A	E	DP	FA
671	586	105	106	.923

George (McFaul), Genevieve "Gene"

Born: Sept. 22, 1927, Regina, Saskatchewan, Canada. 5'3", 110, Catcher, BR, TR. Muskegon Lassies, 1948.

Genevieve George followed in the footsteps of her sister, Mary "Bonnie" Baker, to play one season in the league.

George was 13 when she began playing in a city softball league. When she was 16, her sister and five other Regina softball players went to play in the AAGPBL. She continued to play in Regina until a scout noticed her and gave her her big chance to play the league.

Like her sister, "Gene" was a catcher, a much needed commodity in the league. Yet, the rookie caught in just 14 games during the season. "I didn't get much of a chance down there," she explained. She was not offered a contract by the league the following season.

She came back to Regina and took up playing third base. Gene married Canadian Football League tackle Jim McFaul in 1951. The two fostered boys: Jim and George. She went to the world championships with the team in 1954 and played with Regina until 1959. Her husband passed away in 1994. She now enjoys time with her five grandchildren.

BATTING / FIELDING

G	BA	AB	H	2B	3B	HR	SB	BB	SO	R	RBI		PO	A	E	DP	FA
15	.154	13	2	0	0	0	0	0	4	1	2		19	2	0	0	1.000

Georges, Beulah Ann

Born: May 10, 1923, Columbus, Ohio. 5'5", 129, Pitcher, TR, BR. Chicago Colleens, 1948; Fort Wayne Daisies, 1948.

Beulah Georges was a mediocre pitcher for one season in the league with two teams. She was a chaperone on the player's development tour in 1949. After baseball, she worked in real estate.

PITCHING										BATTING		
W–L	PCT	ERA	G	IP	H	R	ER	BB	SO	BA	AB	H
0–4	.000	5.63	10	48	57	38	30	28	5	.125	16	2

Gianfrancisco, Philomena Theresa "Phil" "Frisco"

Born: April 20, 1923, Chicago, Illinois. Died: Jan. 18, 1992. 5'2", 134, Outfield, BL, TR. Grand Rapids Chicks, 1945–47; Racine Belles, 1948.

Philomena Gianfrancisco had the longest name in the league, but she was a little short on talent with an average bat and glove.

She also was a champion hurdler and toured the country with the Hurricanes in 1938. "Frisco" played amateur softball in Chicago for several years before entering the league. In 1946, she hit a career-best .225 with Grand Rapids.

A knee injury sidelined her for most of 1947 and she underwent surgery to correct the problem. She bounced back in 1948 with Racine and helped them win the pennant.

BATTING												FIELDING				
G	BA	AB	H	2B	3B	HR	SB	BB	SO	R	RBI	PO	A	E	DP	FA
265	.205	877	180	23	5	6	73	106	88	87	94	201	29	11	78	.954

Gilchrist, Jean

Born: June 13, 1926, New Westminister, British Columbia, Canada. 5'5", 125, Catcher, BR, TR. Peoria Redwings, 1946.

Jean Gilchrist was in the league for two months in 1946 with Peoria.

BATTING			
G	BA	AB	H
3	.167	6	1

Gilmore (Hawton), June

Born: June 13, 1922, Peoria, Illinois. Died: Jan. 6, 1980. 5'1", 110, Outfielder. Rockford Peaches, 1944.

June Gilmore was an outfielder for Rockford during the second season of the league.

Glaser, Rose Mary "Hap"

Born: October 22, 1921, Cincinnati, Ohio. 5'10", 145, Outfield, Pitcher. Kenosha Comets, 1944.

BATTING			
G	BA	AB	H
1	.000	3	0

Golden, Thelma

Pitcher. Rockford Peaches, 1943.

One of the original players of the league, Thelma Golden played very little in her only season in the league.

Left: **Fern Shollenberger.** *Right:* **Bethany Goldsmith.**

Goldsmith, Bethany

Born: Oct. 6, 1927, Elgin, Illinois.
5'10", 160, Pitcher, TR, BR.
Kenosha Comets, 1948–50.

Bethany Goldsmith played sandlot ball at age 12 and organized softball as a teenager with McGraw Electric. A former player on her softball team, Charlene Barnett, entered the league in 1947 and talked Goldsmith into attending the next spring training in Opa-locka. She was an outfielder, but she also had a good arm and the league was looking for overhand pitchers. She was taken as a hurler and assigned to Kenosha.

During her three-year run in the league, she recalled throwing a one-hitter but losing to Fort Wayne. Then she pitched the second game of the doubleheader and won. She also recalled a game in which manager Chet Grant left her out on the mound too long and she gave up a lot of runs. "I was out in the jungle that night. I wondered when he was going to take me out," she said.

One of her most memorable trips during her tenure was a Central American tour. She said it was "neat," yet scary at times. "I was never so glad to get back to the United States," she explained.

After baseball, she worked 30 years with AT&T and retired in 1984. She now goes to league reunions and plays golf in her home of Orlando, Florida.

PITCHING										BATTING			FIELDING			
W–L	PCT	ERA	G	IP	H	R	ER	BB	SO	BA	AB	H	PO	A	E	FA
34–34	.500	2.72	87	622	410	251	188	332	246	.160	212	34	31	132	12	.932

Gosbee, Anne

Essex, Massachusetts. Died: Date Unknown. Shortstop, 2nd Base. Grand Rapids Chicks, 1953–54; Rockford Peaches, 1954.

Anne Gosbee played the last two seasons of the league with two different teams. She was with Grand Rapids when it won the league championship in 1953.

BATTING													FIELDING				
G	BA	AB	H	2B	3B	HR	SB	BB	SO	R	RBI		PO	A	E	DP	FA
75	.136	118	16	0	0	0	1	25	11	22	7		89	87	15	17	.922

Graham (Douglas), Mary Lou

Born: Aug. 15, 1936, South Bend, Indiana. 5'7", 149, Pitcher. South Bend Blue Sox, 1953.

Mary Lou Graham was a batgirl with South Bend before she became a player for one season. She married after baseball and now lives in Arizona.

PITCHING	
G	IP
6	8

Grambo (Hundeby), Thelma

Born: Oct. 28, 1923, Domremy, Saskatchewan, Canada. 5'7", 165, Catcher, BR, TR. Grand Rapids Chicks, 1946.

Thelma Grambo played less than ten games with Grand Rapids in 1946.

The Canadian began playing softball at age 8 in public school. In 1942, she joined the Saskatoon Pats and was noticed by the All-American League. Grambo was sent to Pascagoula, Mississippi, for spring training and was assigned to Grand Rapids.

She married Bob Hundley in 1947 and never returned to the league. The couple raised six children: David, Art, Don, Ron, Carol, Larry and Ken. The two now have 16 grandchildren. She went to the league's 50th reunion in 1993. She was named to the Saskatchewan Sports Hall of Fame and the North Battleford Baseball of Fame. She now lives in Elbow, Saskatchewan.

Grant, Olga

Calgary, Alberta, Canada. Outfield, BL, TR. Milwaukee Chicks, 1944.

Olga Grant was an outfielder with the championship Milwaukee Chicks in 1944.

BATTING													FIELDING				
G	BA	AB	H	2B	3B	HR	SB	BB	SO	R	RBI		PO	A	E	DP	FA
21	.247	73	18	1	0	0	9	7	6	6	6		17	0	1	0	.944

Green, Dorothy

Born: April 30, 1921, Natick, Massachusetts. Died: Date Unknown. 5'10", 150, Catcher, BR, TR. Rockford Peaches, 1943–47.

Dorothy Green played five seasons and was the best fielding catcher in 1944 with only 18 errors and a .962 average. She was one of the tallest players in the league. After playing she became a chaperone for six more seasons.

G	BA	AB	H	2B	3B	HR	SB	BB	SO	R	RBI	PO	A	E	DP	FA
								BATTING						FIELDING		
280	.140	767	107	9	6	1	44	103	127	73	43	981	186	49	0	.958

Guest, Geraldine "Jerry"

Flint, Michigan. Died: Date unknown. Outfield. Peoria Redwings, 1951.

Geraldine Guest played a season for Peoria in 1951. She began playing softball at age 15. "Jerry" worked in a spark plug factory before coming to the league.

G	BA	AB	H	2B	3B	HR	SB	BB	SO	R	RBI	PO	A	E	DP	FA
								BATTING						FIELDING		
26	.119	42	5	0	0	0	1	3	12	5	2	15	2	0	1	1.000

Gutz, Julia "Gutzie"

Born: Dec. 4, 1926, Storm Lake, Iowa. 5'5", 155, Catcher, Outfield, BR, TR. Springfield Sallies, 1948; Muskegon Lassies, 1949; Kenosha Comets, 1950.

Julia Gutz was the Cal Ripken of the league as she once played 110 consecutive games without missing an inning. The light-hitting, good-fielding catcher's best season came in 1950 when she hit .203 in 112 games. After baseball, she worked as an electronic technician at Honeywell before she began running a resort in Lake Kabetogama, Minnesota.

G	BA	AB	H	2B	3B	HR	SB	BB	SO	R	RBI	PO	A	E	DP	FA
								BATTING						FIELDING		
235	.175	709	124	13	5	1	14	63	94	62	44	846	238	55	24	.952

Habben, Carol

Born: May 15, 1933, Midland Park, New Jersey. Died: Jan. 11, 1997. 5'5", 135, Outfield, Pitcher, BR, TR. Rockford Peaches, 1953; Kalamazoo Lassies, 1954.

Carol Habben was a solid slugger over the last two seasons of the league.

Habben began playing ball on sandlots at age 12 and joined the Garfield Flashettes two years later. She joined the Berger sisters in going to a league tryout and all three girls made the league. Habben went to Rockford. She spent a year with the Peaches before being traded to Kalamazoo.

When the ball was shrunk to major league size, Habben showed exactly how much power she had in her bat. She slammed out 15 homers in 1954. "I knew I could hit," she said.

Twice during her stay in the league she was called in to pitch a couple of innings after the opposition had a huge lead. "I hit the first batter right in the behind," she recalled. The first batter was one of the best in the league, Betty Foss.

After the league folded, Habben played ASA fast-pitch softball in Linden, New Jersey, until 1973. She worked 37 years for Merck as a credit manager and retired in 1994. She lived in Ringwood, New Jersey, before her death.

BATTING

G	BA	AB	H	2B	3B	HR	SB	BB	SO	R	RBI
190	.240	576	133	10	2	15	13	57	89	64	65

PITCHING

G	IP
2	4

FIELDING

PO	A	E	DP	FA
244	85	39	6	.894

Haefner, Ruby

Pitcher, Catcher. Fort Wayne Daisies, 1948.

Haefner was primarily a catcher, but twice she ventured to the other side of the battery during her year with the Daisies.

PITCHING

W–L	PCT	ERA	G	IP	H	R	ER	BB	SO
0–1	.000	13.51	2	2	6	6	3	0	0

BATTING

G	BA	AB	H	2B	3B	HR	SB	BB	SO	R	RBI
59	.160	156	25	1	0	0	3	15	33	9	8

FIELDING

PO	A	E	DP	FA
195	49	6	3	.976

Hageman (Hargraves), Johanna

Born: Dec. 17, 1918, Chicago, Illinois. Died: February 1984. 5'9", 155, 1st Base, BR, TR. South Bend Blue Sox, 1943–45.

Johanna Hageman was the best fielding first baseman the first year of the league, making only 21 errors and compiling a .983 average. She became a chaperone with Kenosha after her playing days and moved to California.

BATTING

G	BA	AB	H	2B	3B	HR	SB	BB	SO	R	RBI
320	.167	1011	169	14	8	1	58	128	87	79	82

FIELDING

PO	A	E	DP	FA
3220	94	59	93	.983

Haine (Daniels), Audrey "Audie" "Dimples"

Born: May 9, 1927, Winnipeg, Manitoba, Canada. 5'9", 150, Pitcher, TR, BR. Minneapolis Millerettes, 1944; Fort Wayne Daisies, 1945–46; Grand Rapids Chicks, 1946–47; Peoria Redwings, 1947–48; Rockford Peaches, 1951.

Credited with two no-hitters, Audrey Haines was a wild thrower, but she posted good numbers after her first season.

"Audie" got a slow start on the mound as she went 8–20 in her rookie season and led the league in earned runs (124) and wild pitches (29). One of her eight victories was a sparkling no-hitter against Kenosha on Aug. 26. She helped Minneapolis win a pennant and championship that season.

After her rookie year, she settled down some and posted a winning record each season; her best season coming in 1948 when she was 17–14. "Dimples" was credited with a no-hitter on June 15, 1945, in a rain-shortened, six-inning game. She left the league for two years and got married. She returned in 1951 and played under the name of Daniels.

She gave birth to six children after her playing days, including a set of twins. Then she helped start a business. She bowls and plays golf now from her home in Bay Village, Ohio.

PITCHING

W–L	PCT	ERA	G	IP	H	R	ER	BB	SO
72–70	.507	3.48	167	66	851	638	446	835	493

BATTING

G	BA	AB	H	2B	3B	HR	SB	BB	SO	R	RBI
167	.174	426	74	8	1	0	9	30	39	41	29

FIELDING

PO	A	E	FA
77	253	46	.878

Haines, Martha "Marty"

Covington, Kentucky. Kenosha Comets, 1947.

BATTING

G	BA	AB	H
1	.000	1	0

Hanna, Marjorie

Calgary, Alberta, Canada. Pitcher. Kenosha Comets, 1944.

PITCHING

W–L	PCT	ERA	G	IP	H	R	ER	BB	SO
0–1	.000	9.00	1	3	4	8	3	8	0

Harnett, Ann

Born: Aug. 10, 1920, Chicago, Illinois. Died: Date Unknown. 5'6", 139, 3rd Base, Catcher, Outfield, Pitcher, BR, TR. Kenosha Comets, 1943–46; Peoria Redwings, 1947.

The first player to be signed to the league, Ann Harnett was one of the league's best hitters and was named to its first All-Star team. She had the most extra base hits (26) on the season and drove in 69 runs. She also had the best fielding average (.891) among third basemen. Her average dropped off after the first season and she played four more years in the league. After baseball, she became a nun.

BATTING

G	BA	AB	H	2B	3B	HR	SB	BB	SO	R	RBI
314	.231	1532	354	34	28	7	65	96	53	168	171

PITCHING		FIELDING				
G	IP	PO	A	E	DP	FA
1	1	994	660	141	23	.921

Harney, Elise "Lee"

Born: June 22, 1925, Franklin, Illinois. Died: Date Unknown. 5'9", 135, Pitcher, TR, BR. Kenosha Comets, 1943–46; Fort Wayne Daisies, 1946–47.

Elise Harney turned in a losing career record, but tossed two no-hitters and two one-hitters during her five seasons in the league.

Harney was 19–19 her rookie season with Kenosha. The following season she threw her first no-hitter against Fort Wayne on June 14. She repeated the feat in 1945 with a no-hitter against Racine, but she allowed two runs to score. That same year she led the league in earned runs allowed (143).

During her baseball career, she graduated from the University of Wisconsin.

PITCHING										BATTING			FIELDING			
W–L	PCT	ERA	G	IP	H	R	ER	BB	SO	BA	AB	H	PO	A	E	FA
63–85	4.26	2.78	172	1229	991	610	379	449	366	.136	425	58	119	380	59	.894

Harrell (Doyle), Dorothy "Snookie"

Born: Feb. 4, 1924, Los Angeles, California. 5'4", 127, Shortstop, BR, TR. Rockford Peaches, 1944–52.

A four time All-Star, Dorothy Harrell played all of her nine seasons as Rockford's starting shortstop.

Nicknamed "Snookie" by her grandmother when she was born, Harrell started playing baseball with the boys in the playground when she was a little girl. At age 13 she began playing organized softball, but in 1942 the wartime blackouts ended the nightly softball leagues. She

Dorothy "Snookie" Harrell

also got married. Bill Allington, who later became her manager, recruited her and a number of California girls for the league. Harrell remembered arriving in Chicago for spring training on D-Day. "We were bombarded by the pigeons," she recalled.

She was assigned to Rockford after spring training. Harrell had some problems adjusting to the new league, hitting .177 and committing 48 errors. But after that her numbers got better and better. The following season the Peaches won the pennant and the championship with her help. Off the field she divorced her first husband.

In 1946 she had some run-ins with Allington and once received a suspension from the iron-fisted manager. This led her to ask for a trade the following season. The league was about to accommodate her and she attended spring training with Chicago. "It was already arranged for me to play in Chicago," she explained. The league, though, changed its mind and sent her back to Rockford. She nearly quit.

Then in 1947, Harrell came of age. She was named to her first All-Star team. The following season she hit .251, led the team in RBI (58) and helped Rockford win a championship. She continued to lead the team in RBI the next two seasons to gain her a spot on the All-Star team and assist the Peaches in winning the championships.

Harrell recalled a play the Peaches used to perfection in the playoffs. With runners on the corners, the runner on first base lured the pitcher into turning toward second for a pickoff attempt. Meanwhile, Harrell raced home from third for a run. It worked like a charm.

In April 1949 she married David Doyle and played under that name the rest of her career. She quit baseball after the 1952 season and went to college. After receiving a bachelor's degree from Long Beach State, she became a counselor and taught for 26 years, retiring in

1984. Her second husband died in 1960. She now plays golf, goes to reunions and signs autographs at card shows with a group calling themselves the Golden Diamond Girls.

Harrell was one of the lifetime leaders in put outs and assists at shortstop.

BATTING												FIELDING				
G	BA	AB	H	2B	3B	HR	SB	BB	SO	R	RBI	PO	A	E	DP	FA
799	.228	2922	667	56	37	9	229	203	95	326	306	1533	2085	322	0	.918

Hasham, Josephine "Jo"

Waltham, Massachusetts. Pitcher, Outfield, TL, BR. Muskegon Lassies, 1948; Peoria Redwings, 1948; South Bend Blue Sox, 1949; Peoria Redwings, 1950–51; Battle Creek Belles, 1952; Muskegon Belles, 1953; Rockford Peaches, 1954; Grand Rapids Chicks, 1954.

Jo Hasham was a mediocre left-handed hurler for seven seasons in the league.

Hasham began her career in 1948 with Muskegon and Peoria but didn't win a game. She suffered six losses on the season. She bounced back in 1949 with her career-best season, a 12–8 ledger with South Bend. With Peoria in 1950, she led the league in losses (19). She pitched much better the next two seasons before slumping again in 1953 with the most losses in the league (19). She never once played with a pennant-winning team, which is one reason for her losing record. She now lives in Miami, Florida.

PITCHING										BATTING			FIELDING			
W–L	PCT	ERA	G	IP	H	R	ER	BB	SO	BA	AB	H	PO	A	E	FA
58–88	.397	3.15	179	1164	1126	575	407	440	270	.211	629	133	82	357	28	.940

Hatzell (Volkert), Beverly

Born: Jan. 19, 1929, Redkey, Indiana. 5'6", 135, Pitcher, TR, BR. Chicago Colleens, 1949; Racine Belles, 1950; Battle Creek Belles, 1951; Peoria Redwings, 1951.

Beverly Volkert didn't have much luck on the mound and ended up with one of the poorest pitching records in league history.

Volkert played softball in Redkey and Muncie, Indiana, before she tried out for the AAGPBL. After spring training in Angola, Indiana, she was assigned to the Chicago Colleens, one of the league's two traveling teams in 1949. In one exhibition game with the Colleens, she pitched 14 innings and earned a 6–4 victory.

In 1950 she joined the regular league with the Racine Belles. During her first season, she shut out Rockford to end their seven-game win streak.

The following year the Racine franchise was moved to Battle Creek, Michigan. Halfway through the season, Volkert was moved to the Peoria Redwings and finished out the season there. She was not offered a contract for the next season.

After baseball, she went to work at a glass factory. She married in 1959 and moved to Hicksville, Ohio.

PITCHING										BATTING			FIELDING			
W–L	PCT	ERA	G	IP	H	R	ER	BB	SO	BA	AB	H	PO	A	E	FA
5–21	.192	5.26	39	207	197	175	121	180	73	.069	72	5	8	52	5	.923

Havlish, Jean "Grasshopper"

Born: Nov. 23, 1935, St. Paul, Minnesota. 5'6", 130, Shortstop, 3rd Base, BR, TR. Fort Wayne Daisies, 1952–54.

Jean Havlish was an excellent fielding shortstop for Fort Wayne during the waning years of the league.

At 8 years of age, she was watching the older girls play when the shortstop got hurt. She was given an opportunity to play, and after that she played all the time. "I can't even remember not playing baseball," she explained.

When she was a freshman in high school she saw an article about the league in the newspaper. Her father wrote the league, but they received no response. Then they went by bus to the Wrigley Chewing Gum Company, but Wrigley was out of the picture by then. They finally ended up in Kalamazoo, where she took infield practice, but was not signed. She was invited to a tryout and went, but again she was not signed. Then in 1952 she went to a tryout with Fort

Wayne and would have made the team, but Kalamazoo claimed her as their property even though she had never signed a contract with them. Finally, Kalamazoo traded her to the Daisies and she got her chance to play in the league in 1952. "Fort Wayne traded Dottie Schroeder for me — my only claim to fame," she commented. Schroeder was an All-Star shortstop.

The following season she became a starter for the team at either shortstop or third base. She helped Fort Wayne win the pennant.

In the last year of the league, she improved her batting average to .254 and clouted four homers with the major-league sized ball. The team moved the fences back after she hit two homers in the same game. She helped the

Jean "Grasshopper" Havlish

Daisies win a third consecutive pennant. During the season, "Grasshopper" started a triple play when she leaped and caught a line drive.

After the league ended, she played with the Allington All-Stars for a short while before going back to work for an insurance agency. She was a professional bowler for a while, too. Since 1975, she has been a housekeeper for a Catholic priest in her hometown of St. Paul.

			BATTING											FIELDING				
G	BA	AB	H	2B	3B	HR	SB	BB	SO	R	RBI		PO	A	E	DP	FA
193	.218	620	135	17	0	4	23	164	81	74	58		538	593	82	60	.932

Hay, Florence

Chicago, Illinois. Outfield, BR, TR. Chicago Colleens, 1949.

Florence Hay played one season on the player development team.

Haylett, Alice "Al" "Sis"

Born: April 2, 1923, Coldwater, Michigan. 5'6", 155, Pitcher, TR, BR. Grand Rapids Chicks, 1946–49.

Once an All-Star, Alice Haylett's candle burned brightly for one remarkable season that led her to a pitching championship.

Haylett learned baseball in the farm pastures around Coldwater, Michigan. She was playing for Vans Sport Shop in Battle Creek when she tried out for the league. She received an invitation to spring training and was assigned to Grand Rapids.

When "Al" first began the league, she was a mediocre underhand pitcher. She switched to sidearm pitching the following season and found that more to her liking, going 19–11 and leading the Chicks to the championship.

Then in 1948 "Sis" — nickname she picked up from lookalike Alma Ziegler — changed to overhand pitching. She threw a fastball and curveball that baffled batters with remarkable accuracy. She went 25–5 on the season with a 0.77 ERA, leading to her selection as the pitching champion and All-Star team member. In addition, she helped the

Alice "Al" "Sis" Haylett

Chicks win a pennant. She considers a 1–0 victory over South Bend hurler Jean Faut in 20 innings as her greatest victory ever.

Her career ended in 1949. "I got a sore arm and had to quit," she explained.

Haylett worked 30 years for Kellogg's in Battle Creek and retired in 1981. She has attended several league reunions.

PITCHING										BATTING			FIELDING			
W–L	PCT	ERA	G	IP	H	R	ER	BB	SO	BA	AB	H	PO	A	E	FA
70–47	.598	1.92	128	1044	690	303	223	405	390	.173	370	64	57	165	32	.874

Hayslip, Martha

Statesboro, Georgia. Infielder. Kenosha Comets, 1948.

Headin, Irene

Pitcher. South Bend Blue Sox, 1945.

PITCHING		
W–L	G	IP
0–0	1	1

Heafner, Ruby "Rebel"

Born: March 5, 1924, Gastonia, North Carolina. 5'6", 140, Catcher, Pitcher, BR, TR. Rockford Peaches, 1946; Fort Wayne Daisies, 1947–49; Racine Belles, 1950; Battle Creek Belles, 1951.

A clutch hitter, Ruby Heafner played as a catcher in six seasons in the league.

Her mother made softballs for her to play with in her backyard when she was a child. She played organized softball in school and advanced to fast-pitch softball as a teenager. She joined the Army Air Corps and served as a mail clerk during World War II. She saw a Movie-to-News reel on the league and wrote a letter to P.K. Wrigley. She was invited to try out at Pasagoula, Mississippi, in 1946. She was assigned to Rockford after spring training.

Heafner smashed a game-winning triple in the 10th inning of her first game. She once garnered five hits in a doubleheader to help her team with both games. "Rebel" was referred to as the Mickey Cochrane of the AAGPL. She typically played about half the games in a season. Her best year of hitting came in 1950 when she achieved career highs in batting average (.211) and RBI (17).

After baseball, she went to work for McDonald-Douglass as a certified electrician. She wired aircraft and missiles before she quit due to a collapsed right knee in 1980. She was put on disability and walked with the help of crutches for years. Then one day she found God. "I started reading the word of God and put the crutches down. I've been walking ever since," she said. She later coached high school girl's softball in her hometown for a Christian school. She goes to league reunions every two years.

BATTING

G	BA	AB	H	2B	3B	HR	SB	BB	SO	R	RBI
342	.178	959	171	17	4	0	28	124	154	83	57

PITCHING

W–L	PCT	ERA	G	IP	H	R	ER	BB	SO
0–1	.000	13.52	2	2	6	6	3	0	0

FIELDING

PO	A	E	DP	FA
1030	243	52	24	.961

Healy, Dorothy

Outfield. Chicago Colleens, 1948.

Dorothy Healy played one season for the expansion Chicago Colleens in 1948.

BATTING

G	BA	AB	H	2B	3B	HR	SB	BB	SO	R	RBI
12	.122	41	5	1	0	0	0	4	2	2	7

FIELDING

PO	A	E	DP	FA
16	0	3	0	.842

Heim (McDaniel), Kay "Heime"

Born: Aug. 21, 1917, Athabaska, Alberta, Canada. 5'6", 125, Catcher, BR, TR. Kenosha Comets, 1943–44.

An injury stopped the career of Kay Heim, one of the original players in the league, after two seasons.

Heim began playing softball in the fifth grade. "I got behind the plate and never left that position," she said about becoming a catcher. "I never wore a mask, chest protector or shin pads." She joined a city baseball league at age 12 before going into fast-pitch softball. She was playing for the Army-Navy Pats when she received a telegram to play in the new league. She was offered $70 a week, which was more than she was making in a month. She jumped at the opportunity.

Kay "Heime" Heim

The Canadian helped the Comets with the pennant the first year, but the following season she fractured her ankle and was out for the year. She came home, married Ray McDaniel and left baseball behind. She moved to the United States and became a citizen in 1948. The couple had two sons, Raymond and Robert. She bowled and coached softball while they grew up. Now retired from working for a glass company, she lives in Minnesota.

Heim was named to the Albert Hall of Fame in 1987. She still ventures back to her homeland about once a year.

BATTING												FIELDING				
G	BA	AB	H	2B	3B	HR	SB	BB	SO	R	RBI	PO	A	E	DP	FA
58	.154	182	28	0	1	1	25	8	14	17	16	229	40	14	1	.951

Herring, Katherine "Katie"

Born: July 11, 1933, Hedrick, Oklahoma. 5'4", 118. Outfield, TR, BR. Grand Rapids Chicks, 1953.

Hershey, Esther

Born: January 5, 1928, Gap, Pennsylvania. 5'5", 133, Utility, TR, BR. South Bend Blue Sox, 1948.

Hickey, Lillian

Vancouver, British Columbia, Canada. Died: Date Unknown. Outfield, BR, TR. Kenosha Comets, 1946.

BATTING												FIELDING				
G	BA	AB	H	2B	3B	HR	SB	BB	SO	R	RBI	PO	A	E	DP	FA
21	.213	61	13	0	0	0	1	1	13	3	3	11	1	2	0	.857

Hickson, Irene "Choo-Choo" Mae

Born: Aug. 14, 1915, Chattanooga, Tennessee. Died: Nov. 25, 1995, Racine, Wisconsin. 5'2", 116, Catcher, BR, TR. Racine Belles, 1943–50; Kenosha Comets, 1951.

A member of the first All-Star team, Irene Hickson was one of the league's oldest players. She played for nine seasons and set several league records.

Hickson was a boxer and all-around athlete before joining the league in its first season. She also played semi-pro softball in Tennessee, Georgia and North Carolina. In her first season, she led Racine to the pennant and the championship. She hit .417 during the championship playoffs.

On June 13, 1946, she walked five times in a game to set a league record. The unfortunate death of her mother during the season interrupted her playing. When she returned, she broke a finger and was out of the lineup again. Racine won the pennant and championship that season. She helped the team win another pennant in 1948. She went to Kenosha in 1951 but played in only 11 games.

The good-fielding catcher had the most put outs one season (632), which is the second highest total in league history for a season. Her .976 fielding percentage one year ranks third among career leaders for a single season. However, she once had 23 passed balls one year, which is the second highest total for a single season in league history.

BATTING												FIELDING				
G	BA	AB	H	2B	3B	HR	SB	BB	SO	R	RBI	PO	A	E	DP	FA
621	.171	1876	321	23	14	3	319	316	173	296	125	2388	561	130	47	.958

Hill (Westerman), Joyce

Born: Dec. 29, 1925, Kenosha, Wisconsin. 5'5", 150, Catcher, 1st Base, Outfield, BL, TR. Grand Rapid Chicks, 1945; South Bend Blue Sox, 1946; Peoria Redwings, 1947; Racine Belles, 1948–49; Peoria Redwings, 1950–51; South Bend Blue Sox, 1952.

Joyce Hill spent most of her eight-year career behind the plate and was a consistent hitter.

An uncle introduced Hill to baseball when she was 5 years old. She played "street-corner ball" before she started playing organized fast-pitch softball.

In 1945, the AAGPBL held a tryout in Kenosha and Hill was given a chance. She and another of the 60 girls who tried out made the team. She was assigned to the Grand Rapids Chicks as a catcher. "It's the best position on the field. You're in on every play," she said.

While she loved to catch, she also had her share of injuries. She recalled one game in which she had four broken fingers taped on her throwing hand. Needless to say, the other team took advantage and stole many bases. Because her talents behind the plate were needed by many teams, she was moved around the league.

In 1951 she got married to spite her aunt. "She said I would never amount to anything as a wife," she explained. Her days of catching were over and she was put at first base. During her last season, she was on the South Bend team that lost six players near the end of the season. Hill became a hero during a game at the end of the season. She drove in the winning run with two outs in the bottom of the ninth inning.

She retired after the 1952 season to become a mother and raise a family of two daughters, both of whom became ball players. When *A League of Their Own* was filmed, she was one of the women who went to Cooperstown for the last segment of the movie. About her playing days, she said, "We were proud of it. We got to travel and meet friends — things I couldn't do on the farm."

BATTING												FIELDING				
G	BA	AB	H	2B	3B	HR	SB	BB	SO	R	RBI	PO	A	E	DP	FA
531	.228	1515	345	34	14	0	81	292	149	191	167	858	139	51	14	.951

Hlavaty, Lillian

Jessup, Pennsylvania. Outfield. Rockford Peaches, 1951.

						BATTING									FIELDING			
G	BA	AB	H	2B	3B	HR	SB	BB	SO	R	RBI			PO	A	E	DP	FA
47	.189	127	24	3	0	0	7	20	34	13	5			32	6	2	1	.950

Hoffman, Nadine

Peoria Redwings, 1946.

	BATTING		
G	BA	AB	H
2	.000	4	0

Hoffmann, Barbara

Born: Jan. 18, 1931, Bellville, Illinois. 5'6", 133, 3rd Base, 2nd Base, BR, TR. South Bend Blue Sox, 1951–52.

Barbara Hoffmann

Selected to the 1952 All-Star team, Barbara Hoffmann was one of five women who walked off the South Bend team in 1952 to protest the suspension of a fellow player. She never returned to the league.

Hoffmann began playing softball at age 9 and advanced to softball leagues in St. Louis before catching the eye of the league. In her first season she hurt her knee and was temporarily inserted at second base because the pivot was easier. Her .212 average helped the Blue Sox win their first pennant.

The following season she was selected to the All-Star team and hit a home run in the All-Star game, which she considers her greatest individual thrill. Near the end of the season, she walked off the team after Shorty Pryer was suspended. "I guess it was wrong for us to do it. We stood up for our principles," she reflected.

After baseball, she played three years for the Hoosierettes, a South Bend women's basketball team. She also bowled for 25 years, but never professionally. Hoffmann retired in 1985 after 33 years with Bendix. Now she sells baseball cards and antiques in Columbia City, Indiana.

		BATTING												FIELDING				
G	BA	AB	H	2B	3B	HR	SB	BB	SO	R	RBI		PO	A	E	DP	FA
95	.192	271	52	5	4	1	12	45	50	31	22		86	166	35	10	.878

Hohlmayer (McNaughton), Alice

Born: Jan. 19, 1925, Springfield, Ohio. 5'6", 160, Pitcher, 1st Base, TL, BR. Kenosha Comets, 1946–48; Muskegon Lassies, 1949; Kalamazoo Lassies, 1950; Peoria Redwings, 1950–51.

Alice Hohlmayer began her career as a first baseman but ended up as a full-time pitcher in her last season in the league. The Ohio native was good with the bat and when overhand pitching emerged she was used on the mound as well. Her best year as a hurler came in her last season when she went 15–11 for Peoria.

			PITCHING							
W–L	PCT	ERA	G	IP	H	R	ER	BB	SO
33–32	.508	2.58	89	579	533	246	166	141	126

		BATTING											FIELDING			
G	BA	AB	H	2B	3B	HR	SB	BB	SO	R	RBI		PO	A	E	FA
486	.203	1486	301	35	15	3	43	138	192	85	128		4225	254	109	.976

Holda, Mary "Bucky"

Mansfield, Ohio. Died: Date Unknown. Utility Infielder, BR, TR. South Bend Blue Sox, 1943.

Mary Holda was one of the original players of the league and played one season mostly at second and third base.

		BATTING												FIELDING				
G	BA	AB	H	2B	3B	HR	SB	BB	SO	R	RBI		PO	A	E	DP	FA
29	.205	73	15	0	0	0	8	4	11	9	6		30	31	5	2	.924

Holderness, Joan

Born: March 17, 1933, Kenosha, Wisconsin. 5'10", 145, Outfield, BR, TR. Kenosha Comets, 1949–50; Grand Rapids Chicks, 1950–51; Battle Creek Belles, 1951.

Joan Holderness was known as a clutch pinch hitter over three seasons in the league. Her father was a semi-pro player, which is how she was introduced to the game. Her mother took her to a Kenosha game in 1945 and she decided then that she wanted to someday play for the team. She got her "in" with the team in 1947 as the team's first batgirl. She practiced with the team and then was sent to Chicago to play with a farm team of the league when the Comets were on the road.

Holderness finally got her shot with the Comets in 1949 after school was dismissed. She played in 34 games her rookie year. "I was a good pinch hitter at Kenosha. I was pretty proud of that," she said. She said it was nerve racking to play in her hometown because all her relatives would come out and watch her play.

The following season she was sent to Grand Rapids halfway through the season. Then in 1951 she was shipped to Battle Creek. When her younger sister came down with polio late in the season, she came home to help care for her and never returned to the league.

After baseball, Holderness coached and played softball for a few more years. She also went to work for the government. Then she joined the professional bowling tour in 1958. Her highest finish in nine years was second place. She continued to work for the government and retired in 1988 with 32 years to her credit. Now living in Clearwater, Florida, she golfs and goes to league reunions.

BATTING												FIELDING				
G	BA	AB	H	2B	3B	HR	SB	BB	SO	R	RBI	PO	A	E	DP	FA
119	.151	284	43	2	1	0	4	30	21	13	28	79	7	7	4	.925

Holgerson (Silvestri), Marge

Born: Jan. 28, 1927, Mobile, Alabama. Died: March 23, 1990. Pitcher, 2nd Base, TR, BR. Rockford Peaches, 1946–49; Muskegon Lassies, 1949–50; Grand Rapids Chicks, 1950–52.

Marge Holgerson turned into a superb pitcher after a slow start. She also was a member of the 1948 Rockford championship team.

Holgerson was used primarily as a second baseman in her rookie year, but she showed promise on the mound with her sidearm delivery, which the league had converted to in 1946. The following season she became a full-time hurler and was 9–15 on the year.

She married after the 1948 season and played under Silvestri the remainder of her career. Her best season came in 1951 when she was 16–6 with a 1.53 ERA.

PITCHING										BATTING			FIELDING			
W–L	PCT	ERA	G	IP	H	R	ER	BB	SO	BA	AB	H	PO	A	E	FA
76–69	.510	1.94	168	1241	832	393	267	497	599	.172	622	107	52	349	30	.930

Holle, Mabel "Holly"

Born: March 21, 1921, Jacksonville, Illinois. 5'7", 125, 3rd Base, Outfield, BR, TR. South Bend Blue Sox, 1943.

One of the original players of the league, Mabel Holle played a season with South Bend, but her contract was not renewed.

Baseball was in her blood as her father had been a semi-pro pitcher. She played baseball with the boys until one of the first four players who signed with the league put her name in for the tryout at Wrigley Field. She made the final cuts and was assigned to South Bend. She recalled the classes Helen Rubenstein gave on dressing and putting on makeup. "We tried not to laugh, but we did," she said.

One of her most memorable games in the All-American League came when her mother and sister came to see her play. "I got the winning hit," she explained. At the beginning of the next season, the league didn't renew her contract and made her try out again with the rookies. This time she didn't make the cut.

Holle didn't give up playing and went over to the Chicago Chicks to play for a couple more years. She also started teaching school during this time and continued doing so for 47 years. She coached softball and other sports during her teaching career and was inducted into the Illinois Coaches Hall of Fame. She retired in 1990 and now goes to league reunions. She lives in Lake Forest, Illinois.

				BATTING										FIELDING				
G	BA	AB	H	2B	3B	HR	SB	BB	SO	R	RBI		PO	A	E	DP	FA
90	.199	332	66	3	1	0	24	22	33	37	21		145	56	14	2	.942

Hood, Marjorie

Bell Buckle, Tennessee. Outfield. Racine Belles, 1943.

Hoover, Alice "Pee Wee"

Born: Oct. 27, 1928, Reading, Pennsylvania. 4'11", 105, 2nd Base, 3rd Base, BR, TR. Fort Wayne Daisies, 1948.

Alice Hoover played in six games during one season in the league.

Hoover didn't start playing softball until she was age 14 for the Kauffman Maids. Then she was scouted by AAGPBL player Fran Janssen and invited to Opa-locka, Florida, for spring training. She was assigned to Fort Wayne, where she didn't see much action. "The rookies didn't play much," she said.

The following season she decided not to go back—a move she now regrets. "I wish I would have gone back, but I didn't know what to do with my life," she explained. Instead, she went to work in a shirt factory for the next 33 years. Then she switched careers and went to work for AT&T for nearly 16 years. She retired in 1993 and lives in Lauredale, Pennsylvania.

	BATTING		
G	BA	AB	H
6	.000	4	0

Horstman, Catherine "Katie"

Born: April 14, 1935, Minster, Ohio. 5'7", 150, Pitcher, Catcher, Outfield, Shortstop, 3rd Base, TR, BR. Kenosha Comets, 1951; Fort Wayne Daisies, 1951–54.

An All-Star third baseman in 1953, "Katie" Horstman was a versatile player who could pitch and field. She helped Fort Wayne win three straight pennants. In 1954, she was 10–4 on the mound and pounded out 16 home runs.

PITCHING

W–L	PCT	ERA	G	IP	H	R	ER	BB	SO
29–11	.725	2.50	49	313	202	129	87	122	140

BATTING												FIELDING				
G	BA	AB	H	2B	3B	HR	SB	BB	SO	R	RBI	PO	A	E	DP	FA
308	.286	1057	302	42	14	23	28	104	61	164	150	343	491	74	1	.919

Hosbein, Marion

Born: Jan. 29, 1937, Coloma, Michigan. 5'8", 138, Outfield, BR, TR. South Bend Blue Sox, 1954.

Marion Hosbein played in less than ten games in the league. After baseball, she became a letter carrier for the U.S. Postal Service. Now she lives in Kalamazoo.

Hunter, Dorothy "Dottie"

Born: Jan. 28, 1916, Winnipeg, Manitoba, Canada. 5'6", 155, 1st Base, BR, TR. Racine Belles, 1943.

One of the original players of the league, Dorothy Hunter played one season before becoming a chaperone. She helped Racine win a pennant and championship in 1943. "Dottie" was one of the oldest players to enter the league at 27. Her father was a prominent soccer player and manager.

BATTING												FIELDING				
G	BA	AB	H	2B	3B	HR	SB	BB	SO	R	RBI	PO	A	E	DP	FA
82	.224	254	57	6	5	1	9	16	18	27	28	736	15	21	16	.973

Hutchison, Anna May "Hutch"

Born: May 1, 1925, Louisville, Kentucky. 5'7", 149, Pitcher, Catcher, TR, BR. Racine Belles, 1944–48; Muskegon Lassies, 1949.

Anna May Hutchison was one of the best sidearm pitchers in the league and holds the season record for most game appearances.

Hutchison grew up in Louisville and played softball during her high school years. AAGPBL scout A.J. Hamilton spotted her and talked to her parents about joining the league. She went to spring training in 1944 and was placed on the Racine Belles as a catcher.

"Hutch" also had another nickname, but it came from opposing fans who called her "Ryecrisp" after the diet cracker, because Hutchison was on the chunky side. The group even came to Racine to see her once. She took it in stride. "Racine was the best ball park in the league. It had great fans and great turnouts," she said.

In 1946 the league decided to move from underhand to sidearm pitching. Pitchers were needed and Hutchison was taken from behind the plate to in front of it. She responded with a 26–14 record and more appearances (51) than any other pitcher in the league's history in helping her team win the league championship.

Hutchison became one of the best pitchers when the league went strictly sidearm the next season. She won the most games (27), threw the most innings (360), complete games (36) and shutouts (12). However, she also gave up the most hits (230).

As the league went to sidearm or overhand pitching in 1948, Hutch's record dropped off to below 500 for the next two seasons. She recalled how tough a grind the league was — daily games with doubleheaders on Sunday. The league traveled mostly by bus, but later plane rides became more common for road trips. She remembered being paid $60 to $70 a week and staying in private homes, which made her feel like being part of a family.

After baseball she became a teacher. She taught driver's education, golf and elementary school. She retired in Racine in 1985. "There will never be another league like ours. We were at the right place at the right time," she explained.

PITCHING

W–L	PCT	ERA	G	IP	R	ER	SO	BB	HB	WP
64–45	.587	1.82	134	885	265	179	257	252	53	12

BATTING												FIELDING				
G	BA	AB	H	2B	3B	HR	SB	BB	SO	R	RBI	PO	A	E	DP	FA
212	.153	511	78	52	0	0	5	29	47	26	31	214	291	53	2	.891

Jackson, Lillian "Bird Dog"

Born: Aug. 4, 1919, Nashville, Tennessee. 5'6", 125, Outfield, BL, TL. Rockford Peaches, 1943; Minneapolis Millerettes, 1944; Fort Wayne Daisies, 1945.

Lillian Jackson was one of the original players of the league. Her career ended prematurely, as did some others, when the league switched to sidearm pitching in 1946 and pitchers dominated the batters.

The Nashville native was a late bloomer compared to most players because she didn't begin playing softball until she was 18 in high school. However, she adapted quickly and was recognized by a league scout in her hometown. She was making just $18 a week, and she was offered $65 a week to play in the new league. Jackson didn't hesitate and went to Chicago to try out with some 200 other women at Wrigley Field. She was in awe of the Cubs' home. "We went to Helen Rubenstein classes every morning and practiced every afternoon. Mr. (P.K.) Wrigley wanted ladies, not tomboys," she explained.

When the cut was made she was selected to play with 13 others on the Rockford Peaches. The short fielder was converted to outfield on the new league and played little her first season.

Jackson was sent to Minneapolis the second year of her playing career. Her teammate, Faye Dancer, was a clown and was always acting up. Dancer told Jackson one day that she ran just like a "Bird Dog." The nickname stuck. Jackson played in 58 games in 1944 and hit .201, a respectable average for the league. She stole 24 bases and scored 23 runs for the Millerettes.

Lillian "Bird Dog" Jackson

The following season the franchise folded and was moved to Fort Wayne. She seldom played but in one game remembered going after a foul ball and running into the bleachers. She caught the ball put paid the price with four stitches to close a split lip.

When the league moved to complete sidearm pitching the next season, she decided to quit. "I couldn't follow the ball," Bird Dog said.

Jackson went to a softball league in Chicago and played five more years before giving up the game. She went to work for the Sunbeam Corporation and became a manager before she retired after 31 years at the appliance company.

When the players got together to form a player's association, Jackson volunteered to help. She was elected to the Board of Directors. Jackson was one of the women who helped in the filming of *A League of Their Own*. "You know it took those girls six months to learn how to play the game," she commented. Today, she lives in Green Valley, Arizona.

			BATTING										FIELDING				
G	BA	AB	H	2B	3B	HR	SB	BB	SO	R	RBI		PO	A	E	DP	FA
120	.161	367	59	2	3	1	31	27	39	47	31		110	13	11	2	.918

Jacobs (Badini), Jane "Jake"

Born: June 16, 1924, Cuyahoga Falls, Ohio. 5'4", 130, Pitcher, TR, BR. Racine Belles, 1944–45, 47; Peoria Redwings, 1946.

Jane Jacobs fell victim to sidearm pitching when the league converted over to it. One bright spot in her career came when she threw a one-hitter.

Jacobs started playing softball at age 11. A few years later her coach was in Cleveland and approached a scout from the league. He got her an invitation to a tryout in 1943. She was assigned to Racine, but she came down with the mumps and her season was over before it began.

The following season "Jake" finally received her chance to play and was 9–16 on the season for the Belles. She threw an in-curve, out-curve, upshoot and a drop. She had good control but not a great fastball, which was her downfall. While she was playing, her brother Jimmy died in World War II, which was a blow to the young girl.

When the league switched to sidearm in 1946, it spelled the end of Jacobs' career. "I was afraid I'd ruin my arm," she explained.

She came home and went into her own dry cleaning business for 40 years. She married Mario Badini in 1973. He was a pipe fitter and passed away in 1989. Jacobs went through a cancer operation in 1994 that nearly killed her, she said. She now runs a ceramics business and plans to retire soon.

PITCHING

W–L	PCT	ERA	G	IP	H	R	ER	BB	SO
24–43	.358	2.65	88	590	581	292	174	189	52

BATTING												FIELDING			
G	BA	AB	H	2B	3B	HR	SB	BB	SO	R	RBI	PO	A	E	FA
204	.118	204	24	0	0	1	10	11	29	7	9	20	170	19	.909

Jacobs (Murk), Janet "Jay Jay"

Born: Oct. 31, 1928, Englewood, New Jersey. 5'4", 120, Shortstop, Outfield, BB, TR. Racine Belles, 1945.

Janet Jacobs spent a season with Racine before going on to college.

Jacobs switched to swimming after her year in the league and graduated with a bachelor's degree from Purdue University. She got married in 1950 and raised a family of four children: Vicki, Doug, Wendy and Larry. The chemist also played tennis and competed in the Senior Platform Tennis Championships in the 1980s. Now she lives in Franklin Lakes, New Jersey.

Jameson, Shirley

Born: March 19, 1918, Maywood, Illinois. Died: Dec. 29, 1993. 4'11", 105, Outfield, BR, TR. Kenosha Comets, 1943–46.

One of the original players of the league, Shirley Jameson played for the Kenosha Comets for four seasons.

Before she began playing in the league, she earned a bachelor's degree at the University of Illinois. The diminutive outfielder with good bat and speed on the bases helped the team to its only pennant in 1943.

After baseball, she obtained a master's degree at Northwestern University in 1947. She became the athletic director at Triton College and retired in 1971.

BATTING												FIELDING				
G	BA	AB	H	2B	3B	HR	SB	BB	SO	R	RBI	PO	A	E	DP	FA
385	.229	1368	313	16	17	8	401	279	38	278	73	698	57	26	9	.967

Jamieson, Janet "Jamie"

Born: April 3, 1927, Minneapolis, Minnesota. 5'3", 136, Catcher, BR, TR. South Bend Blue Sox, 1948.

Janet Jamieson was an excellent softball player on a championship team, but her baseball career never materialized. She was also a nationally ranked table tennis player. She went into banking after baseball.

BATTING

G	BA	AB	H
1	.000	1	0

Janssen, Frances
"Big Red" "Little Red"

Born: Jan. 25, 1926, Remington, Indiana. 5'11", 155, Pitcher, TR, BR. South Bend Blue Sox, 1948; Grand Rapids Chicks, 1948; Chicago Colleens, 1949; Peoria Redwings, 1950; Kalamazoo Lassies, 1950; Fort Wayne Daisies, 1950–51; Kalamazoo Lassies, 1951; Battle Creek, Belles, 1951–52.

Frances Janssen was a journeywoman relief pitcher who played with seven different teams in her five years in the league.

Janssen's parents immigrated from Germany to the farmlands of Indiana before she was born. She first played organized softball in high school. She graduated from a business college in 1944 and began working in an office. Several players from her local softball team had been picked for the league, so she gave it a try in 1946 but didn't make the grade.

The tall, red-haired basketball player tried out again in 1948 as an outfielder, but the league liked her arm enough to send her to spring training as a pitcher. After spring training, she was assigned to South Bend for a couple of days before being sent to Grand Rapids. After a month, she was released. "I got released because I couldn't throw a curveball," she explained.

She didn't give up on the league and was put on one of the traveling teams in 1949. She came along fine and pitched a one-hitter in Texas. She was paid $25 a week plus $3 a day for meals.

"Big Red," or "Little Red" as she was called, was assigned to Peoria at the beginning of the season and ended up pitching for Fort Wayne in the playoffs, which the Daisies lost.

The following season she was sent to Peoria and to her it felt like "the end of the world." The same season she went to Battle Creek and Kalamazoo. She spent the 1952 season with Battle Creek and was used mainly in relief, a seldom used role in the league. She was released after the season. "We never realized the financial condition the league was in, but we always got paid," she said.

After baseball, the near six-footer played center for the South Bend Rockettes, an amateur women's basketball team with several former players, and volleyball with the South Bend Turners. She went to work for an insurance agency for 25 years and retired in 1991. Now she helps the league research information at the Northern Indiana Historical Society.

PITCHING										BATTING			FIELDING			
W–L	PCT	ERA	G	IP	H	R	ER	BB	SO	BA	AB	H	PO	A	E	FA
13–18	.419	3.74	61	289	283	178	120	143	67	.162	105	17	7	129	9	.938

Jaykoski, Joan

Menasha, Wisconsin. Pitcher, Outfield. Kenosha Comets, 1951; Grand Rapids, 1952.

Joan Jaykoski was a marginal pitcher-outfielder for two seasons in the league.

PITCHING

W–L	PCT	ERA	G	IP	H	R	ER	BB	SO
1–3	.250	7.81	10	30	32	42	26	44	4

BATTING

G	BA	AB	H	2B	3B	HR	SB	BB	SO	R	RBI
45	.120	83	10	0	0	0	2	14	19	7	5

FIELDING

PO	A	E	DP	FA
41	1	0	1	1.000

Jenkins, Marilyn "Jenks"

Born: Sept. 18, 1934, Grand Rapids, Michigan. 5'6", 140, Catcher, BR, TR. Grand Rapids Chicks, 1952–54.

Marilyn "Jenks" Jenkins

Marilyn Jenkins saw limited action over three seasons as a catcher for Grand Rapids.

A batgirl for the Chicks when she was 10 years old, Jenkins had an inside track to making it into the league. When she was a young teen, they allowed her to practice with them. She caught batting practice, which prepared her to become a catcher. "I learned a lot and idolized them, of course," she recalled.

Her father died when she was 13 and the Chicks were very supportive of her and her mother. By the time she was 17, she was big enough to start playing with the team. In her second season with the team, "Jenks" raised her batting average up to .207. Then about halfway through the 1954 season — the last year of the league — the league started using the major-league sized ball. In her first at-bat with the new ball, she hit one over the wall for the only home run in her career, which was cut short due to a health problem.

Jenkins went into the health care field as an X-ray technician. She switched careers some years later to become a paralegal. Then she began an estate sales business in 1980 and has run it ever since. She now loves to play golf.

"I learned a lot about life in the league," she said of her baseball career.

BATTING												FIELDING				
G	BA	AB	H	2B	3B	HR	SB	BB	SO	R	RBI	PO	A	E	DP	FA
141	.192	365	70	8	2	1	11	50	43	38	33	346	63	17	11	.960

Jewett (Beckett), Christine

Born: Aug. 3, 1926, England. 5'6", 145, Outfield, BR, TR. Kenosha Comets, 1948–49; Peoria Redwings, 1949.

Christine Jewett was a good hitting outfielder for two seasons in the league with two teams. Before joining the league she played for the Bombers in Regina, Canada. After baseball, she married in 1949. She had three sons and now has five grandchildren.

BATTING												FIELDING				
G	BA	AB	H	2B	3B	HR	SB	BB	SO	R	RBI	PO	A	E	DP	FA
202	.213	677	144	7	4	3	68	43	73	70	50	186	22	25	3	.893

Betsy "Sock'um" Jochum

Jochum, Betsy "Sock'um"

Born: Feb. 8, 1921, Cincinnati, Ohio. 5'7", 140, Outfielder, 1st Base, Pitcher, TR, BR. South Bend Blue Sox, 1943–48.

Betsy Jochum, one of the original players in the AAGPBL, won the batting championship in 1944 with a .296 average. She led the league in several hitting categories the first two years of the league.

Jochum began playing sandlot baseball at the age of 8. It was not until she was 12 that she played organized softball. The outfielder had a good arm and proved it playing softball. "In a softball game in Chicago, I one hopped it to the catcher and threw a gal out," she said.

A scout for the league spotted her and she was given a tryout in Cincinnati. She was picked to go on to Chicago for another tryout. She remembered staying in the Belmont Hotel.

In the inaugural season of the AAGPBL, "Sock'em" Jockum, as her fans used to call her, led the league in hits (120), singles (100) and doubles (12). She finished fifth in the league in hitting (.273). Her defensive abilities were almost as good as her offensive skills: She once caught a fly ball barehanded. Her excellent arm also led to many put outs in the outfield.

The following season the outfielder — she played left and center — had her career year in stroking the most singles (120) and hits (128). She also led the league in batting average.

When South Bend led the league in hitting (.213) in 1945, Jockum contributed with a .237 average, 11th best in the league. She continued to hit well and in 1946 had the fewest strikeouts (10) in the league.

In 1947, the league traveled to Cuba for spring training. It was her first ride in an airplane. As pitching switched to sidearm and then overhand, Jockum's average started to slide. It dropped to .211 in 1947.

In 1948, when league pitching went to overhand and the ball was shrunk to 10⅜ inches, the strong-armed Jochum was a natural to become a pitcher. "It was more fun pitching," she admitted. In her debut as a pitcher, she whipped Fort Wayne on a two-hitter. She allowed only four batters to get on base and struck out five.

At one point during the 1948 campaign, she was 13–6, but she ended the season with a 14–13 mark. Her batting average dropped off to .195. When she wasn't on the mound, manager Marty McManus used the veteran to fill in at any position and pinch hit.

After baseball, Jochum obtained a degree in physical education from Illinois State and a master's degree from Indiana University. She taught in South Bend for 25 years and still lives there today.

PITCHING

W–L	PCT	ERA	G	IP	H	R	ER	BB	SO
14–13	.519	1.51	29	215	154	61	36	58	103

BATTING												FIELDING				
G	BA	AB	H	2B	3B	HR	SB	BB	SO	R	RBI	PO	A	E	DP	FA
645	.246	2401	591	43	29	7	358	177	104	307	232	888	76	48	13	.953

Jogerst, Donna

Freeport, Illinois. Pitcher. Rockford Peaches, 1952.

PITCHING

G	IP
1	1

Johnson (Noga), Arleene "Johnnie"

Born: Jan. 1, 1924, Regina, Saskatchewan, Canada. 5'4", 137, 3rd Base, Shortstop, BR, TR. Fort Wayne Daisies, 1945; Muskegon Lassies, 1946–48; Fort Wayne Daisies, 1948.

"Good fielder, weak hitter" could have been the scouting report on Arleene Johnson during her four seasons in the league.

She played a year of softball in Canada before assigned to the league. She was the best fielding third baseman two years in a row. She also had the dubious distinction of leading the league in strikeouts (67) in 1946. She helped the Lassies win a pennant in 1947. After baseball, she worked for the Canadian government for 30 years.

"Johnnie" was named to the Saskatchewan Baseball and Sports Hall of Fame. She got married and has one daughter, Carol Lee, and one son, Rob.

BATTING												FIELDING				
G	BA	AB	H	2B	3B	HR	SB	BB	SO	R	RBI	PO	A	E	DP	FA
354	.164	1119	183	14	13	3	123	113	224	103	91	465	870	95	50	.934

Jones, Doris

Born: 1924, Sellersburg, Indiana. 5'7", 125, Outfield, BR, TR. South Bend Blue Sox, 1945.

Doris Jones, who wore number 4 and played right field, saw action in six games for South Bend in 1945.

BATTING			
G	BA	AB	H
6	.000	15	0

Jones (Davis), Marguerite "The Lady"

Born: Nov. 3, 1917, Windthorst, Saskatchewan, Canada. Died: May 9, 1995. 5'9", Pitcher, TR, BR. Minneapolis Millerettes, 1944; Rockford Peaches, 1944

Marguerite Jones pitched for one season in the league without much success.

She returned to Canada to marry Gordon Davis in 1945 and left the league behind. She played softball in Regina for several years before raising a family of four children: Ron, Jerry, Carol and Tom. In 1958, the family moved to Moose Jaw. Her husband passed away in 1985. "The Lady" attended the 1988 reunion of players in Cooperstown.

In her later years, she developed Alzheimer's disease and died in 1995. "As her short-term memory failed, her longer-term memory actually improved for awhile. Among her most cherished memories was her time in the AAGPBL and the sport she loved," said her son, Ron.

PITCHING										BATTING			FIELDING			
W–L	PCT	ERA	G	IP	H	R	ER	BB	SO	BA	AB	H	PO	A	E	FA
6–12	.333	3.70	28	175	150	72	16	24	1	.162	68	11	10	71	7	.920

Jones (Doxey), Marilyn C. "Jonesy"

Born: April 5, 1927, Providence, Rhode Island. 5'5", 135, Pitcher, Catcher, TR, BR. Kenosha Comets, 1948; Fort Wayne Daisies, 1949; Chicago Colleens, 1949; Rockford Peaches, 1950–51; Battle Creek Belles, 1951–52; Muskegon Belles, 1953; Fort Wayne Daisies, 1954.

Marilyn Jones was a back-up catcher at first, but she was moved to pitcher and once pitched a no-hitter during her seven years in the league.

Jones began playing softball at age 12. She played her first organized ball at age 16 with the Monowatt Electric Company, where she also worked. Then she moved to the Riverside Townies. The manager of the team contacted her parents about her playing in the AAGPBL and they consented to her trying out. She tried out in New Jersey in March 1948 and was picked to go to Opa-locka, Florida, for spring training. She came into the league as a utility fielder, but she became a second-string catcher because she wasn't hitting well.

In her first season, she was the back-up catcher for the Kenosha Comets and appeared in 25 games. She hit only .040 on the season, managing just 2 hits in 50 at-bats. The following season she was assigned to the barnstorming Chicago Colleens to get more hitting experience.

"Jonesy" was still considered a rookie in 1950 with Rockford, which earned her more playing time under the rookie rule (a team had to have a rookie in the defensive lineup at all times). Just before the end of the season, the regular catcher broke her leg and Jones was called on to catch in the championships that Rockford won.

In 1952, she was traded to Battle Creek in June. Because the team had two injured pitchers, she was asked to pitch. Ironically, the second game she pitched came against her old teammates on July 10, 1952. She bit the hand that once fed her by no-hitting the Daisies. She racked up a 9–7 record on the season with a 1.69 ERA.

Marilyn C. "Jonesy" Jones

The franchise moved to Muskegon the following season and she had another good year on the mound with a 14–11 record. When the Lassies folded up at the end of the season, she was sent to Fort Wayne, where she went 8–8 and helped the Daisies win a pennant.

After the league folded, she went to work for Michigan Bell and played for the Kalamazoo Lassies, a basketball team in the city league made up of several All-Americans. In 1969, she married Bud Doxey, a softball umpire and former player. "He always said I had a Class A arm and a Class D head," she said. Marilyn retired in 1983 and now the two play golf together.

PITCHING

W–L	PCT	ERA	G	IP	H	R	ER	BB	SO
31–26	.544	2.31	69	577	415	213	148	149	191

BATTING | FIELDING

G	BA	AB	H	2B	3B	HR	SB	BB	SO	R	RBI	PO	A	E	DP	FA
222	.158	481	76	7	0	0	4	66	79	43	28	167	180	53	3	.868

Junior, Daisy

Born: July 10, 1920, Regina, Saskatchewan, Canada. 5'6", 140, Outfield, BR, TR. South Bend Blue Sox, 1946–48; Springfield Sallies, 1948; Fort Wayne Daisies, 1949.

Daisy Junior was a good-fielding, light-hitting outfielder for four seasons in the league. After baseball she took up golf and married. She still lives in Regina and spends winters in Arizona.

BATTING | FIELDING

G	BA	AB	H	2B	3B	HR	SB	BB	SO	R	RBI	PO	A	E	DP	FA
454	.152	847	129	10	3	0	77	81	125	70	51	455	27	15	3	.970

Jurgensmeier (Carroll), Margaret "Jurgy"

Born: Sept. 2, 1934, Freeport, Illinois. 5'7", 130, Pitcher, TR, BR. Rockford Peaches, 1951.

Margaret Jurgensmeier played in less than ten games during her only season in the league.

She recalled playing baseball when she was only 4 years old. She was 16 when she joined the league. "I was scared to death being away from home," she remembered when she went to spring training in Peoria, Illinois.

The rookie wasn't given much of a chance to pitch and appeared in just nine games during the 1952 season with Rockford.

"Jurgy" got married the following year and left the league behind. She became busy as a housewife and raised three children: Mike, Steve and Dave. She now lives in Roscoe, Illinois.

PITCHING

W–L	PCT	ERA	G	IP	H	R	ER	BB	SO
1–1	.500	7.96	9	26	23	31	23	37	7

Kabick, Josephine

Born: March 27, 1922, Detroit, Michigan. Died: Date Unknown. 5'7", 142, Pitcher, TR, BR. Milwaukee Chicks, 1944; Grand Rapids Chicks, 1945–46; Kenosha Comets, 1946; Peoria Redwings, 1947.

Josephine Kabick was an underhand pitcher in her four years on the mound.

Kabick logged the most innings (366) and tied for the most games pitched (45) in her rookie season. She also had the most wins on the year, which turned out to be her best season.

She continued to put in a lot of innings and allowed the most hits (283) and runs (131) in 1946. She also gave up the most runs (101) in 1947, her last year. The league turned to overhand and sidearm pitching the next season.

PITCHING										BATTING			FIELDING			
W–L	PCT	ERA	G	IP	H	R	ER	BB	SO	BA	AB	H	PO	A	E	FA
74–72	.507	2.33	151	1213	948	481	314	403	245	.158	322	51	75	381	83	.846

Kamenshek, Dorothy "Dottie" "Kammie"

Born: Dec. 21, 1925, Cincinnati, Ohio. 5'6", 136, 1st Base, Outfield, BL, TL. Rockford Peaches, 1943–51, 53.

One of the original players of the league, Dorothy Kamenshek was named to seven All-Star teams during her decade in the league. She twice won the batting crown and was the career leader in several categories.

Kamenshek grew up in Cincinnati, Ohio, and first started playing organized softball at age 12. Two years later she was playing for H.H. Meyers Packing Company in the national championships. "You were supposed to be 16," she explained.

Then in 1943 the Chicago Cubs sent a scout to Cincinnati and her coach gathered up 54 girls for a tryout. Six made the cut, including Kamenshek, and were sent to Wrigley Field for another tryout. Of the six who went to Chicago, Kamenshek and Betsy Jochum were selected for the new league.

Kamenshek was assigned to Rockford, where she would remain for the rest of her career. The Peaches would not let go of their best player and they even paid her bonuses "under the table" to keep her satisfied. She eventually became

Dorothy "Dottie" "Kammie" Kamenshek

one of the highest paid players in the league with a weekly salary of $125 at one point, not including the "bonus" money.

"Kammie's" impact on the team was almost immediate as the leadoff hitter boasted one of the highest averages in the league — .271. She struck out only 6 times in 395 at bats, swiped 42 bases and scored 58 times. She was selected for the first All-Star team, which played a doubleheader in Wrigley Field.

The following season she led the league in the fewest strikeouts (6) and most at bats (447), but she was more interested in her team winning than with individual statistics. "It was the winning that made the game enjoyable," she said.

"Dottie" got her wish in 1945 when she helped Rockford to its first pennant and championships. She scored the most runs (80) and recorded the most at bats (419) in the league. She likely would have been named to the All-Star teams in 1944 and 1945, but the league didn't name a team during those years.

The league switched to sidearm pitching and a smaller ball in 1946, and "Kammie" ate it up, recording career highs in hits (129) and stolen bases (109), while leading the league with a .316 average. The All-Star team selection was back and she won it hands down at first base.

The 1947 season was a mirror image of 1946 for the slugger, who compares her hitting to former major league hitter Rod Carew of the Minnesota Twins. "I could hit to all fields, but I had no power. I wouldn't swing for the fences," she explained. She again led the league in hitting with a .306 average.

For the next three seasons, Kamenshek continued to hit well and be ranked among the league leaders. More importantly, she helped Rockford win three successive league championships and a pennant in 1950. She recalled hitting three homers in one championship playoff game! She hit just 13 homers during her whole career, making this feat even more miraculous.

Her years of playing began to take its toll on her back so she decided to quit after the 1951 season, although she had a career high .345 batting average during the season and was named to her seventh All-Star team. However, her fans talked her into coming back in 1953 to play just home games. "That was a mistake," she said. She found it difficult to keep in shape and keep sharp while the team was away. She still hit a respectable .293 average, one point above her career total.

After baseball, she finished a college career at Marquette University and received a bachelor's degree in physical therapy. She spent the next 25 years working for the Los Angeles County Cripple Services. Then she worked five more years before retiring in 1985. She turned her attention toward attending league reunions and signing autographs. In 1991, she joined with three other players to form a company called "The Legendary Ladies of Baseball." The former players attend card shows and charity events, signing autographs for money or for free. "We're not out there just to make money," she explained.

Kamenshek is the league's career leader in hits (1,090), putouts (10,440) and double plays (360). She ranks second in at-bats (3,736) and runs scored (667). Remarkably, she struck out only 81 times in her career.

BATTING												FIELDING				
G	BA	AB	H	2B	3B	HR	SB	BB	SO	R	RBI	PO	A	E	DP	FA
1012	.292	3736	1090	89	41	13	657	492	110	667	304	10,440	284	193	360	.982

Kaufmann, Joan "Jo"

Born: Nov. 9, 1935, Rockford, Illinois. 5'4", 120, 2nd Base, 3rd Base, BR, TR. Rockford Peaches, 1954.

"It was a life-long dream," said Joan Kaufmann about her one season in the league. She joined the league in its last year and filled in on the left side of the infield.

When Kaufmann was a small child, she would visit her grandmother who lived close to the Rockford Peaches. "You could hear the sounds and see the lights on the field," she recalled. Then began her desire to play baseball for the team when she grew up.

At the age 12, she joined a girl's softball team. Then at 15 she hooked up with the Rockford Coeds, the next best opportunity to joining the Peaches. "Jo" tried out for the Peaches in 1953, while she was still in high school. The Peaches told her to come back next year; she did that and made the club. However, the team was already having financial problems. At the end of the season, she never did receive her last check.

After baseball, she joined the Air Force as a personnel clerk. She spent the next 20 years in the military and retired in 1975 as a master sergeant. She bought a gift shop in 1978, which she runs today. Severe arthritis has stopped her from participating in any more sports.

				BATTING									FIELDING				
G	BA	AB	H	2B	3B	HR	SB	BB	SO	R	RBI		PO	A	E	DP	FA
43	.134	97	13	3	0	0	0	9	13	3	5		49	77	20	12	.863

Kazmierczak, Marie

Born: Feb. 14, 1920, South Milwaukee, Wisconsin. 5'4", 145, Outfield, BR, TR. Kenosha Comets, 1944; South Bend Blue Sox, 1944; Milwaukee Chicks, 1944.

Marie Kazmierczak stayed in the league for only one season. "I didn't like riding the bench," she explained. She returned to her home to play softball full time without getting paid. She played softball up until 1954 and then took up golf. She worked in an air conditioning plant before retiring to raise Siberian huskies at her home in Three Lakes, Wisconsin.

				BATTING									FIELDING				
G	BA	AB	H	2B	3B	HR	SB	BB	SO	R	RBI		G	PO	A	E	DP	FA
16	.032	31	1	0	0	0	2	4	4	3	2		13	5	0	1	0	.833

Keagle, Merle

Born: March 21, 1923, Phoenix, Arizona. Died: Date Unknown. 5'2", 144, Outfield, Pitcher, BR, TR. Milwaukee Chicks, 1944; Grand Rapid Chicks, 1945–48.

Merle Keagle hammered out the league's most home runs (7) during her rookie season and was selected to the All-Star team in 1946. Keagle was primarily an outfielder, but she was called on to pitch occasionally during her career. As a rookie, she also led the league in total bases (145); in 1946 she had the most doubles (15). She helped the Chicks win the league championship in 1947 and the pennant in 1948.

BATTING

G	BA	AB	H	2B	3B	HR	SB	BB	SO	R	RBI
337	.266	1238	329	33	18	12	314	153	86	216	133

PITCHING										FIELDING				
W–L	PCT	ERA	G	IP	H	R	ER	BB	SO	PO	A	E	DP	FA
7–5	.583	2.82	16	102	73	46	32	66	22	498	200	34	22	.954

Keller, Rita

Born: January 21, 1933, Kalamazoo, Michigan. 5'3", 115. Shortstop, TR, BR. Kalamazoo Lassies, 1951.

Kelley (Savage), Jackie "Scrounge" "Babe"

Born: Nov. 11, 1926, Lansing, Michigan. Died: May 12, 1988. 5'7", 140, Pitcher, Utility fielder, BR, TR. South Bend Blue Sox, 1947; Chicago Colleens, 1948; Peoria Redwings, 1949; Rockford Peaches, 1950–53.

Jackie Kelley was a versatile performer during her seven years in the league.

She grew up with Alice Deschaine and both were sent to spring training in Cuba in 1947. The two played together on the Peaches later in their careers. "Scrounge's" best year on the mound came in 1952 when she went 12–11 and led the league in runs allowed (91), earned runs allowed (67) and walks (132). Her best season at the plate came in 1950 when she collected a career-high 85 hits, 14 doubles, 6 triples and 52 RBI.

After baseball, Kelley joined the Marines and met her husband. She died of lung cancer in 1988.

BATTING

G	BA	AB	H	2B	3B	HR	SB	BB	SO	R	RBI
426	.207	1307	270	42	18	5	70	105	166	112	131

PITCHING										FIELDING				
W–L	PCT	ERA	G	IP	H	R	ER	BB	SO	PO	A	E	DP	FA
15–18	.455	3.46	53	310	259	157	119	216	115	699	5476	116	42	.915

Kellogg, Vivian

Born: Nov. 6, 1922, Jackson, Michigan. 5'7", 149, 1st Base, Catcher, BR, TR. Minneapolis Millerettes, 1944; Ft. Wayne Daisies, 1945–50.

After the league was inducted into the National Baseball Hall of Fame in 1988, President

GERALD R. FORD

November 19, 1988

Dear Vivian:

Betty and I congratulate you on your induction
into the Baseball Hall of Fame as a former star
in the All American Girls Professional Baseball
League. This is recognition you richly deserve
because of your outstanding record.

I vividly recall the League when it played its
games at the old South High School field in
Grand Rapids. I was an avid fan. It was
excellent baseball.

Again, our highest compliments.

Warmest best wishes,

Gerald R. Ford

Ms. Vivian C. Kellogg
104 Sheridan
Brooklyn, MI 49230

Vivian Kellogg

Gerald Ford sent Vivian Kellogg a personal letter, which she considers her most prized possession.

Kellogg was a sandlot baseball player in her youth but didn't start playing organized softball until she was 16. When she was 18 she was approached by an AAGPBL scout after a state tournament. She signed a contract in 1943, but didn't end up playing in the league until 1944 with Minneapolis.

The following season she went to the Fort Wayne Daisies where she played five seasons. During the 1948 season she had the most at-bats in the league (472) and played more games at first base (126) than any other player. Sometimes she even filled in behind the plate. She recalled trying to throw someone out stealing third but ending up hitting the player in the head. They wore no batting helmets in those days. Kellogg also remembered hitting a homer once that won a game. "They all were exciting games," she claimed.

After baseball she worked for a dentist for 30 years, retiring in 1979. She has been inducted into the Jackson Bowling Hall of Fame and was named as grand marshal in a parade. A softball complex has been named after Kellogg in her hometown of Brooklyn, Michigan. "A little boy called me and asked me to come out and watch him play at the field," she said. Now she goes to league reunions.

G	BA	AB	H	2B	3B	HR	SB	BB	SO	R	RBI		PO	A	E	DP	FA
						BATTING									FIELDING		
747	.221	2709	600	66	39	8	86	160	156	219	264		6844	222	158	240	.978

Kemmerer, Beatrice "Betty"

Born: Feb. 23, 1930, Center Valley, Pennsylvania. 5'3", 145, Catcher, Shortstop, BR, TR. Fort Wayne Daisies, 1950; South Bend Blue Sox, 1950–51.

Beatrice Kemmerer played in less than ten games in both of the seasons she was in the league. She now lives in Breman, Indiana.

Keough, Lavina

Walworth, Wisconsin. Pitcher. South Bend Blue Sox, 1945–46.

Lavina Keough wore number 7 and played with South Bend.

Keppel, Evelyn

Catcher. South Bend Blue Sox, 1945.

Evelyn Keppel, who wore number 15, played in less than ten games with South Bend in 1945.

Kerrar, Adeline "Addie"

Born: Aug. 31, 1924, Milwaukee, Wisconsin. **Died:** July 4, 1995. 5'2", 130, Shortstop, 3rd Base, Catcher, BB, TR. Rockford Peaches, 1944.

Adeline Kerrar played in a few games for Rockford in 1944. One time she scored the winning run by stealing home, but because she wasn't told to steal home she was fined. She served as an area representative for the AAGPBL Players Association for a number of years.

BATTING

G	BA	AB	H
8	.167	18	3

Kerrigan, Marguerite "Kerry"

Born: July 24, 1931, Ridgeway, Minnesota. 5'9", 150, Pitcher, Utility, BR, TR. Rockford Peaches, 1950–52.

Marguerite Kerrigan was with Rockford for three seasons, but she saw limited action.

Kerrigan was raised on a farm and played with her cousins as a child. Her first organized softball came when she was in high school. While attending the College of St. Theresa, she played for Zahn Sheet Metal. "I had a friend in Rockford and he convinced me to try out in 1950," she explained. The Peaches took her, but didn't use her much over three seasons.

After baseball, she played for R.H. Hall in Florida and went to several world championships.

She also worked with Delta Airlines in reservation sales for 24 years. She retired in 1987 and lives in Largo, Florida.

PITCHING

G	IP
1	1

Kerwin, Irene "Pepper"

**Born: Nov. 3, 1925, Peoria, Illinois.
5'7", 150, 1st Base, Catcher, BR, TR.
Peoria Redwings, 1949.**

Irene Kerwin played one season with her hometown team in 1949.

Kerwin began playing softball between eighth grade and high school with the Farrow Chix. She played with them for a couple of years before working at and playing with the Catapillar Diselettes. That led her hometown team, the Peoria Redwings, to ask her to join them. She did for the 1949 season.

The following year the Redwings offered her another contract, but she knew the team didn't have much of a future. She decided to go to Chicago to play professional softball and go to college. Peoria folded after the 1951 season.

Kerwin received her degree through Illinois State University and played a few more years of softball with the Pekinlettes "We drew fantastic, between 3,000 and 10,000 fans," she said about the team. "If the All-America League could have drew that many it would still be around."

She went on to teaching and coaching for the next 30 years and retired in 1983. She has been named to three local halls of fame.

Irene "Pepper" Kerwin

						BATTING								FIELDING				
G	BA	AB	H	2B	3B	HR	SB	BB	SO	R	RBI		PO	A	E	DP	FA
27	.137	73	10	0	0	0	2	7	12	2	1		166	7	6	6	.966

Helen Ketola

Ketola (LaCamera), Helen

Born: Sept. 30, 1931, Quincy, Massachusetts. 5'4", 129, 3rd Base. Fort Wayne Daisies, 1950.

Helen Ketola enjoyed a season with Fort Wayne in 1950, but she decided to call it quits when the team sent her a contract the next season.

Ketola played sandlot ball at age 9 before she joined a softball team in high school as a sophomore. Mary Pratt, who played in the league in the mid–1940s, became her coach and took her to a league tryout in Everett, Massachusetts. She made the cut there then traveled to South Bend to compete with some 400 women trying to make the league. The league took 40 of the players and she was one of them.

Manager Max Carey installed her at third base and she played frequently until Betty Foss arrived with her big bat and sent her to the bench. The following year she met Joseph LaCamera and they fell in love. She decided not to go back to the league. The two married in 1955 and had two children, Paul and Jean.

While her children were in school, she decided to drive a school bus. After the children left home, she retired and the couple moved to Florida. Then in 1992, she decided to go back to driving a bus. She reflected on her time in the league, "Other than my husband and children, it was one of the most enjoyable times of my life."

BATTING												FIELDING				
G	BA	AB	H	2B	3B	HR	SB	BB	SO	R	RBI	PO	A	E	DP	FA
31	.131	61	8	0	0	0	0	11	14	8	9	20	48	8	6	.895

Keyes, Erma "Erm"

Born: Aug. 1, 1926, Frazier, Pennsylvania. 5'5", 135, Outfield, BR, TR. Battle Creek Belles, 1951; Peoria Redwings, 1951.

Erma Keyes was a fair fielding and hitting outfielder for one season with two teams. She graduated from Ursinus College, Collegeville, Pennsylvania.

BATTING												FIELDING				
G	BA	AB	H	2B	3B	HR	SB	BB	SO	R	RBI	PO	A	E	DP	FA
89	.212	316	67	0	0	0	7	20	23	23	23	120	13	9	1	.937

Kidd, Sue

**Born: Sept. 2, 1933, Choctaw, Arkansas.
5'8", 165, Pitcher, 1st Base, TR, BR.
Peoria Redwings, 1950; Muskegon
Lassies, 1950; South Bend Blue Sox,
1950–54; Battle Creek Belles, 1951.**

Sue Kidd helped the South Bend Blue Sox to two titles during her five-year career in the league as a pitcher and first baseman.

From the time she could sit up, Kidd was playing with a ball. Her father was a player-manager on a semi-pro team and her three brothers played baseball. When the traveling Springfield team stopped in Arkansas in 1949, she tried out and was taken. She pitched a no-hitter with the Sallies during the exhibition tour.

Kidd began league play in 1950, but not with much success; her record was 1–10. She landed on the South Bend team in 1951 and received much more run support. Her 11–7 record helped the team win the pennant. In the playoffs, she was untouchable and recorded a perfect game.

The following season there was a rift in the team and she debated on leaving with some players who walked off the team. "I called my father for advice and he said I better not," she recalled. She stayed with the team and helped them win the playoffs by playing first and pitching on the 12-member team.

In 1953 she pitched both ends of a doubleheader and won both, yet she ended the season with a losing record (13–15). She had the most innings pitched (258) in the league and tied for the most games started (29).

After the league ended, Kidd played until 1960 for the South Bend Rockettes, a women's basketball team.

Sue Kidd

She then went to college as a promise to her father and graduated with a degree from Arkansas State Teachers College. She then taught for 25 years in Logansport, Indiana. She continued to play softball until 1975. She now has dog grooming businesses in Arkansas and Indiana.

PITCHING										BATTING			FIELDING				
W–L	PCT	ERA	G	IP	H	R	ER	BB	SO	BA	AB	H	PO	A	E	DP	FA
47–45	.511	2.49	117	857	634	353	237	185	270	.201	563	113	465	341	26	29	.969

Kimball (Purdham), Mary Ellen

Born: April 1, 1929, Kalamazoo, Michigan. 5'7", 148, Outfield, Pitcher. Racine Belles, 1948.

Mary Ellen Kimball didn't get much playing time during her one season in the league. Racine also tried to turn her into a pitcher. She now lives in Irons, Michigan.

	BATTING		
G	BA	AB	H
2	.000	5	0

King, Nancy

Chicago, Illinois. Outfielder. Kenosha Comets, 1951.

Kissel (Lafser), Audrey "Pigtails" "Kiss"

Born: Feb. 27, 1926, St. Louis, Missouri. 5'3", 120, 2nd Base, BR, TR. Minneapolis Millerettes, 1944.

Audrey Kissel played a single season in the league and gave it up for married life.

Kissel learned to play baseball from her three brothers. Then she played in a prep league in St. Louis until she was 18. All-American player Lois Florreich talked her into joining

Audrey "Pigtails" "Kiss" Kissel

the league in 1944. She went to spring training in LaSalle, Illinois, and was assigned to Minneapolis. "Kiss," as her teammates called her, became the regular second baseman for the team. The press called her "Pigtails" because of way she wore her hair.

During the off-season, she received devastating news: Her sailor boyfriend had been listed as killed in action after being shot down. "They had given up on him and sent his clothes home," she explained. However, he survived and returned home to her before she signed a contract to play in 1945. "If he had come back a week later, I would have signed it," she said.

She married Fred Lafser and the two raised five children: Kathleen, Frederick Jr., Eileen, Daniel and Colleen. She took up teaching in Sunday School and became the superintendent for the last 25 years. She now is busy with her nine grandchildren and goes to league reunions. Also she was named to the Hancock Sports Hall of Fame.

BATTING												FIELDING				
G	BA	AB	H	2B	3B	HR	SB	BB	SO	R	RBI	PO	A	E	DP	FA
102	.189	360	68	1	3	1	47	32	12	47	19	261	182	37	20	.923

Kline (Randall), Maxine "Max"

Born: Sept. 16, 1929, North Adams, Michigan. 5'7", 130, Pitcher, TR, BR. Fort Wayne Daisies, 1948–54.

As one of the best overhand hurlers in the league, Maxine Kline led the league in wins twice on her way to becoming the third most winningest pitcher in the league's existence. The four time All-Star helped Fort Wayne win three straight pennants.

Kline grew up on a farm with nine sisters and brothers. She played softball, but no baseball. She was an excellent basketball player in high school. Her basketball coach was so confident of her skills that he and her principal took her to a tryout in Fort Wayne. "When I got back home from my senior trip, I had a contract. I had three days to report," she reminisced.

She first got her chance to play when Fort Wayne was riddled with injuries. Kline, an outfielder with an excellent arm, was put in to pitch.

Maxine "Max" Kline

She responded with two shutouts in her first two starts, which earned her a spot in the rotation.

The following season she really came of age when she pitched a 5–0 no-hitter against Grand Rapids on June 12. She relied on her fastball, but also had a changeup and curveball. "My biggest asset was that I had good control," she said. She ended her sophomore year with a 14–11 mark.

In 1950, "Max" posted a 23–9 record, which was the most wins in the season by any hurler. She was named to her first All-Star team. Her winning percentage was even better the following season as she went 18–4 (.818). Her spot on the All-Star team was secure.

In 1952, Fort Wayne had amassed the best hitters in the league. Kline remembered the three Weaver sisters as the heart of the lineup. She continued her dominance on the mound, too. She helped the Daisies win their first pennant with a 19–7 record, which included six shutouts.

Kline had an off year in 1953. She posted a 16–14 mark, but the Daisies still won the pennant for the second year in a row and it didn't stop the sports writers from picking her for the All-Star team. However, the Daisies lost in the playoffs. "I don't know why we didn't win the playoffs," she explained.

The last year of the league saw Kline pitch her second no-hitter on June 20, once again against Grand Rapids. She had particularly good luck against the Chicks and once tossed a 17-inning shutout against them. She led the league in wins (18), games pitched (28), complete games (24), innings pitched (1,518) and shutouts (6). She wasn't picked for the All-Star team probably because of her performance the year before.

After the league folded, she joined on with Bill Allington's All-Americans for four summers. "We would play against men's teams, like the Colorado Silver Bullets," Kline, who wore number 3, commented.

After her barnstorming days ended, she moved back to her hometown and married Robert Randall in 1973. That's when she quit working for Jonesville Products, an automotive products company. He retired in 1992 and the couple enjoy farming. Kline stays close to home due to back problems. The town erected a sign in her honor that reads: "The Home of Maxine Kline, HOFer."

PITCHING										BATTING			FIELDING			
W–L	PCT	ERA	G	IP	H	R	ER	BB	SO	BA	AB	H	PO	A	E	FA
116–65	.641	2.34	196	1518	1244	538	394	389	495	.194	592	115	155	505	19	.972

Klosowski, Delores

Born: April 28, 1923, Detroit, Michigan. 5'4", 134, 1st Base, BL, TL. Milwaukee Chicks, 1944; South Bend Blue Sox, 1945.

Delores Klosowski was a member of the Milwaukee Chicks during their 1944 Championship year. She also played for South Bend the next season, filling in at first base. Now she lives in Washington, Michigan.

BATTING												FIELDING					
G	BA	AB	H	2B	3B	HR	SB	BB	SO	R	RBI	G	PO	A	E	DP	FA
39	.197	137	27	2	0	0	10	12	15	8	16	37	390	16	15	19	.964

Klosowski, Theresa

Muskegon Lassies, 1948.

BATTING

G	BA	AB	H
2	.000	3	0

Knezovich (Martz), Ruby

Born: March 18, 1918, Hamilton, Ontario, Canada. Died: Aug. 1, 1995, Regina, Saskatchewan, Canada. 5'2", 130, Catcher. Racine Belles, 1944–45.

Ruby Knezovich shared the catching duties with two other players during her two seasons in the league with Racine.

BATTING | FIELDING

G	BA	AB	H	2B	3B	HR	SB	BB	SO	R	RBI	PO	A	E	DP	FA
17	.146	41	6	0	0	0	1	3	3	4	2	29	16	2	1	.958

Kobuszewski, Theresa

Born: July 15, 1920, Wyandotte, Michigan. 5'4", 165, Pitcher, TR, BR. Kenosha Comets, 1946–47; Fort Wayne Daisies, 1947; Muskegon Lassies, 1948.

Theresa Kobuszewski was an underhand pitcher for three seasons in the league.

Kobuszewski used to shag flies when she was a child before breaking into a city league in the late 1930s. She then went to play in Detroit before the war. When World War II started, she signed up and was put into aircraft warning. When she was shipped to Europe, the Wac was switched to an ordinance battalion.

After the war ended, she returned to the United States to find some of her former friends had joined the All-American League. She tried out and was taken as an underhand pitcher, although the league was phasing out that pitching style. She was assigned to Kenosha. She recalled one game in South Bend where some 5,000 fans had showed up. She was nervous, but she still won the game. "Marge Stefani came out to me after the game and asked, 'What are you throwing today?'" she remembered. She was a "spot pitcher," which meant she was able to throw to the spots the catcher called. She also had a drop, in-shoot and riser.

Kobuszewski didn't get much run support from the Comets and ended her rookie year with a 3–9 record. The following season she started in Kenosha, but ended up at Fort Wayne with another losing season, 11–15. In 1948, the league decided to discard all of its underhand pitchers, so she was released. She went over to the National League in Chicago and played pro softball for three more years.

In 1951, Kobuszewski joined the Air Force during the Korean War. She was an administrative worker during her long military career and traveled all over the world. She continued to play softball and in 1974 threw in an exhibition against the King and His Court. She retired as a chief master sergeant, the highest enlisted rank, in 1975. She attended a league reunion in 1993, but a heart attack prevented her from attending the 1995 reunion.

PITCHING										BATTING			FIELDING			
W–L	PCT	ERA	G	IP	H	R	ER	BB	SO	BA	AB	H	PO	A	E	FA
14–24	.368	2.53	51	331	254	160	93	108	103	.242	124	30	36	126	21	.885

Koehn, Phyllis "Sugar"

Born: Sept. 15, 1922, Marshfield, Wisconsin. 5'5", 120, Pitcher, Utility Fielder, TR, BR. Kenosha Comets, 1943–45; South Bend Blue Sox, 1945–48; Peoria Redwings, 1948; Racine Belles, 1948–49; Fort Wayne Daisies, 1949; Grand Rapids Chicks, 1950.

Phyllis Koehn played just about every position during her eight-year career in the league.

Like many league players, she began playing baseball in the sandlots and advanced to organized softball when she was in high school. Then she began playing for a factory team, the Red Dot Potato Chip Company, which won two state championships.

Her father saw that the league had tryouts, but Koehn missed them and went to Wrigley Field instead, where she landed a contract for $60 a week and became one of the first players in the league. "That was big money," she said of the contract, which was twice as much as she was getting with the factory team.

She started out as a utility fielder with the Comets and played seven different positions. In her rookie season, she hit for power — 4 homers and 15 extra-base hits — and had a solid .238 average. She also had the first homer at the team's Lakefront Stadium.

"Sugar," as she was called by her teammates, recalled one game in Kenosha in which she missed a bunt sign and was fined $5. But the next night she made a miraculous catch in the outfield and the manager told her to forget the fine.

In 1946, the league began switching to sidearm pitching and South Bend experimented with her as a pitcher because she had a good arm. She responded by becoming one of the best pitchers in the league. She compiled a 22–15 record, and the following season she threw in 34 games and ended up with a 16–16 mark.

In 1948, she spent time with three teams and either pitched or played the field. The hop-scotching played havoc on her performance. Pitching took a toll on her arm and her record dropped to an all-time low of 2–11. She hardly pitched at all in her last season. She decided to quit the league because her arm was spent. By the time she quit, she was making a $125 week.

After baseball, she went on to work for Zenith for 34 years and retired in 1983. She now plays golf and goes to AAGPBL reunions.

PITCHING									
W–L	PCT	ERA	G	IP	H	R	ER	BB	SO
48–54	.471	2.55	124	886	631	393	251	413	234

BATTING												FIELDING				
G	BA	AB	H	2B	3B	HR	SB	BB	SO	R	RBI	PO	A	E	DP	FA
587	.200	1946	390	37	21	6	116	97	143	199	195	687	541	106	18	.921

Kolanko, Mary Lou "Klinky"

Born: May 16, 1932, Weirton, West Virginia. 5'2", 124, Outfield, BL, TL. Peoria Redwings, 1950; Springfield Sallies, 1950.

Mary Lou Kolanko played in less than ten games with Peoria before being sent down to the barnstorming Springfield Sallies for further development in her only season in the league.

Kolanko grew up with five brothers, so she had plenty of help learning how to play ball. She played in the city leagues during high school. Then she saw an article in the newspaper and wrote the league. She was invited to a tryout in McKeesport, Pennsylvania. After passing the test, she was sent to South Bend for another tryout. She wasn't out of school yet, so she had to go back home to take her finals before she could report to Peoria.

The Redwings decided she wasn't ready for the league just yet, so she was reassigned to Springfield. She hit .285 in 45 games with the Sallies, where she was known for her speed, stealing and bunting.

After baseball, she earned degrees at St. Louis University and Webster College. She then taught for 38 years and retired to Tampa, Florida, in 1989.

Mary Lou "Klinky" Kolanko

Kotil, Arlene

1st Base. Muskegon Lassies, 1950; South Bend Blue Sox, 1950–51.

BATTING													FIELDING					
G	BA	AB	H	2B	3B	HR	SB	BB	SO	R	RBI		G	PO	A	E	DP	FA
83	.205	244	50	5	1	0	10	30	64	21	21		82	177	20	19	33	.977

Kotowicz, Irene K. "Ike"

Born: Dec. 10, 1919, Chicago, Illinois. 5'5", 128, Pitcher, Outfield, TR, BR. Rockford Peaches, 1945; Fort Wayne Daisies, 1946–47; Kenosha Comets, 1947; Chicago Colleens, 1948; Racine Belles, 1949–50.

Irene Kotowicz was plagued by wildness at the beginning of her pitching career, but she settled down and became an average pitcher.

She played for the Rockolas in Chicago before joining the league. In her first season, "Ike" played outfield for the championship Rockford Peaches. Her best season in the league came in 1948 with her hometown Colleens as she went 18–17.

After baseball, she was a buyer of men's clothing for Sears for 33 years. She now lives in Elk Grove, Illinois.

PITCHING

W–L	PCT	ERA	G	IP	H	R	ER	BB	SO
42–47	.472	2.73	96	702	503	299	213	413	315

BATTING												FIELDING				
G	BA	AB	H	2B	3B	HR	SB	BB	SO	R	RBI	PO	A	E	DP	FA
188	.141	518	73	6	3	0	21	54	52	45	32	53	142	31	1	.863

Kovalchick (Roark), Helen "Dot"

Born: December 31, 1925, Sagamore, Pennsylvania. 5'2", 125. Outfield, Third Base, TR, BR. Fort Wayne Daisies, 1945.

Kramer (Hartman), Ruth "Rocky"

Born: April 26, 1926, Limekiln, Pennsylvania. 5'1", 110, Relief Pitcher, 2nd Base, TR, BR. Racine Belles, 1946; Fort Wayne Daisies, 1947.

Ruth Kramer was a relief pitcher in a league that expected the starter to finish the game, so she played in less than ten games in both seasons. She was used more as a batting practice pitcher. After baseball, she taught physical education for 29 years. She also got married and had one daughter.

Krick, Jaynne "Red"

Born: Oct. 1, 1929, Auburn, Indiana. 5'11", 150, Pitcher, Outfield, 3rd Base, TR, BR. South Bend Blue Sox, 1948–49; Battle Creek Belles, 1951; Peoria Redwings, 1951; Grand Rapids Chicks, 1951–53.

Jayne Krick was a wild pitcher who hit the most batters (15) in 1951.

In one game during the '51 season, she hit Connie Wisniewski, one of the best players in the league, four times. The next day "Red" was traded to Grand Rapids. After baseball, she worked for Motorola and owned a gas station in Moose Jaw, Canada. She became a security guard after retirement. She now lives in Arlington, Texas.

PITCHING										BATTING			FIELDING			
W–L	PCT	ERA	G	IP	H	R	ER	BB	SO	BA	AB	H	PO	A	E	FA
8–22	.267	3.37	61	315	286	207	118	189	97	.195	524	102	111	301	19	.956

Kruckel, Marie "Kruck"

Born: June 18, 1924, Bronx, New York. 5'4", 130, Utility, Pitcher, BR, TR. South Bend Blue Sox, 1946; Fort Wayne Daisies, 1947; South Bend Blue Sox, 1948; Muskegon Lassies, 1948–49.

Marie Kruckel was a utility player and average pitcher for four seasons in the league. She started playing softball in grade school in the Bronx. In high school, she played organized ball on the weekends. When she attended East Stroudsburg State Teacher's College, Kruckel played with a team in Yorktown, New York. She wrote a letter to the league in 1945. "They sent me a contract after I graduated," she commented.

Because she taught school, "Kruck" couldn't go to spring training, so she was used as a utility player during her first two years in the league. Then in 1948, the Blue Sox tried her as a pitcher and she displayed a good curveball and changeup. In 1949 the mound was moved back another five feet, but she couldn't adjust. She was let go after the season.

After baseball, she taught and coached for 38 years at Clay High School in South Bend. Now she goes to league reunions.

BATTING

G	BA	AB	H	2B	3B	HR	SB	BB	SO	R	RBI
98	.248	236	35	1	1	0	7	42	35	16	16

PITCHING / FIELDING

W–L	PCT	ERA	G	IP	H	R	ER	BB	SO		PO	A	E	DP	FA
10–11	.476	2.11	34	205	165	86	48	64	27		82	52	6	2	.958

Kunkel (Huff), Anna "Kunk"

Born: March 18, 1932, Wescosville, Pennsylvania. 5'2", 112. BR, TR. South Bend, 1950–51.

Anna Kunkel's playing career ended early because of a knee injury. She had surgery and came back, but the knee didn't hold up. After baseball, she worked as a counselor for the Arizona Department of Corrections. She now lives in Tucson.

Kurys, Sophie "Soph" "Flint Flash"

Born: May 14, 1925, Flint, Michigan. 5'5", 115, 2nd Base, Outfield, Pitcher, BR, TR. Racine Belles, 1943–50; Battle Creek Belles, 1952.

Sophie Kurys stole a phenomenal 80 percent of the time she was on base. In one season of 112 games, she swiped 201 bases in 203 attempts. Seven times she led the league in steals, and six times she led in runs scored. She is the lifetime leader in stolen bases and runs scored.

An empty field catercorner from her house became a ball field for the youngster while growing up in Detroit. Her best friend was named "Squirt" and they would play baseball in the morning, because the bigger kids would take over in the afternoon. She advanced to women's softball and played with the Michigan state champions in 1939.

Then in 1943 a scout from the league came by her town. Her friends called her up and told her of the tryout. She thought they were crazy, since it was snowing outside. The tryout was down the street in a fieldhouse. Her friends picked her up and she tried out in a skirt and sweater. The scout liked her and sent her parents a contract. Her father heard about it in the newspaper and did not want his 17-year-old daughter going away to Chicago. Her mother, though, signed the contract and sent her on a train to Chicago. "I had never been out of Michigan. I was as green as the grass," she recalled. When she arrived in Chicago it was pouring down rain and she became homesick, but the scout talked her into staying.

After spring training she was allocated to Racine, a city she had never heard of. She played second base and hit .271 on the season with 44 stolen bases, helping Racine win the pennant and championship.

In her sophomore year, "Soph" began to steal bases on a regular basis. "They give a sign whether they're going to pitch the ball or throw over to first. Most of the time I would pick up their sign," she explained. She also had quick jump. Kurys stole seven bases on September 3 to tie a league record for most steals in one game. She ended up swiping a league record 166 bases on the year and leading the league in runs scored (87).

After slowing down to 115 steals in 1945, the "Flint Flash" earned her nickname in 1946. She became a threat to steal any base at any time, including home, which she swiped a few times in her career. Besides stealing 201 bases, she set two team records for highest batting average (.286) and most hits in one season (112). She also led the league in walks (93) and runs scored (117). Her fantastic year earned her Player of the Year honors and a spot on the All-Star team. She also helped the Belles win a pennant and championship, which gave her more satisfaction than the individual records. In her first five seasons, she played in every inning of every game for Racine.

For the next four seasons she led the league in stolen bases and runs scored and was selected on the All-Star team each year, except for 1950. In 1950 she also led the league in hits (130) and home runs (7). In 1952 she was traded to Battle Creek and played in 17 games before being injured.

Kurys holds the all-time records for stolen bases (1,114) and runs scored (688). She's third lifetime in hits (859) and walks (522). She holds single season records for stolen bases (201), runs scored (117) and base on balls (93).

She jumped to a Chicago league in 1953 and played second base for the Admiral Music Maids. Then in 1955 she moved to Arizona to play shortstop for the A-1 Queens. She quit playing softball and became part owner in Apex Machine Products until she retired in 1972. Then she worked part-time another 10 years.

Sports Illustrated ran a photo of her next to Rickey Henderson after he broke the career stole base record. "They (the press) scoff at that (the records) because it was only a women's league," she explained. Now retired, she lives in Scottsdale and attends league reunions.

BATTING

G	BA	AB	H	2B	3B	HR	SB	BB	SO	R	RBI
914	.260	3298	859	71	39	22	1114	522	204	688	278

PITCHING

G	IP
1	2

FIELDING

PO	A	E	DP	FA
2407	1641	190	173	.957

Ladd, Jean
Kenosha Comets, 1951.

Lake, Joyce

Muskegon Belles, 1953.

Lawson, Mary

Norfolk, Virginia. Outfield. Peoria Redwings, 1946.

			BATTING											FIELDING				
G	BA	AB	H	2B	3B	HR	SB	BB	SO	R	RBI		PO	A	E	DP	FA
25	.105	57	6	2	0	0	1	1	3	3	1		27	3	2	1	.938

Leduc (Alverson), Noella "Pinky"

Born: Dec. 23, 1933, Graniteville, Massachusetts. 5'5", 130, Pitcher, Outfield, TR, BR. Peoria Redwings, 1951; Battle Creek Belles, 1952; Muskegon Belles, 1953; Fort Wayne Daisies, 1954.

Noella Leduc, a pitcher-outfielder, played for four seasons and helped Fort Wayne win a third consecutive title in 1954.

Leduc began playing sandlot ball with the boys at age 5. When she went to high school she had to play softball, but after school she played with the boys again. One day she came home from school and hit shags to the outfield of the boy's team. Someone told her about the league and to contact Rita Briggs after the season was over. She tried out for Briggs and was sent to spring training in Peoria. "Pinky"—the nickname Briggs gave her—signed a contract with Battle Creek.

She went 3–4 with the Belles in her rookie season. In one game, she pitched 14 innings and scored the winning run after doubling.

Noella "Pinky" Leduc

In her final season, she was picked up by Fort Wayne. The Daisies played the All-Star team that year and Pinky was the winning pitcher. She gave up the most earned runs (84) on the season; however, the Daisies gave her plenty of run support and her record (9–10) was much better than her ERA (6.05). The Daisies again won the pennant.

After baseball, her father passed away and she took care of her mother for awhile. In 1964 she married George Alverson, who was in the Navy. The retired couple have one daughter, Betsy, and now live in Leonardo, New Jersey.

PITCHING

W–L	PCT	ERA	G	IP	H	R	ER	BB	SO
15–23	.395	4.96	67	303	331	218	167	146	66

BATTING												FIELDING				
G	BA	AB	H	2B	3B	HR	SB	BB	SO	R	RBI	PO	A	E	DP	FA
144	.195	267	52	6	0	2	4	23	45	33	21	85	100	5	1	.974

Annabelle "Lefty" Lee

Lee (Harmon), Annabelle "Lefty"

Born: Jan. 22, 1922, Los Angeles, California. 5'2", 120, Pitcher, 1st Base, TL, BB. Minneapolis Millerettes, 1944; Fort Wayne Daisies, 1945; Peoria Redwings, 1946–47; Grand Rapids Chicks, 1947; Fort Wayne Daisies, 1948; Peoria Redwings, 1949–50.

Although credited with a perfect game and a no-hitter, Annabelle Lee was one of those pitchers who had a fine ERA but never had a winning season partly because she was never on a championship team.

Lee's father had been a semi-pro player in Hollywood, California, and taught her the basics. "I never played with dolls; I always played with balls and bats," she recalled. At age 15, she began playing with the factory teams in her hometown area. Her first team was the Hollywood Curlers in 1937. For the next seven years, she played on several teams and then was noticed by Bill Allington, who recruited her for the All-American League.

She was assigned to Minneapolis, which was a new franchise in 1944. She had played mostly first base before coming to the league, but the Millerettes needed her as a pitcher, too. On July 29 against Kenosha, she pitched the first perfect game in league history against the Kenosha Comets. "I didn't even know I had a perfect game," she said. "Lefty" ended the season with an 11–14 mark.

The following season, the league sent her to another new franchise in Fort Wayne. On July 7 she again had a dazzling performance when she pitched a one-hitter against Grand Rapids. She lowered her ERA to 1.56, but she still ended up with a losing (13–16) record. She was also the best fielding pitcher in the league, committing just five errors on the season.

In 1946 she was again assigned to another new franchise in Peoria. The Redwings had the worst batting average in the league and Lee suffered through a 12–23 season. The league decided to switch to sidearm pitching during the season, and Lee was one of the few pitchers who successfully made the transition. "My dad always said I needed to have a 'true arm' and be able to throw the ball every way," she explained. He made her throw underhand, sidearm and overhand to a mattress with the strike zone marked on it or through a tire.

While in Peoria, manager Johnny Gottselig told her he'd never trade her, but after a horrible game in Racine, he sent her to Fort Wayne. She ran back to Peoria to get her belongings and then raced to Fort Wayne. She was sent in to pitch that evening and threw a shutout. "It always makes you stronger to have something adverse happen to you," she said. She lived by that philosophy.

By 1948, the league had switched to overhand or sidearm delivery and Lee continued to pitch. Then in 1950 she was hurt sliding into home. She hit the back of her head on the plate and suffered partial paralysis due to the head injury. She was out for the rest of the season and decided to call it quits.

After a year away from the game, she went back to playing softball until 1957. She then married Lloyd Harmon and worked in the electronics field until 1987. Baseball runs in her family as nephew Bill Lee became a pitcher for the Boston Red Sox and Montreal Expos.

Lee now cares for her 95-year-old mother and a garden when she's not out signing autographs with a group of women called the Golden Diamond Girls. She also attends league reunions.

PITCHING

W–L	PCT	ERA	G	IP	H	R	ER	BB	SO
63–96	.396	2.25	186	1322	1073	543	331	415	271

BATTING												FIELDING				
G	BA	AB	H	2B	3B	HR	SB	BB	SO	R	RBI	PO	A	E	DP	FA
230	.147	510	75	7	0	0	23	86	31	36	20	233	359	45	3	.929

Lee (Dries), Dolores "Pickles"

Born: April 21, 1935, Jersey City, New Jersey. 5'6", 130, Pitcher, 2nd Base, TR, BR. Rockford Peaches, 1952–54.

Rockford's Rookie of the Year in 1953, Dolores Lee was a pitcher and second baseman during the waning years of the league.

Lee started playing ball when she was 4 years old with the boys on the street. "I was one of the guys," she explained. She started playing softball with the girls when she was 12. Her manager was the father of AAGPBL player Joan Berger, so she had an inside track to the league and made the Peaches' roster in 1952.

"Pickles"—a name she picked up back home because some men couldn't remember her name—threw all the pitches, but her fastball was her bread-and-butter pitch. She recalled one game that was very interesting. "I remember I had the bases loaded three times. I got out of it each time," she explained. She once appeared on the television show *What's My Line?* They guessed incorrectly that she was a softball player.

After the league, she married in 1960 and had one son. She also became a police detective in Jersey City and retired in 1978. She now lives in Deming, New Mexico, and has one grand-daughter. She has attended several league reunions.

PITCHING

W–L	PCT	ERA	G	IP	H	R	ER	BB	SO
23–22	.511	3.01	53	371	340	177	124	168	130

BATTING													FIELDING				
G	BA	AB	H	2B	3B	HR	SB	BB	SO	R	RBI		PO	A	E	DP	FA
93	.159	246	39	0	2	0	9	10	21	20	9		109	207	21	10	.938

Lee, Laurie Ann

Born: Jan. 3, 1931, Racine, Wisconsin. 5'7", 131, Pitcher, TR, BR. Racine Belles, 1948.

Laurie Lee was a local product of Racine and practiced with the team before being signed by the league and assigned to the Belles. She suffered a broken finger during spring training and did not pitch much after that.

Lenard, Jo "Bubblegum"

Born: Sept. 2, 1921, Chicago, Illinois. 5'4", 130, Outfielder, BR, TR. Rockford Peaches, 1944–45; Muskegon Lassies, 1946–49; Peoria Redwings, 1949; Kenosha Comets, 1950–51; South Bend Blue Sox, 1952–53.

Jo Lenard spent a decade with the league on three championship teams and was once selected to an All-Star team.

Lenard played on Chicago softball teams in her youth. When she wasn't playing ball, she was ice skating. She won a national speed skating championship. After high school, she fell in love with a pilot and they became engaged. He was shot down in the war and died six months later. Lenard went to work in a defense plant in 1943 before being lured to the league in 1944.

Jo "Bubblegum" Lenard

Her first team was the Rockford Peaches and she hit .211 the first season while roaming left field. She showed right away she had speed by leading the league in triples (10). She also swiped 68 bases. "I was pretty fast," she explained. "If I got on base, I wasn't afraid to steal."

The stealing took toll on her posterior. "I used to ride side saddle for all the scabs I had from sliding on the other side," she recalled.

In her second season she led all outfielders in fielding (.993) and helped lead Rockford to a pennant and playoff win. She picked up the nickname "Bubblegum" because she snuck kids into the ballpark for a piece of bubblegum, which she chewed incessantly.

The league moved her to Muskegon in 1946, which was an off year for Lenard. She got on track with a .261 average the next season in leading Muskegon to the pennant. Her efforts also earned her a spot on the All-Star team, but the game wasn't played that year.

Lenard played in Kenosha for two seasons, 1950–51. She was traded to South Bend in 1952 and hit a solid .259 in leading the Blue Sox to their second playoff win in a row. She finally left the league after the 1953 season.

Lenard obtained a teaching degree from Chicago Teacher's College and taught high school in her hometown. On April 5, 1968 — the day after Martin Luther King, Jr., died — she was assaulted by an African American girl. She was hit in the forehead and suffered eye damage that left her nearly blind. She retired from teaching after 25 years because of the injury.

She obtained a seeing-eye dog in 1995 to help her around. She named the dog "Homer" because she hit only one home run in the league. She now lives in Williams Bay, Wisconsin.

						BATTING										FIELDING		
G	BA	AB	H	2B	3B	HR	SB	BB	SO	R	RBI		PO	A	E	DP	FA
1000	.221	3420	756	73	31	1	520	481	234	465	351		1467	90	64	21	.961

Leonard (Linehan), Rhoda "Nicky"

Somerset, Massachusetts. 5'5", 115, 2nd Base, Outfield, BL. Fort Wayne Daisies, 1946.

Rhoda Leonard didn't get much of a chance to play in her only season in the league. After baseball, she married Edmund Linehan and had two children, Mark and Maggie. She became an elementary school teacher. Leonard was inducted into the Somerset High School Hall of Fame.

BATTING			
G	BA	AB	H
9	.095	21	2

Lequia (Barker), Joan "Joanie"

Born: March 13, 1935, Negaunee, Michigan. 5'2", 120, 3rd Base, TR, BR. Grand Rapids Chicks, 1953.

Joan Lequia played in less than ten games for the Chicks in 1953.

"Joanie" began playing fast-pitch softball at age 14. Grand Rapids picked up the infielder in 1953. She left in mid-season to return home to fix financial problems there. She continued playing fast-pitch softball.

She got married in 1975. After 36 years with AT&T, she retired in 1989. Today she is still a big sports fan.

Lessing, Ruth

Born: Aug. 15, 1925, San Antonio, Texas. 5'5", 128, Catcher, BR, TR. Minneapolis Millerettes, 1944; Fort Wayne Daisies, 1945; Grand Rapids Chicks, 1946–49.

A three time All-Star, Ruth Lessing was one of the best fielding catchers the league ever had. For three successive seasons she led the league in fielding. She was a dependable hitter as well.

G	BA	AB	H	2B	3B	HR	SB	BB	SO	R	RBI	PO	A	E	DP	FA
						BATTING								FIELDING		
559	.191	1840	351	31	8	2	98	178	187	164	161	2597	219	87	56	.973

Lester, Mary Louise

Born: Jan. 19, 1921, Monterey, Tennessee. Died: Date Unknown. 5'3", 138, 2nd Base, BR, TR. Kenosha Comets, 1943–44; South Bend Blue Sox, 1944.

One of the league's original players, Mary Lester, played two seasons in the league.

G	BA	AB	H	2B	3B	HR	SB	BB	SO	R	RBI	PO	A	E	DP	FA
						BATTING								FIELDING		
112	.186	345	64	4	3	0	25	50	29	43	33	190	124	31	11	.910

Liebrich, Barbara "Bobbie"

Born: Sept. 30, 1922, Providence, Rhode Island. 5'9", 145, 2nd Base, 3rd Base, BR, TR. Rockford Peaches, 1948.

Barbara Liebrich didn't get much playing time, but she became a player-manager of one of the traveling teams and later served as a chaperone.

Liebrich was a late bloomer and didn't start playing softball until after she graduated from high school in 1940. She played for a local team that worked its way to the nationals in Detroit one year. Then one of her teammates heard about the league and they attended a try-out in New Jersey. She signed and went to Opa-locka, Florida, for spring training. She was assigned to Rockford but played in only three games during the season.

Following the season, the league decided it would have two teams—the Springfield Sallies and the Chicago Colleens—go on a traveling tour to scout out talent and give rookies more experience. "Bobbie" became the player-manager of the Sallies. The tour began in Illinois and took on a counterclockwise route through Texas, the South, the East Coast and back to the Midwest. "We were accepted all over the country," Liebrich explained. "We played for charity only. We were the 'good-will ambassadors' of the league." During the tour, tryouts were held in every city and quite a few players were subsequently signed. The two barnstorming teams held a repeat performance in 1950 and Liebrich just managed.

Liebrich then became a chaperone for the Kalamazoo Lassies before the league folded in 1954. She went to work as an accountant and eventually as an office manager for a printing company, retiring in 1989. She served on the Board of Directors for the Players Association in the 1980s and she now attends league reunions.

Barbara "Bobbie" Liebrich

BATTING

G	BA	AB	H
3	.250	4	1

Lionikis, Kay "Irene"

New Brunswick, New Jersey. Died: Date Unknown. 2nd Base, TR, BR. Peoria Redwings, 1948; Grand Rapids Chicks, 1948; Chicago Colleens/Springfield Sallies, 1949; Fort Wayne Daisies, 1950.

Kay Lionikis was in the league for three years, but she saw little action. She was on the player development tour in 1949.

BATTING

G	BA	AB	H
2	.000	4	0

Little, Alta

Born: May 21, 1923, Gas City, Indiana. 5'10", 1st Base, Pitcher, TR, BR. Muskegon Lassies, 1947; Fort Wayne Daisies, 1948.

Alta Little's timing in trying to crack the lineup as a regular first baseman wasn't right during her two years in the league.

When she was growing up in Michigan, her sisters played on a softball team. "I wanted to play, but the coach said I was too young," she explained. Then one day the team was short of players and she was given her chance at age 11. She was in the lineup thereafter.

She was playing in a Muskegon factory league when the league signed her to a contract and she went to Opa-locka, Florida, for spring training. She was assigned to her hometown team, but she was never given playing time because the team had a regular first baseman. She was reassigned to Fort Wayne the next season and the same thing occurred, so she quit the league.

Little went into managing bowling lanes and is now semi-retired near Dallas, Texas.

PITCHING			BATTING		
G	IP		BA	AB	H
1	1		.128	47	6

Little (Bend), Olive "Ollie"

Born: May 7, 1917, Poplar Point, Manitoba, Canada. Died: Feb. 2, 1987. 5'3", 135, Pitcher, TR, BR. Rockford Peaches, 1943, 45–46.

One of the original players of the league, Olive Little pitched the first no-hitter in league history and was named to the first All-Star team.

Little, whose name was Bend before she married, learned how to play ball from her father at the age of 10. Her father was a softball coach. He would spend an hour with her every night fielding balls and pitching. By the time she joined the Norwood Collegiates in 1937, she was further along than most and soon became the top pitcher on the team. She threw a no-hitter in her first season.

In 1942 she was touring the United States with the Moose Jaw Royals and was noticed by league scouts. Later, she was offered a contract for $100 a week, one of the richest offered by the league. She had planned on marrying George Little and teaching, but the pay was too much for her to pass up. She took the offer and joined the Rockford Peaches.

Early in the season on June 10, she tossed a no-hitter against Rockford

Olive "Ollie" Little

to make league history as the first pitcher with a no-hitter, although she did allow two unearned runs. Her no-hitter earned her a spot on the All-Star team that played a double-header at Wrigley Field under the lights.

Later that season, she also tossed a seven-inning no-hit game on August 15 against South Bend. Her 21–15 record in her rookie year was one of the best in the league. She was also among the league leaders in strikeouts.

She took the 1944 season off to deliver the couple's first child, Bobbi. Her husband was in the armed forces in 1944 as well. Little came roaring back in 1945 and pitched even better than she had in her first season. Her third no hitter came on July 10, 1945, against Fort Wayne. She ended the season with a 22–11 record and helped Rockford win pennant and championship. The following season the league was switching to sidearm pitching, so she called it quits after a 14–17 mark.

She went on to raise another daughter, Frankie, and both played softball like their mom. In 1983, she was inducted into the Canadian Softball Hall of Fame and, in 1985, she was added to the Manitoba Sports Hall of Fame.

PITCHING

W–L	PCT	ERA	G	IP	H	R	ER	BB	SO
57–43	.570	2.16	112	858	650	249	206	383	381

BATTING | | | | | | | | | | | FIELDING

G	BA	AB	H	2B	3B	HR	SB	BB	SO	R	RBI		PO	A	E	FA
113	.148	294	43	4	0	0	5	25	32	22	19		67	220	35	.891

Lobrovich, Claire

Campbell, California. Outfield, BR, TR. Kenosha Comets, 1947; Rockford Peaches, 1948.

Claire Lobrovich played outfield for two seasons in the league, including a year with the championship Rockford Peaches in 1948.

BATTING | | | | | | | | | | | FIELDING

G	BA	AB	H	2B	3B	HR	SB	BB	SO	R	RBI		G	PO	A	E	DP	FA
81	.209	258	54	3	2	0	15	23	27	22	21		77	69	7	6	0	.927

Lonetto, Sarah "Tomato"

Born: June 9, 1922, Detroit, Michigan. 5'3", 120, Outfield, Pitcher, BB, TR. Racine Belles, 1947; Muskegon Lassies, 1948–49.

Sarah Lonetto was a pitcher-outfielder for three seasons in the late 1940s. "Tomato" went to spring training in Havana, Cuba. She also went on the South American tour in 1948. She played with the Bomberettes in Detroit before joining the league. She now lives in Southfield, Michigan.

BATTING

G	BA	AB	H	2B	3B	HR	SB	BB	SO	R	RBI
102	.142	225	32	2	1	1	8	20	37	25	5

PITCHING										FIELDING				
W–L	PCT	ERA	G	IP	H	R	ER	BB	SO	PO	A	E	DP	FA
3–9	.250	2.78	20	109	88	48	30	57	12	50	8	3	1	.951

Lovell (Dowler), Jean "Grump"

Conneaut, Ohio. Died: Jan. 1, 1992. Catcher, Pitcher. Rockford Peaches, 1948–49; Kalamazoo Lassies, 1950–54; Kenosha Comets, 1951.

Jean Lovell played both battery positions, but was a much better receiver. She was a member of the championship Rockford Peaches in 1948 and 1949 and championship Kalamazoo Lassies in 1954. Her best year as a hitter came in 1954 when the ball was reduced to major league size. She hit 21 home runs, drove in 69 runs and also had a career high .286 batting average.

BATTING

G	BA	AB	H	2B	3B	HR	SB	BB	SO	R	RBI
470	.229	1376	315	39	6	25	11	1440	131	174	174

PITCHING										FIELDING				
W–L	PCT	ERA	G	IP	H	R	ER	BB	SO	PO	A	E	DP	FA
3–10	.231	4.18	18	113	103	83	52	60	17	1376	253	77	33	.955

Lovett, Frances

Pitcher. Peoria Redwings, 1946.

PITCHING								BATTING		
W–L	PCT	G	IP	H	R	BB	SO	BA	AB	H
0–1	.000	1	7	13	12	2	0	.000	2	0

Luckey, Lillian

Born: May 9, 1919, Niles, Michigan. 5', 126, Pitcher, TR, BR. South Bend Blue Sox, 1946.

PITCHING										FIELDING		
W–L	PCT	ERA	G	IP	H	R	ER	BB	SO	BA	AB	H
2–4	.333	3.44	8	54	51	37	21	48	10	.133	15	2

Luhtala, Shirley

1st Base. Racine Belles, 1950; Battle Creek Belles, 1951; Rockford Peaches, 1951.

Shirley Luhtala played first base for two seasons in the league with two teams. She was involved in a rare triple play in 1951.

												BATTING / FIELDING				

BATTING

G	BA	AB	H	2B	3B	HR	SB	BB	SO	R	RBI
30	.167	96	16	1	0	0	1	7	13	6	5

FIELDING

PO	A	E	DP	FA
152	4	9	3	.945

Luna (Hill), Betty Jean

Born: May 1, 1927, Dallas, Texas. 5'5", 133, Pitcher, Outfield, TR, BR. Rockford Peaches, 1944; South Bend Blue Sox, 1945–46; Rockford Peaches, 1947; Chicago Colleens, 1948; Fort Wayne Daisies, 1949–50; Kalamazoo Lassies, 1950.

Betty Jean Luna tossed two no-hitters during her seven seasons in the league. The first came against Grand Rapids on Aug. 6, 1945; the other came in 1947. Her best season came in 1946 when she went 23–13 for South Bend. She was one of the few pitchers in the league to make the conversion from underhand to overhand pitching.

PITCHING

W–L	PCT	ERA	G	IP	H	R	ER	BB	SO
74–70	.514	2.12	162	1207	768	429	284	524	430

BATTING

BA	AB	H
.218	1378	300

FIELDING

PO	A	E	FA
492	388	70	.926

Lyman (Kelly), Esther

Peoria, Illinois. Died: Date Unknown. Catcher. South Bend Blue Sox, 1946.

McCarty, Mary "Mick"

Born: June 8, 1931. 5'6", 180. Outfield. Peoria Redwings, 1951.

Mary McCarty played three years of softball and a year of baseball before coming to the league for one season with Peoria.

BATTING

G	BA	AB	H	2B	3B	HR	SB	BB	SO	R	RBI
72	.169	207	35	6	2	0	9	20	49	20	24

FIELDING

PO	A	E	DP	FA
83	9	9	4	.922

Joanne McComb

McComb, Joanne

Born: March 1, 1933, Avonmore, Pennsylvania. 5'7", 130, 1st Base, TR, BR. Springfield Sallies, 1950.

Joanne McComb barnstormed with the Springfield Sallies for a season before deciding the league wasn't for her.

McComb never played softball or baseball with any organized team before trying out for the league in 1949 at age 15. She didn't make the grade that year, but the next year she was selected at a tryout. She was going to be late for the beginning of the season, so she was assigned to Springfield to tour the country and get more experience.

She specially enjoyed the games in Griffith and Yankee Stadium. "I really enjoyed meeting people at the various towns we played in," she reflected.

After the season, she decided to go to college. "I was going nowhere in the league," she explained. She went to Slippery Rock University and obtained a teaching degree. After teaching 26 years, she retired in 1986. She now does much volunteer work for the Red Cross.

BATTING

G	BA	AB	H	2B	3B	HR	SB	BB	SO	R	RBI
69	.141	242	34	1	0	0	9	37	43	32	19

McCormick, Judy

Pitcher. South Bend Blue Sox, 1954.

PITCHING

G	IP
1	4

McCreary, Ethel

Died: Date Unknown. Outfield. Rockford Peaches, 1943; Kenosha Comets, 1943.

One of the original players in the league, Ethel McCreary was a good hitting outfielder.

						BATTING									FIELDING			
G	BA	AB	H	2B	3B	HR	SB	BB	SO	R	RBI		PO	A	E	DP	FA
71	.251	231	58	6	1	1	11	18	7	29	36		57	8	4	1	.942

McFadden (Rusynyk), Betty "Mac"

**Born: Oct. 22, 1924, Savanna, Illinois.
5'7", 135, Pitcher, BR, TR.
South Bend Blue Sox, 1943.**

Betty "Mac" McFadden

Betty McFadden was one of the original players signed in the league, but she wasn't offered a contract after the inaugural year of the AAGPBL.

She was 11 when she started playing softball. She read about tryouts for the league in the newspaper and went to Wrigley Field. "The day I went it was raining, so we tried out under the bleachers. I was the best player on concrete," she recalled. She tried out as a third baseman, but due to a shortage of pitchers she was taken for mound duty.

During the season, "Mac," as players liked to call her, spent more time on the bench than on the mound. She remembers starting about five games and appearing in both games of a doubleheader once. However, she played in less than ten games, which is why her statistics weren't recorded.

The following season she was not offered a contract and went back to work shipping munitions for the war effort. She married Michael Rusynyk in 1945 and had three children: Gary, David and Lynn. After working at Sears & Roebuck for 23 years, she retired in 1993. She now enjoys golf, bowling and travel. She also attends some of the league reunions.

Machado (Van Sant), Helene "Chow"

Born: April 17, 1926, Venice, California. 5'11", 148, Outfield, BR, TR. Peoria Redwings, 1946; Fort Wayne Daisies, 1947.

Helene Machado picked up the unusual nickname of "Chow" in Cuba after she collected scraps of food from the players for the street dogs during spring training in 1947.

Machado was an excellent softball player who played on two championship teams in the early 1940s. She also played basketball and tennis. The league began recruiting her in 1942, but didn't sign her until 1946 because her father wouldn't let her go to the league.

When her father became sick, she left the game and never returned. She later got married and had three sons and three daughters. She also went to college and received a degree in psychology. She retired in 1991 and lives in San Bernadino. She had seven grandchildren at last count.

BATTING													FIELDING				
G	BA	AB	H	2B	3B	HR	SB	BB	SO	R	RBI		PO	A	E	DP	FA
163	.204	553	113	13	4	0	33	35	32	39	37		261	14	17	2	.942

McKenna, Betty

Lisbon, Ohio. Died: Feb. 24, 1992. 3rd Base. Fort Wayne Daisies, 1951; Peoria Redwings, 1951; Battle Creek Belles, 1951–52; Muskegon Belles, 1953.

Betty McKenna was a part-time third baseman for three teams in three years with the league. She worked at her local library after baseball and played basketball.

BATTING													FIELDING				
G	BA	AB	H	2B	3B	HR	SB	BB	SO	R	RBI		PO	A	E	DP	FA
166	.186	478	89	14	2	0	25	95	77	53	42		201	384	57	18	.911

McKinley (Uselmann), Therese "Terry"

Born: Feb. 28, 1928, Chicago, Illinois. 5'6", 135, Outfielder, BR, TR. Muskegon Lassies, 1949.

Therese McKinley was an excellent player in the minors, but didn't get much of a chance to play during her season in the sun.

McKinley began playing with 14-inch softball in the park district in Chicago when she was 9 years old. She saw an advertisement in the *Chicago Tribune* and tried out for the All-American League in 1948. She was put on one of the four teams that were like a minor league in Chicago. There the outfielder hit .402 and stole bases with her good speed.

The following season "Terry" was moved up to the league and assigned to Muskegon. The rookie had problems hitting the curveball and struggled behind the plate. However, in the field she possessed a good glove. She recalled one of her two errors on the season: an easy flyball she should have caught. She got better as the season wore on and the manager put her in the lineup during the playoffs.

After her season, she played more softball in Chicago before joining the Navy during the Korean War. Then she attended DePaul University and received a bachelor's degree in physical education. In 1960 she married Duane Uselmann. The couple raised five children: Mary, Frances, Jean, Carol and Patrick. She also taught 18 years and retired in 1995. She now has four grandchildren and lives in Park Ridge, a suburb of Chicago. She has attended several league reunions.

BATTING													FIELDING				
G	BA	AB	H	2B	3B	HR	SB	BB	SO	R	RBI		PO	A	E	DP	FA
37	.099	101	10	0	0	0	7	9	18	10	4		38	3	2	2	.953

MacLean (Ross), Lucella "Frenchy"

Born: Jan. 3, 1921, Lloydminster, Saskatchewan, Canada. 5'2", 135, Catcher, Outfield, BR, TR. South Bend Blue Sox, 1943–44.

Lucella MacLean, one of the original members of the AAGPBL, is best remembered for starting the league's first triple play in 1944.

She began playing "scrub" ball in 5th grade in her native Canada. She played on the senior team at her high school all four years. After high school, she joined the best town team in Saskatchewan.

When the AAGPBL was scouting players in Canada, they wanted the top pitcher on her team, but she insisted on not going to the new league without her battery mate — MacLean. "Frenchy," as her teammates called her, went to South Bend and became the backup catcher. She really enjoyed the people. "The people were wonderful to us. The owner of the newspaper would loan us his car to go to the beach," she recalled.

Lucella "Frenchy" MacLean

On May 30, 1944, MacLean was catching in a game where the opposing team had runners on first and second base. "The batter was trying to punt the ball. It popped a little. I threw it to first and she threw it to second for the triple play. The runners had been off with the pitch," she explained.

In 1945, she didn't like the contract that was sent to her by Max Carey, so she took the summer off. The following season she signed with the Chicago National League, where she got paid $65 a week. She married her first husband, Roger Moore, in 1950 and played in Chicago through the 1952 season.

She moved to Detroit and worked as an advertising clerk for the *Detroit Free Press* for several years. Her first husband passed away and she returned home to Canada. She married Mervyn Ross in 1950 and went to work for the Canadian government for several years.

She visited the National Baseball Hall of Fame when the league was inducted in 1988. The Saskatchewan Baseball Hall of Fame inducted her in 1991.

BATTING													FIELDING				
G	BA	AB	H	2B	3B	HR	SB	BB	SO	R	RBI		PO	A	E	DP	FA
101	.149	402	60	4	1	0	62	28	17	34	25		243	36	14	8	.952

Dorothy "Mickey" Maguire

Maguire (McAlpin), Dorothy "Mickey"

Born: Nov. 12, 1918, LaGrange, Ohio. Died: Aug. 2, 1981. 5'5", 145, Catcher, Outfield, BR, TR. Racine Belles, 1943; Milwaukee Chicks, 1944; Grand Rapids Chicks, 1945; Muskegon Lassies, 1946–49.

Dorothy Maguire was one of the original All-Americans and played seven seasons in the league.

She started playing softball at age 11. She then joined Erin Brew team, which won the world championship in 1936 and 1938.

Maguire joined the All-American League when it began and helped Racine win a pennant and championship in her first season by hitting a career high .269 average. She was tagged with the nickname "Mickey" because her play was reminiscent of major leaguer Mickey Cochrane. She was shipped to Milwaukee the next season and they won the pennant.

In 1945 with Grand Rapids, she tied a league record with three sacrifices in one game. She went to Muskegon the following season and the Lassies won a pennant in 1947 with her help. After the season, she got married. She played another full season before retiring on June 5, 1949.

She went on to marry again and foster five boys and a girl. Her son, Richard, tried out for the Kansas City Royals, but couldn't follow in his mother's footsteps. She trained horses before her death in 1981.

	BATTING												FIELDING				
G	BA	AB	H	2B	3B	HR	SB	BB	SO	R	RBI		PO	A	E	DP	FA
.595	.194	1906	370	30	16	3	243	206	149	222	185		1922	525	190	56	.928

Mahon, Elizabeth "Lib"

Born: Nov. 18, 1919, Greenville, South Carolina. 5'7", 135, 2nd Base, Outfield, BR, TR. Kenosha Comets, 1944; South Bend Blue Sox, 1945–52.

A two time All-Star, Elizabeth Mahon was one of the best clutch hitters in the league during her nine year career.

Mahon was age 6 when she first began playing baseball with the boys in Greenville. "The boys would ask me to play with them," she recalled. Her mother didn't take kindly to her playing with the boys and criticized her.

After high school, she went to Winthrop University and graduated with a teaching degree. She was only getting paid $90 a month to teach, so she went to work for the U.S. Postal Service for 65 cents an hour. Meanwhile, she played ball with the Springfield Spinners.

In May 1944, AAGPBL scout Jimmy Gaston spotted her and signed her and Viola Thompson to a contract for $60 a week, which was much more than the post office paid. She went to spring training with Minneapolis. "I hurt my arm in spring training and never did throw as well after that," she said.

Kenosha manager Marty McManus saw her in spring training and liked what he saw so he traded for her. The following season McManus went to the Blue Sox and traded for Mahon again, because he liked her hitting. Once during her career, she outscored the other team and the headline read the next day: "Racine Gets 2, Lib Gets 4." During the season she tied the league record by hitting safely in 13 consecutive games from July 27–August 9.

She had her best year and was named to the All-Star team in 1946. She led the league in RBI (72), total bases (326) and runs scored (90). She also led the league in RBI (60) in 1949. She was the best fielding outfielder in 1950 with only one error.

One of her most interesting times in the league came during 1947

Elizabeth "Lib" Mahon

spring training in Cuba. "It was beautiful training weather," she recalled. However, some players weren't used to all the sun and suffered some severe burns. They had to watch their equipment carefully or otherwise the poor Cubans would steal it.

Her greatest thrill in the league came in 1951 when she helped South Bend win the pennant and playoffs. She also was named an All-Star player in 1949.

Her career ended abruptly in 1952 when she joined five others in walking out on the Blue Sox after manager Karl Winsch suspended Shorty Pryer with a week left in the season. She had already planned to quit at the end of the season, though. "I hated for my ball playing to end that way," she reflected.

Mahon's career 400 RBI is third best in league history. She twice led the league in RBI.

After baseball, she taught school for 36 years before retiring in 1981. She still calls South Bend her home and goes to AAGPBL reunions. She also loves to play golf.

				BATTING									FIELDING				
G	BA	AB	H	2B	3B	HR	SB	BB	SO	R	RBI		PO	A	E	DP	FA
837	.281	2562	721	84	34	8	364	358	150	432	400		1190	236	58	28	.961

Mahoney, Marie "Red"

Born: Sept. 21, 1924, Houston, Texas. 5'3", 135, Outfield, BR, TR. South Bend Blue Sox, 1947–48; Fort Wayne Daisies, 1948.

With a nickname that matched her hair color, Marie Mahoney roamed the outfield for two seasons in the league.

Mahoney took up softball when she was 9 years old. She also competed in volleyball, basketball and tennis while she grew up in Houston. At age 16 she joined a women's softball team and invited to join the league. She went to spring training in Havana, Cuba.

"Red" played about half the time during her two seasons in the league with the Indiana teams. She later played softball in Houston. She worked for Eastman Kodak as a microfilm technician for 32 years and retired in 1983. In 1993, she was diagnosed with breast cancer, but she recovered from it and still golfs today in Houston.

BATTING												FIELDING				
G	BA	AB	H	2B	3B	HR	SB	BB	SO	R	RBI	PO	A	E	DP	FA
103	.177	254	45	3	7	1	27	16	41	31	14	96	5	7	2	.935

Malach (Webb), Kay

Born: May 30, 1926, Knoxville, Tennessee. 5'5", 135, Outfield, BR, TR. Fort Wayne Daisies, 1947.

BATTING			
G	BA	AB	H
1	.000	1	0

Mandella, Lenora "Smokey"

Born: May 4, 1931, McKeesport, Pennsylvania. 5'7", 145, Pitcher, TR, BR. South Bend Blue Sox, 1949; Springfield Sallies, 1950; Peoria Redwings, 1951.

Lenora Mandella wasn't given much of a chance to pitch in her three seasons, but one of her three career victories was a one-hitter. After baseball, she managed softball teams and became a security guard. She was an avid bowler and was once the best duck pin bowler in the United States and Canada. She now lives in Herminie, Pennsylvania.

PITCHING										BATTING			FIELDING			
W–L	PCT	ERA	G	IP	H	R	ER	BB	SO	BA	AB	H	PO	A	E	FA
3–4	.429	4.28	17	80	75	66	38	71	23	.111	27	3	2	26	2	.933

Mansfield (Kelley), Marie "Boston"

Born: Nov. 4, 1931, Boston, Massachusetts. 5'7", 140, Pitcher, 1st Base, Outfield, TR, BR. Rockford Peaches, 1950–54; Battle Creek Belles, 1952.

Marie Mansfield helped the Rockford Peaches win a pennant and championship during

Marie "Boston" Mansfield

her rookie year with a dazzling 16–8 record and a 2.85 ERA. Her pitching career took a nose dive after that, though. She went 3–14 the following season, and in 1953 she led the league in walks and strikeouts. Mansfield began playing softball at age 12. She was a key punch operator after baseball. She now lives in Jamica Plain, Massachusetts.

PITCHING

W–L	PCT	ERA	G	IP	H	R	ER	BB	SO
34–42	.447	3.33	92	611	424	321	226	505	369

BATTING

G	BA	AB	H	2B	3B	HR	SB	BB	SO	R	RBI
253	.130	623	81	10	1	0	16	69	140	54	38

FIELDING

PO	A	E	DP	FA
376	224	28	8	.957

Marks, Gloria

Born: 1923, San Diego, California. 5'6", 130, Pitcher, TR, BR. Racine Belles, 1943.

One of the original players of the league, Gloria Marks pitched one season and helped Racine win a pennant and championship. She pitched for championship teams in San Diego before joining the league.

PITCHING										BATTING			FIELDING			
W–L	PCT	ERA	G	IP	H	R	ER	BB	SO	BA	AB	H	PO	A	E	FA
11–9	.550	4.03	29	166	145	123	75	117	29	.265	68	18	18	63	15	.844

Marlowe (Malanowski), Jean "Mal" "Jeanie"

Born: Dec. 28, 1929, Scranton, Pennsylvania. 5'6", 135, Pitcher, 1st Base, 2nd Base, Outfield, TR, BR. Springfield Sallies, 1948; Kenosha Comets, 1949–51; Kalamazoo Lassies, 1952–54.

Jean Marlowe, whose last name is really Malanowski, acquired her last name in the league as a result of a misspelling, but it didn't matter to her because all she wanted to do was play ball.

Her coal miner father and uncle were ball players and taught her how to play when she was growing up. She read about the league in the newspaper and went to Allentown for a try-out with some 200 other girls. Marlowe tried out as an infielder and outfielder, but the league liked her arm and saw her as a future pitcher, so she was invited to spring training in Opa-locka, Florida.

"Mal" was assigned to a new franchise, the Springfield Sallies. The team didn't give her much run support and she got off to a poor start in her first season by losing the most games (22) and allowing the most earned runs (96) and runs (141) in 1948.

"Jeanie" greatly improved her record the next two seasons to .500. Then she had three more losing seasons. She was the best fielding pitcher in 1952 with no errors. She issued the most walks (114) in 1954. One of her greatest thrills was her team winning the last championship of the league. "To me, every game was great," she said.

After baseball, she continued to play softball and worked for B.F. Goodrich. She then went to Schottglass Technologies and worked there until retirement in 1987. She now goes to league reunions.

PITCHING

W–L	PCT	ERA	G	IP	H	R	ER	BB	SO
56–79	.415	3.18	133	953	840	474	337	433	274

BATTING												FIELDING				
G	BA	AB	H	2B	3B	HR	SB	BB	SO	R	RBI	PO	A	E	DP	FA
314	.199	838	167	17	6	7	28	86	98	83	68	347	348	38	13	.971

Marrero, Mirtha

Havana, Cuba. Pitcher, TR, BR. Chicago Colleens, 1948–49; Kalamazoo Lassies, 1950; Fort Wayne Daisies, 1951; Battle Creek Belles, 1952; Muskegon Belles, 1953.

Mirtha Marrero was one of the Cubans who came to the league in 1948 after the league had held spring training in Cuba the season before. She never materialized into the pitcher the league had hoped for when they recruited her, though. After a slow start in 1948 in which she went 4–21, she spent a season on the traveling team in hopes of improving. She did have a 17–8 record in 1951 with Fort Wayne, but she then fell to a 4–14 mark the next season.

PITCHING										BATTING			FIELDING			
W–L	PCT	ERA	G	IP	H	R	ER	BB	SO	BA	AB	H	PO	A	E	FA
32–62	.340	3.42	119	774	693	437	294	396	252	.191	278	53	40	222	34	.885

Marshall, Theda "T"

Born: April 24, 1925, Canton, South Dakota. 5'7", 133, 1st Base, BR, TR. South Bend Blue Sox, 1947–48; Chicago Colleens, 1948.

Theda Marshall spent two seasons in the league before being offered more money to play softball in Arizona.

Marshall came from a large family of seven brothers and sisters. She began playing softball in school at age 12, she recalled. Then at 15 she played on one of the two girl's softball teams in town. A few years later a scout from the league stopped by the town and her coach recommended her for the league. "My ball coach got $50 out of the deal," she said.

Spring training was in Havana, Cuba, that year and she almost didn't make it there. "We had a horrible snowstorm and we almost didn't get off the ground," she explained. She finally made it to Cuba, which was an experience in itself. "There was a revolution for two days and we couldn't leave the hotel. We had to lower buckets so they could send us up Cokes," she remembered.

"T" was assigned to South Bend. She had trouble hitting the overhand pitching and led the league with 79 strikeouts in 1947. Her numbers were better in her second year, but her batting average was below par. However, she was a good fielder. The league sent her to the new Chicago Colleens team in 1948 where she finished out her short career. When a softball team in Arizona offered her more money the next season, she jumped at the chance.

After her playing days ended, she went to work for the government

Theda "T" Marshall

as a computer technician. She worked at the Air Force Accounting and Finance Center in Denver, Colorado, for 30 years, retiring in 1981. Then she took up newspaper delivery to "keep busy," which she has been doing ever since in Denver. In 1992, she had to have her right rotator cuff removed from injuries suffered during her baseball and softball days. Now she has only 50 percent mobility in the arm and has become a lefty.

			BATTING												FIELDING			
G	BA	AB	H	2B	3B	HR	SB	BB	SO	R	RBI		PO	A	E	DP	FA
238	.141	754	106	16	9	0	34	59	139	53	48		2607	61	80	95	.971

Mason, Pat

Cedar Rapids, Iowa. Grand Rapids Chicks, 1953.

Matlack (Sagrati), Ruth "Matty"

Born: Jan. 13, 1931, Cromwells Heights, Pennsylvania. 5'2", 127, Pitcher, TL, BL. Fort Wayne Daisies, 1950.

Ruth Matlack was a better hitter than pitcher during her only season in the league.

Matlack learned to play ball from her father. She first started playing organized softball in the eighth grade. After graduation from high school, she went to play in Norristown. Then she went to a league tryout in Allentown and was invited to spring training in Cape Giradeau, Missouri. She was assigned to Fort Wayne as a pitcher. "I had a natural curveball, a changeup, but not much of a fastball," she explained.

"Matty" was used mainly as a relief pitcher. She hit .361, but couldn't win a game on the mound. Over the winter she was dealt to Kalamazoo, but she was homesick and didn't want to go back to the league.

After baseball, she worked at a restaurant before becoming a factory supervisor. She got married in 1970, but it didn't work out. Then she married again in 1985 to John Sagrati. Retired now in Quartetown, Pennsylvania, she golfs and works part-time.

PITCHING

W–L	PCT	ERA	G	IP	H	R	ER	BB	SO
0–4	.000	3.54	14	61	37	34	24	65	6

BATTING						FIELDING			
G	BA	AB	H	R	RBI	PO	A	E	FA
21	.361	36	13	3	2	2	11	3	.813

Mattson (Baumgart), Jacqueline

Born: Nov. 16, 1928, Waukegan, Illinois. 5'5", 100, Catcher, BR, TR. Chicago Colleens/Springfield Sallies, 1950; Kenosha Comets, 1951.

Jacqueline Mattson was a backup receiver who played two seasons in the league.

The youngest of eight children, she grew up with a fascination for baseball and played with her brother as a child. She played organized softball on the playgrounds of Milwaukee. In 1945 she helped West Allis, Wisconsin, to the state championship.

While barnstorming in 1950 with the player development tour, she hit .200 in 48 games; however, when she reached the regular league, she managed to teach just half of that average as a backup receiver.

BATTING											FIELDING				
G	BA	AB	H	2B	3B	HR	SB	BB	SO	R	RBI	PO	A	E	DP	FA
51	.098	51	5	0	0	0	1	7	7	6	3	67	9	4	1	.950

Maturzewski, Joan

Milwaukee, Wisconsin. Outfield. South Bend Blue Sox, 1953.

BATTING												FIELDING				
G	BA	AB	H	2B	3B	HR	SB	BB	SO	R	RBI	PO	A	E	DP	FA
28	.162	99	16	2	1	0	3	15	14	15	2	32	1	5	0	.868

Mayer, Alice

Outfield. South Bend Blue Sox, 1948.

BATTING												FIELDING				
G	BA	AB	H	2B	3B	HR	SB	BB	SO	R	RBI	PO	A	E	DP	FA
37	.211	90	19	0	2	0	9	7	15	6	13	13	0	2	0	.867

Meacham, Mildred "Meach"

Born: May 5, 1924, Charlotte, North Carolina. 5'8", 160, 1st Base, BR, TR. Fort Wayne Daisies, 1947; Racine Belles, 1947; Springfield Sallies, 1948.

Mildred Meacham was the starting first baseman for the Springfield Sallies in 1948. She spent two seasons in the league. She played in the Chicago National League before joining the AAGPBL. The sure-handed fielder was a good base stealer. She still lives in Charlotte.

BATTING												FIELDING				
G	BA	AB	H	2B	3B	HR	SB	BB	SO	R	RBI	PO	A	E	DP	FA
97	.179	291	52	4	3	0	24	32	37	26	10	984	32	26	20	.975

Measner, Hazel

Rockford Peaches, 1946.

BATTING		
G	BA	AB	H
1	.000	1	0

Meier, Naomi "Sally"

Born: Nov. 17, 1926, Fort Wayne, Indiana. Died: Date Unknown. 5'10", 148, Outfield, BR, TR. Rockford Peaches, 1946–47; Fort Wayne Daisies, 1947; Peoria Redwings, 1948; Chicago Colleens, 1948; Kalamazoo Lassies, 1950; Fort Wayne Daisies, 1950–52; Battle Creek Belles, 1952; Muskegon Belles, 1953.

Naomi Meier was a good hitting and fielding outfielder for seven different teams in eight seasons in the league.

Meier grew up in Fort Wayne and played sandlot ball until she was discovered by the league. She was assigned to Rockford, but was sent back to her hometown to play during her second season in the league.

Then in 1948 she was sent to the newly formed Chicago Colleens. "Sally" led the team with a career high 100 hits, 54 runs and 47 RBI. After a stop in Kalamazoo, she was sent back to Fort Wayne. In 1951 she suffered a season-ending compound fracture of her right ankle by sliding into second base. Near the end of the next season the Daisies traded her to Battle Creek.

	BATTING												FIELDING				
G	BA	AB	H	2B	3B	HR	SB	BB	SO	R	RBI		PO	A	E	DP	FA
710	.258	2456	560	33	14	4	206	219	277	265	234		1106	47	73	9	.941

Melin, Berith

Rockford, Illinois. Died: Date Unknown. Outfield, BR, TR. Rockford Peaches, 1943.

Berith Melin was one of the original members of the league who spent a single season with her hometown Rockford Peaches.

	BATTING												FIELDING				
G	BA	AB	H	2B	3B	HR	SB	BB	SO	R	RBI		PO	A	E	DP	FA
56	.158	146	23	2	2	0	4	5	25	7	4		27	4	3	1	.912

Menheer (Zoromapal), Marie

Kenosha, Wisconsin. 5'5", 142, Pitcher. Kenosha Comets, 1945.

PITCHING					BATTING			
W–L	PCT	G	IP		G	BA	AB	H
0–0	.000	1	6		1	.000	3	0

Metesh, Bernice

Born: Aug. 9, 1929, Joliet, Illinois. 5'6", 132, Pitcher. South Bend Blue Sox, 1948; Rockford Peaches, 1948.

Bernice Metesh was with the league for one season. She returned to Joliet after baseball and pitched for an all-male team.

	BATTING		
G	BA	AB	H
2	.000	3	0

Metrolis, Norma "Trolley"

Born: Dec. 5, 1925, Kettery, Maine. 5'6", 135, Catcher, BR, TR. Muskegon Lassies, 1946; Racine Belles, 1947; South Bend Blue Sox, 1948–49; Fort Wayne Daisies, 1950.

Norman "Trolley" Metrolis

A knee injury prevented Norma Metrolis from keeping a starting role during her five seasons in the league.

Born in Maine, Metrolis began playing softball at age 13 in Sarasota, Florida. Her father was reassigned to Orlando, where she continued to play softball. Then in 1945 she was picked as the outstanding player in the league and thus won a free trip to a tryout in Racine with the All-Americans. "I was in a position to stay there and I turned it down. It was the end of the season and I couldn't afford to lose my job," she explained. She was then earning $15 a week as a cashier in a drugstore.

"Trolley" came back to spring training the next season and was picked up by Muskegon as a backup receiver. She played in 15 games during the season. The following season, after spring training in Cuba, she was assigned to Racine, where she was again the backup catcher.

Her best year was 1948. She won the starting job behind the plate, but early in the season she "tore up the knee" and lost her opportunity. She was backup receiver again in 1949 with the Sox. Trolley ended up with Fort Wayne in 1950. They put her on waivers and nobody picked her up. She went home to work in a juice plant. The league invited her back in 1951, but she had a regular job.

Metrolis went on to become an inspector of fruit and vegetables for 31 years with the U.S. Department of Agriculture. She retired in 1986 and now frequently plays golf in the Sunshine State.

BATTING												FIELDING				
G	BA	AB	H	2B	3B	HR	SB	BB	SO	R	RBI	PO	A	E	DP	FA
60	.160	131	21	0	0	0	7	13	11	7	8	182	19	14	4	.935

Meyer (Petrovic), Anna "Pee Wee"

Born: Nov. 17, 1928, Aurora, Illinois. 5'3", 105, Shortstop, BR, TR. Kenosha Comets, 1944; Minneapolis Millerettes, 1944

Anna Meyer was one of the youngest players to sign a contract with the league at age 15.

Anna "Pee Wee" Meyer

Meyer had five brothers and learned to play baseball before she can remember. When she grew up, she wanted to play on a team. "I kept saying to my dad that there had to be a league somewhere," she said. Her father read about the league in a Cincinnati paper and talked to the parents of player Betsy Jochum. She was invited to a tryout and made the league only after her father lied about her age. The league minimum was 16.

The young player was inexperienced with baseball, so she didn't get much playing time with Kenosha. She decided to jump to the Chicago Bluebirds to get more playing time and nearly as much money. She liked it more because she didn't have to travel and could hold down a job. She played in the Chicago league for five more years. She married photographer George Petrovic in 1950, and they raised two sons, David and George, Jr. She now lives in Tucson, Arizona, and works full-time in a supermarket.

BATTING

G	BA	AB	H	2B	3B	HR	SB	BB	SO	R	RBI
17	.107	28	3	0	0	0	3	5	7	3	1

Meyer (Moellering), Rita "Slats"

Born: Feb. 12, 1927, Florissant, Missouri. Died: Date Unknown. 5'10", 145, Shortstop, Pitcher, BR, TR. Peoria Redwings, 1946–49.

Rita Meyer was a good fielding shortstop and average hitter for four seasons in the league.

The oldest of six children, Meyer tried out for the league at spring training in Pascagoula, Mississippi, and was assigned to the Redwings in 1946. She quickly earned the nickname "Slats" because she reminded other players of Slats Marion, a shortstop for the St. Louis Cardinals. In 1947 she was briefly used as a pitcher.

Her best season came in 1948 when she hit .232 with a dozen doubles and a career high 45 stolen bases and 68 RBI.

She married Robert Moellering on Feb. 26, 1949, and left after the 1949 season. Her hobbies included collecting emblems, poems and Dick Tracy comics.

BATTING

G	BA	AB	H	2B	3B	HR	SB	BB	SO	R	RBI
399	.205	1385	284	24	7	3	76	83	96	121	140

PITCHING

W–L	PCT	ERA	G	IP	H	R	ER	BB	SO
3–6	.333	3.12	13	75	45	41	26	48	56

FIELDING

PO	A	E	DP	FA
13	30	4	60	.915

Mickelson, Darlene "Mickey"

Kenosha, Wisconsin. Died: Date Unknown. Outfield. Kenosha Comets, 1943; South Bend Blue Sox, 1945.

Darlene Mickelson, who wore number 12, was one of the original players of the league and played one lackluster season.

BATTING

G	BA	AB	H	2B	3B	HR	SB	BB	SO	R	RBI
50	.200	165	33	1	2	0	10	19	18	20	29

FIELDING

PO	A	E	DP	FA
34	3	4	0	.902

Middleton (Gentry), Ruth

Born: Aug. 25, 1930, Winnipeg, Manitoba, Canada. 5'2", 115, Outfield, BR, TR. Chicago Colleens, 1950; Battle Creek Belles, 1951–52; Muskegon Belles, 1953.

Ruth Middleton was a light-hitting outfielder for four seasons in the league. She hit .226 in 1950 with the traveling Chicago Colleens, but when she came to the regular league she hit poorly. She now lives in Hamilton, Indiana.

BATTING

G	BA	AB	H	2B	3B	HR	SB	BB	SO	R	RBI
122	.134	232	31	3	0	0	8	31	41	25	12

FIELDING

PO	A	E	DP	FA
205	9	10	2	.955

Miller, Pauline "Polly"

Kenosha Comets, 1948.

"Polly" Miller played in one game with Kenosha in 1948.

BATTING

G	BA	AB	H
1	.000	0	0

Miller, Ruth

Rockford Peaches, 1943. Catcher.

Ruth Miller was not one of the original players of the league, but she played in 1943 as a backup receiver.

Moczynski, Betty "Moe"

Born: June 30, 1926, Milwaukee, Wisconsin. 5'3", 120, Outfield, BR, TR. Rockford Peaches, 1943.

An original player in the league, Betty Moczynski spent one season at Rockford before jumping to a rival softball league.

Moczynski was 8 years old when she began playing sandlot ball in her hometown. At age 14 she joined her first organized softball team in West Allis, a suburb of Milwaukee. The owner of the league was a scout for the AAGPBL and invited her to the tryouts for the league at Wrigley Field.

She was assigned to Rockford and played the outfield. During one game she drove in five runs, one short of the record held by Dottie Kamenshek at the time. "Moe," as players called her, also had one home run during the year. "I swung hard and it went over the left fielder's head," she recalled. A local dairy gave her $5 for hitting the homer.

The following season she was offered a contract, but she went to the National League Chicago Bluebirds instead for the same amount of money. She said she did it because there would be less traveling and she could go home to Milwaukee more often. "A lot of girls came over to the National League," she explained.

Moe played for four seasons in the National League as a catcher and outfielder. She totaled 16 years of professional softball. She went to work for General Motors for 38 years and retired in 1987. She now enjoys bingo and fishing.

BATTING												FIELDING				
G	BA	AB	H	2B	3B	HR	SB	BB	SO	R	RBI	PO	A	E	DP	FA
59	.173	208	36	1	2	1	13	17	13	15	27	75	7	4	0	.953

Moffet, Jane

Born: July 2, 1930, Pirtman, New Jersey. 5'10", 151, 1st Base, Outfield, Catcher, BR, TR. Springfield Sallies, 1949–50; Kalamazoo Lassies, 1951–52; Battle Creek Belles, 1952.

Jane Moffet made the league by mistake and played for four seasons.

Moffet was a freshman at East Stroudsborg University when she was dragged to a league tryout by a friend who didn't want to go alone. She made the league but her friend didn't. "I really felt badly about that," she said.

She was put on the traveling Springfield Sallies for two years to gain more experience. In 1950, she played 21 games mostly at catcher and hit .161. She then moved on to the regular league.

After baseball, she finished her master's degree at Rutgers University. She became a high school principal, and after 42 years in the teaching profession, she retired in 1994. She was named to the East Stroudsborg University Hall of Fame. She now lives in Toms River, New Jersey.

BATTING

G	BA	AB	H	2B	3B	HR	SB	BB	SO	R	RBI
150	.210	463	97	13	4	0	31	47	53	48	37

FIELDING

PO	A	E	DP	FA
326	28	23	11	.939

Jane Moffet

Montalbano, Rose "Monty"

Staten Island, New York. 2nd Base. South Bend Blue Sox, 1951–53; Battle Creek Belles, 1952; Muskegon Belles, 1953.

Rose Montalbano saw limited action at second base with three teams during three seasons in the league.

BATTING													FIELDING				
G	BA	AB	H	2B	3B	HR	SB	BB	SO	R	RBI		PO	A	E	DP	FA
38	.221	95	21	2	0	0	3	15	20	13	9		35	38	14	3	.839

Montgomery, Dorothy "Monty"

Born: Feb. 6, 1924, Asheville, North Carolina. 5'3", 110, Utility infielder, BL, TR. Muskegon Lassies, 1946.

Dorothy Montgomery was cut twice from the league, but she still played one season with Muskegon as an infielder.

Montgomery was working for Peerless Wool Mills and playing for its semi-pro team, the Wollenettes, when she was scouted by the league. She received an invitation to try out for league. On her way to spring training with Racine in 1945, she stopped in Chicago to have lunch with league president Max Carey. Both loved blueberry pie, but the cafeteria had only one piece left, so Carey gave it to her. "He was a nice fella," she said.

She practiced with Racine, but they cut her before the season began. "They sent me back home because I was a little green," she explained. The following year she was invited back and this time she passed the test at spring training and was allocated to Muskegon. "Monty" played at several infield positions during the season.

In 1947 she left college early to attend spring training in Havana, Cuba. When the league returned to the United States, she was cut. "I didn't have my heart in playing ball," she now admits.

Montgomery finished her bachelor of science degree and taught some before going to work at hospitals. She couldn't return to playing softball for five years after her league play. Then she played until she was 68. She set up a pap smear laboratory at the Wilburn Clinic in Evansville before retiring in 1991. She now lives in her parent's home in Chattanooga, Tennessee.

	BATTING												FIELDING				
G	BA	AB	H	2B	3B	HR	SB	BB	SO	R	RBI		PO	A	E	DP	FA
26	.208	53	11	0	0	0	3	7	3	5	2		29	20	5	4	.908

Moon, Dorothy

Belleville, Michigan. Pitcher. Rockford Peaches, 1946.

Dorothy Moon was a mediocre pitcher for Rockford for one season.

	PITCHING										BATTING			FIELDING			
W–L	PCT	ERA	G	IP	H	R	ER	BB	SO		BA	AB	H	PO	A	E	FA
2–6	.250	6.89	15	63	64	66	49	64	17		.167	30	5	2	13	7	.682

Moore, Dolores "Dee"

Born: Oct. 27, 1932, Chicago, Illinois. 5'7", 153, 1st Base, 2nd Base, BR, TR. Grand Rapids Chicks, 1953–54.

Dolores Moore played the last two seasons of the league as an infielder for Grand Rapids.

Moore remembered playing sandlot ball with her brother when she was 5 years old. Later during her youth she was playing at Hubble Park when Rogers Hornsby told her she should play in the All-American League. She was too young for the league, though. When Dolores was 16, she was recruited for the league, but her mother wouldn't let her go because

Dolores "Dee" Moore

of all the travel. She instead played softball with the Chicago National League for four seasons. Then Woody English went to the league as a manager and invited her to come along.

"Dee" was a solid hitter and fielder in the league. In one game she knocked in six runs. She helped the Chicks win the championship in 1953. After the league folded, she received a contract to play with Bill Allington's traveling team, but she turned it down. She went to work and started playing other sports. She played briefly with Refiner's Pride, a women's professional basketball team that played exhibition games before the Harlem Globetrotters and NBA teams. She also bowled, fished and golfed.

Moore worked for the Chicago Department of Education as a playground teacher for 31 years before retiring in 1993. She now volunteers at a local hospital.

BATTING												FIELDING				
G	BA	AB	H	2B	3B	HR	SB	BB	SO	R	RBI	PO	A	E	DP	FA
149	.239	477	114	8	0	3	10	33	39	46	57	921	105	27	64	.974

Moore (Walker), Eleanor "Ellie"

Born: Nov. 1, 1933, Long Point, Illinois. 5'10", 165, Pitcher, 1st Base, TR, BR. Chicago Colleens, 1950; Kalamazoo Lassies, 1951; Fort Wayne Daisies, 1951–52; Grand Rapids Chicks, 1952–54.

Eleanor Moore broke into the All-Star team roster in 1953, the same year she recorded 17 wins and tied Jean Faut for the most victories. The following season she hurled a no-hitter and had the most complete games (21). When she wasn't pitching in 1954, she was playing first base and had the best fielding percentage (.988) while committing just 11 errors. She also had the most triples (5).

PITCHING										BATTING			FIELDING			
W–L	PCT	ERA	G	IP	H	R	ER	BB	SO	BA	AB	H	PO	A	E	FA
43–40	.518	2.74	111	703	607	315	214	304	296	.260	315	82	55	222	13	.955

Moore, Mary

California. Pitcher. Rockford Peaches, 1948.

PITCHING										BATTING		
W–L	PCT	ERA	G	IP	H	R	ER	BB	SO	BA	AB	H
2–3	.400	4.00	8	45	31	23	20	40	5	.222	18	4

Moore, Mary Ann "Sis"

Born: June 7, 1932, Detroit, Michigan. 5'5", 145, 2nd Base, BR. Springfield Sallies, 1950; Battle Creek Belles, 1951–52.

Injuries hampered the career of Mary Moore and led her to quit the league after two seasons.

Mary A. "Sis" Moore

Moore was 15 when she first started playing softball by joining Wyandott Chemicals, an industrial team. Her high school English teacher introduced her to the All-American League. She went to South Bend for a tryout and was assigned to the traveling Springfield Sallies in 1950. She led the team in home runs (3), total bases, runs scored (65), RBI (48) and walks (61) while barnstorming the country. Her greatest thrill was playing in Yankee Stadium and meeting Yankee greats Joe DiMaggio, Yogi Berra, Billy Martin and Phil Rizzuto. At the end of the tour she was drafted by Battle Creek.

Before her first spring training, Moore was working in an automobile plant and had several fingers partially cut off in a punch press. Her injury was reminiscent of major leaguer Mordecai "Three-Finger" Brown, who had his fingers damaged in a corn grinder. The injury didn't stop the determined ballplayer from going to spring training four months later. She practiced but team officials decided she just wasn't ready to start the season. Toward the end of the season, she was put in several games, but retained her rookie status.

The following season, "Sis" finally got more of an opportunity to play, but her hand hampered her performance. Then on August 18, she hit her first double of the season and sprained her ankle sliding into second base. Her season was over.

Moore was offered a contract for the 1953 season, yet she decided not to go back. "I was so disappointed in my stats and my play because of my injury," she explained. It was hard for her to walk away from it because she loved to play ball.

After baseball, she worked for AT&T for 35 years, retiring in 1989. She now loves to play softball, golf, bowl and go to league reunions.

BATTING

G	BA	AB	H	2B	3B	HR	SB	BB	SO	R	RBI
42	.148	88	13	1	0	0	5	20	31	11	0

Moraty, Mary

St. Charles, Missouri. Pitcher. Fort Wayne Daisies, 1946.

PITCHING								BATTING		
W–L	PCT	G	IP	H	R	BB	SO	BA	AB	H
0–2	.000	6	28	34	24	22	5	.182	11	2

Morris, Carolyn

Born: Sept. 28, 1925, Phoenix, Arizona. Died: February 20, 1996, Scottsdale, Arizona. 5'8", 145, Pitcher, TR, BR. Rockford Peaches, 1944–46.

Named to the 1946 All-Star team, Carolyn Morris was one of the best underhand hurlers in the league for three seasons.

In her first season, she pitched two no-hitters: the first was a seven-inning affair on August 6 against Milwaukee, and the second came against South Bend on September 6. She was 23–18 her rookie year.

Morris' record improved to 28–12 the following season and she tossed the second perfect game in league history on July 6. She helped Rockford win its first-ever pennant and league championship.

In her final season, she went 29–13 and threw a seven-inning no-hitter at Peoria on August 4. Her 15 shutouts in a single season is the third best total in league history.

PITCHING										BATTING			FIELDING			
W–L	PCT	ERA	G	IP	H	R	ER	BB	SO	BA	AB	H	PO	A	E	FA
80–43	.650	1.55	134	1032	556	266	178	286	471	.165	248	41	83	251	38	.898

Morrison (Gamberdella), Esther "Schmattze"

Born: May 26, 1931, Chicago, Illinois. 5'1", 125, Outfield, Catcher, Pitcher, BR, TR. Springfield Sallies, 1950.

Esther Morrison spent less than a season barnstorming with the league before she became ill and had to retire.

Morrison was playing at Thillen's Stadium in Chicago when the league approached her about playing in 1949. She joined the league the following year and played for Springfield. While the Sallies were touring in the South, she became sick. "I had to quit because every time I bent over, I got a bloody nose," she explained. She was never asked to come back by the league.

She continued to play softball with the Chicago Bluebirds the following season and later played for other softball teams. She worked for Motorola for 14 years before joining the U.S. Postal Service for another 18 years.

Morrison nearly met her death in 1988 in a freak car accident in which she was run over twice. She suffered brain, nerve and tissue damage and nearly died five times, but was revived each time. She feels fortunate now to be alive in Rogue River, Oregon.

BATTING									
G	BA	AB	H	2B	3B	HR	SB	R	RBI
13	.204	59	12	0	1	0	2	11	9

Moss, Glenora

Infielder. Racine Belles, 1943.

Glenora Moss was added to Racine's roster during the 1943 season and played in less than ten games in her only season.

Nancy "Smudgie" Mudge

Mudge (Cato), Nancy "Smudgie"

Born: Oct. 3, 1929, Bridgeport, New York. 5'2", 120, 2nd Base, Shortstop, BR, TR. Chicago Colleens/Springfield Sallies, 1950; Kalamazoo Lassies, 1951–52; Battle Creek Belles, 1952; Muskegon Belles, 1953; Kalamazoo Lassies, 1954.

Once an All-Star, Nancy Mudge played four seasons in the league and helped Kalamazoo win a championship.

Mudge grew up in a small town where there was no baseball or softball for girls. "I played softball and football with the boys ever since I can remember," she said. When she was sophomore in college, she played overhand pitch in a summer league, which was sort of a modified baseball game. She was spotted by a scout from the league and recruited. Mudge was assigned to the traveling teams and hit .308 in 40 games.

The impressive statistics earned her a spot in the league with Kalamazoo the next season. Between seasons she taught school. From there she went to Battle Creek, which was moved to Muskegon in 1953. During "Nancy Mudge Night" at the stadium, she hit her career first home run.

Her home run power continued into the next season and earned her a spot on the All-Star team. In fact, the whole infield of the All-Star squad was from Kalamazoo. "Smudgie" helped the Lassies win the league playoffs over the powerful Fort Wayne Daisies. She ended up with seven home runs on the season and a career best .232 batting average.

She continued playing softball after the league folded, but her "heart was never in it." She married Mark Cato in 1956 and they had one child, Kim. She went on to a long, illustrious teaching career at Hillsdale College and the University of Minnesota and retired in 1979. The couple now have four grandchildren and live in Elk River, Minnesota. She's been to some league reunions.

				BATTING										FIELDING				
G	BA	AB	H	2B	3B	HR	SB	BB	SO	R	RBI		PO	A	E	DP	FA
350	.183	1094	200	25	3	8	97	204	233	186	55		826	623	109	111	.935

Mueller (Bajda), Dolores "Champ"

Born: May 31, 1931, Chicago, Illinois. 5'3", 155, Pitcher, BR, TR. South Bend Blue Sox, 1949.

Dolores Mueller spent a season with the South Bend Blue Sox in 1949 and played in less than ten games.

Mueller began playing softball when she was 8 on the playgrounds of Chicago. She joined one of the league's farm teams in 1948. At the end of the season, "Champ" tried out for the league and played in 1949. "I didn't play that much. I was a rookie," she explained.

After baseball, she got married in 1954 and became a bookkeeper and mother. She and her husband had two daughters and four grandchildren. Mueller retired in 1990. She went through an operation and had one kidney removed. She is now an honorary member of Chicago's "Old Timers Baseball Association."

Dolores "Champ" Mueller

Mueller, Dorothy "Sporty" "Dottie"

Born: Dec. 25, 1925, Cheviot, Ohio. Died: June 2, 1985. 5'11", 160, Pitcher, 1st Base, TR, BR. Peoria Redwings, 1947–49; South Bend Blue Sox, 1950–52.

An All-Star pitcher in her rookie year, "Dottie" Mueller was an excellent sidearm pitcher who helped lead South Bend to two championships.

Originally a catcher, Mueller played ten years of softball before joining the league. She was taken as a pitcher because of her sidearm delivery, which had an underhand whip to it. She had 21 victories while appearing in a season high 48 games her rookie season, which earned her an All-Star berth. The following year her record was even better at 21–9, including a no-hitter.

Dorothy "Sporty" "Dottie" Mueller

In 1949, Peoria and "Sporty" fell on hard times. She ended up with the most losses (16) in the league, although her ERA was 1.89. She made a great comeback the next two years with South Bend and posted a 10–2 mark, which tied her for the best winning percentage (.833) on the season. Her outstanding record helped the Sox win the pennant and championship in 1951.

In 1952, she played first base at the beginning of the season before going back to the mound. She was 5–7 before she walked off the team to protest the suspension of Shorty Pryer.

Born on Christmas Day, she was highly superstitious when she pitched and used to make sure not to step on the baseline.

PITCHING										BATTING			FIELDING				
W–L	PCT	ERA	G	IP	H	R	ER	BB	SO	BA	AB	H	PO	A	E	DP	FA
92–63	.594	1.80	186	1409	974	435	282	336	657	.211	856	181	841	503	57	35	.959

Murray, Margaret "Marge"

Joliet, Illinois. Catcher, Outfield. Springfield Sallies, 1948–49.

Margaret Murray joined the Springfield Sallies in 1948 when it was a regular part of the league. She continued with the team the next year when it became a barnstorming player development team. She now lives in Green Valley, Arizona.

Naum (Parker), Dorothy "Dottie"

Born: Jan. 5, 1928, Dearborn, Michigan. 5'4", 112, Catcher, 2nd Baseman, Shortstop, Pitcher, BR, TR. South Bend Blue Sox, 1946; Kenosha Comets, 1947–50; Kalamazoo Lassies, 1951–53.

"I'd do it all over again for nothing!" That's how Dottie Naum feels about her eight-year experience in the league.

Naum's two brothers perked her interest for the game at an early age. She didn't begin playing organized softball until she was 12. When she turned 18, her coach turned her name into the league and she was offered a tryout. Her coach advised her to try out as a catcher, because the league didn't have enough good ones. Naum admittedly wasn't strong enough to be a good hitter.

Dorothy "Dottie" Naum

She broke into the league as a catcher, but later was moved to the middle infield positions. Then in 1950 with Kenosha she innocently began pitching. It occurred one game when her team was down 10–1. She turned to her manager and asked him, "Why don't you let me try to pitch?" He did, and she didn't allow any more runs, which earned her a spot in the rotation. She finished the season with a 6–4 record.

The following season she was used periodically as a pitcher and tied for the league lead with a 1.14 ERA in 12 appearances. Her fastball was below average, but she had good control of her curveball and changeup.

In 1953, she helped Kalamazoo reach the playoffs with her 14–7 mark. She considers a playoff win against Fort Wayne as her best performance on the mound. Going into the eighth inning, the Lassies were down 1–0 with her due up to bat. She figured her manager was going to pinch hit for her, but he didn't. She stepped up to the plate and hit one over the wall for a home run, which even surprised her. That tied the game and the Lassies added another run in the inning to go ahead. She set down the Daisies in the ninth inning for the victory.

After the away game, her manager flew her and Gloria Cordes back to Kalamazoo in a private plane so they could have plenty of rest for the final round of the playoffs. The gesture surprised the two women, but it didn't help the team win.

Following the season, Naum married Ron Parker. He was going to allow her to play the final season of the league, but she became pregnant with her first son. In all, she had two sons, Craig and Robert.

BATTING

G	BA	AB	H	2B	3B	HR	SB	BB	SO	R	RBI
578	.181	1620	293	18	3	0	127	225	93	184	72

PITCHING									FIELDING				
W–L	PCT	ERA	G	IP	H	R	ER	BB	SO	PO	A	E	DP	FA
27–19	.587	2.01	64	439	274	155	98	149	160	1383	808	118	75	.949

Neal, Doris

Born: Aug. 30, 1928, Lincoln Park, Michigan. 5'4", 128, 3rd Base, Outfield, TR, BR. Springfield Sallies, 1948; Grand Rapids Chicks, 1949.

Doris Neal was a light-hitting outfielder-third baseman during her two seasons in the league. She now lives in Sarasota, Florida.

BATTING												FIELDING				
G	BA	AB	H	2B	3B	HR	SB	BB	SO	R	RBI	PO	A	E	DP	FA
180	.130	584	76	7	6	0	27	72	81	38	39	239	383	71	19	.898

Nearing (Buntrock), Myrna "Toddy"

Born: June 13, 1943, Eland, Wisconsin. 5'4", 125, Pitcher, TR, BR. Kenosha Comets, 1943.

Myrna Nearing was a mid-season replacement player during the first season of the league.

Her father painted a figure on a brick wall to show her how to pitch when she was 6 years old. At age 10 she began playing organized softball in school. Her mom used to call her "Tommy," but someone misunderstood it to be "Toddy," so she stuck with that. She was playing amateur softball in West Allis, Wisconsin, when a scout signed her to play in the league to replace an injured pitcher on the Kenosha team.

After the season ended, she decided not to go back to the league. "I didn't know how long it was going to last, and I didn't want to give up my job," she explained. She worked at a department store that also gave her room and board in exchange for babysitting duties in the evenings. In 1947 she was married, but she got divorced six years later. She continued to play softball for a decade after she left the league. She also went on to work at Briggs and Stratton for 30 years and retired in 1985.

PITCHING											BATTING			FIELDING			
W–L	PCT	ERA	G	IP	H	R	ER	BB	SO		BA	AB	H	PO	A	E	FA
0–1	.000	7.40	5	19	31	22	15	13	0		.000	8	0	2	8	1	.909

Nelson, Doris "Dodie"

Born: Dec. 12, 1923, Des Moines, Iowa. 5'7", 136, Outfield, BR, TR. Rockford Peaches, 1944.

"Dodie" Nelson was a good-hitting outfielder for Rockford for one season.

BATTING												FIELDING				
G	BA	AB	H	2B	3B	HR	SB	BB	SO	R	RBI	PO	A	E	DP	FA
99	.231	373	86	5	1	1	70	36	28	51	23	181	9	12	3	.941

Nelson (Sandiford), Helen "Nellie"

Born: June 13, 1919, Logie Easter, Scotland. Died: Feb. 6, 1993, Wheeling, Illinois. 5'1", 100, Catcher, BR, TR. Rockford Peaches, 1943.

Helen Nelson was one of the original All-Americans and played in one season before jumping to the Chicago professional softball league.

In the summer of 1942, Nelson was playing amateur softball in Toronto when one of the league's scouts spotted her and invited her to a tryout at Wrigley Field. She made the cut and was contracted to play with Rockford.

Nelson fielded well at catcher and hit with some power, considering her small size. She was known for her constant chatter behind the plate that gave encouragement to her pitchers.

After one season in the AAGPL, she switched to the Chicago professional softball league, where the money was just as good and the travel was a lot less. She went to work for Walgreens as a secretary and continued playing softball at night and on the weekends. She moved up to executive secretary for a senior vice president and worked at the job until she died in 1993.

BATTING												FIELDING				
G	BA	AB	H	2B	3B	HR	SB	BB	SO	R	RBI	PO	A	E	DP	FA
83	.210	214	45	4	0	0	15	35	16	36	20	204	49	19	7	.930

Nelson, Mary "Nelly"

Born: June 2, 1938, Angola, Indiana. 5'6", 105, Second Base, TR, BR. Fort Wayne Daisies, 1954.

Nesbitt (Wisham), Marie "Choo-Choo"

Born: Feb. 1, 1925, Greenville, South Carolina. 5'8", 155, Pitcher, 1st Base, Outfield, TL, BL. Racine Belles, 1943–45; Peoria Redwings, 1947–48, 50.

A member of the 1943 All-Star team, Marie Nesbitt was one of the original league members of the AAGPBL. Besides being a top-notch pitcher, she was one of the best hitters during her tenure.

Her beginnings in baseball began when she played at age 12 in a fast-pitch softball league. She played with some championship teams in Florida. Nesbitt was playing on a men's team in Chattanooga, Tennessee, when scout Jimmy Hamilton found her. "I just couldn't believe it. I couldn't believe there was a league," she said about her first encounter with the scout. Hamilton signed her up and she was off to Chicago for tryouts.

"Choo-Choo" was instrumental in helping Racine win the first championship in the first year of the league. Her knuckleball led her to a 26–13 record, one of the best in the league. She stayed on the mound until she broke her collarbone in 1945. She lost her control, so she was switched to first base. She hit .319 and shared the batting crown in 1945 with Helen Callaghan.

Nesbitt didn't play in 1946 after getting married, but she returned the next season with Peoria and played four more years. Choo-Choo was Peoria's best hitter in 1948 and led the league in extra base hits (39) and doubles (24). During the 1950 season, she became pregnant and later delivered her first son in December, which ended her career.

Nesbitt had four children: David, Luree, Mary Elizabeth and Todd. She played softball up until she was 65. She pulled a hamstring and decided her playing days were over. She drove a school bus for 22 years and retired in 1990.

She also played under the name of Crews.

PITCHING

W–L	PCT	ERA	G	IP	H	R	ER	BB	SO
65–49	.570	2.44	129	935	633	380	253	388	249

BATTING

G	BA	AB	H	2B	3B	HR	SB	BB	SO	R	RBI
498	.282	1488	419	55	36	13	161	209	117	209	186

FIELDING

PO	A	E	DP	FA
3092	522	88	3	.976

Nicol (Fox), Helen "Nicki"

Born: May 9, 1920, Ardley, Alberta, Canada. 5'3", 130, Pitcher, TR, BR. Kenosha Comets, 1943–47; Rockford Peaches, 1947–52.

Helen Nicol was the Cy Young of the league with 163 wins, the most by any pitcher. She set many career records and was one of the few hurlers to pitch all three styles in the league.

The Canadian first learned how to play softball in grammar school. At 13 she was the youngest player in the senior league and became a starting pitcher. She played for the Edmonton Pats, Parkhill Vics and Old Harold. "I remember one time back home when I had 21 strikeouts and lost the game 1–0," she said.

She saw an article about the "glamour" league in the newspaper, but ignored it because Chicago was a long way away. Soon after reading the article, she received a telegram from P.K. Wrigley. "It was the biggest wire I had ever seen," she said. The telegram offered her $85 a week, which was more than three times what she made for the Hudson Bay Company. She answered the call and came to the United States.

Nicol showed the league she was worth every penny of her contract in her first season. The experienced underhand pitcher compiled a 31–8 record and led Kenosha to a pennant. She led the league in ERA (1.81), winning percentage (.795), strikeouts (220), games pitched (47) and innings pitched (348). She was named to the first All-Star team and as Pitcher of the Year.

She lowered her ERA to 0.93 the following season to retain the Pitcher of the Year honor. She tossed a no-hitter and four one-hitters during the season in compiling a 17–11 record. She continued to thwart batters in 1946 with a 24–19 record and a 1.34 ERA. She was not named to All-Star teams in these two seasons because the league didn't name teams.

The league decided to convert to sidearm pitching in 1946, which sent many underhand pitchers to other leagues. Since "Nicki" naturally threw sidearm on her pickoff attempts to first base, she stayed with the league and gave it a try. She was 15–17 the first season and 6–16 the next year. Her struggle over the two seasons was compounded by a marriage to Gordon Fox that lasted just over a year. She began playing under the name of Fox.

The league went to sidearm or overhand pitching in 1948 and she adjusted well to the style. She bounced back to post winning records the next three seasons in helping Rockford win three consecutive pennants.

After an 18–7 record in 1951, she played only home games in 1952 because of her job with Illinois Gas and Electric. She went 8–7 on the year and decided to quit. She continued to play another five years with the Rockford Co-eds, which was like a farm club of the Peaches. She also became an American citizen.

In 1960 she went to work for American Motors in Kenosha for a dozen years before moving to Motorola and retiring in 1982. She now lives in Arizona and goes to baseball card shows to sign autographs.

Her decade of pitching produced all-time records in strikeouts (1,076), games pitched (313), innings pitched (2,382), hits allowed (1,579), losses (118) and earned runs allowed (499).

PITCHING

W–L	G	IP	H	R	ER	BB	SO
163–118	313	2382	1579	778	499	895	1076

BATTING | FIELDING

G	BA	AB	H	2B	3B	HR	SB	BB	SO	R	RBI	PO	A	E	FA
320	.145	892	137	9	8	4	24	37	105	66	49	231	522	53	.934

Niemiec (Konwinski), Dolores "Dolly"

Born: May 27, 1931, Chicago, Illinois. 5'4", 115, 2nd Base, 3rd Base, BR, TR. Springfield Sallies/Chicago Colleens, 1949; Grand Rapids Chicks, 1950–51.

Dolores Niemiec's baseball career was cut short by an automobile accident after three years in the league as an infielder.

Niemiec's father had her out on the softball field when she was 6 years old. She didn't play organized ball until 1948, when she played baseball for one of the four Chicago teams that were considered as the league's farm system. The following season she was elevated to the traveling teams that toured the country.

In 1950, "Dolly" was allocated to Grand Rapids and started at third base. When Alma Ziegler pitched, she filled in at second base. The next season her batting average dipped to .092 and she didn't get as much playing time.

Before the start of the 1952 season, she was injured in an automobile accident. "My leg was banged up bad," she explained. The injury ended her playing career.

Niemiec went to work at General Motors and took up bowling. In 1955, she married Bob Konwinski and began to raise a family. She became a charter member of the professional bowling tour in 1958. After bowling, she became a full-time mother and raised four children: Susan, Robert Jr., Tom and Patty. She took up umpiring full-time and called high school and college games. Dolly had a speaking part in *A League of Their Own*, but it ended up on the cutting room floor. She retired in 1992 and now enjoys golfing. She attends league reunions when she's not spending time with her six grandchildren from her home in Caldonia, Michigan.

Dolores "Dolly" Niemiec

			BATTING										FIELDING			
G	BA	AB	H	2B	3B	HR	SB	BB	SO	R	RBI		PO	A	E	DP	FA
78	.146	212	31	3	0	0	1	24	31	20	10		78	128	29	12	.877

Nobine, Sally

South Bend Blue Sox, 1947.

Helen "Nordie" Nordquist

Nordquist, Helen "Nordie"

Born: March 23, 1932, Malden, Massachusetts. 5'6", 160, Pitcher, Outfield, TR, BR. Kenosha Comets, 1951; Rockford Peaches, 1952–53; South Bend Blue Sox, 1954.

Helen Nordquist was a pitcher-outfielder for four seasons in the league and once led outfielders in assists.

Nordquist starting playing ball with the boys when she was 8 years old. She began playing organized softball in high school. Right after graduation she saw an article about the league in the *Boston Herald* and went to Alexandria, Virginia, for a tryout. She was taken and assigned to Kenosha. In her rookie season the right fielder led all outfielders in assists. "I could throw out runners at first base," she explained.

"Nordie" went to Rockford the next season and was converted into a pitcher. She had a fastball and a good curveball. However, she gave up too many runs and was more effective as a hitter. Between seasons she once played for the Miami Beach Belles of the International League, but the league lasted only one season.

After baseball she was a telephone operator and an accountant. She also coached softball and played up until she was 55. She retired in 1994. Now she lives in Alton, New Hampshire.

PITCHING

W–L	PCT	ERA	G	IP	H	R	ER	BB	SO
6–20	.231	5.43	44	209	222	197	126	189	57

BATTING | FIELDING

G	BA	AB	H	2B	3B	HR	SB	BB	SO	R	RBI	PO	A	E	DP	FA
177	.189	434	82	14	4	4	11	46	70	43	31	104	91	26	8	.882

Normine, Cynthia

Everett, Massachusetts. Rockford Peaches, 1950.

Norris, Donna

Culver City, California. Fort Wayne Daisies, 1953; South Bend Blue Sox, 1953.

BATTING

G	BA	AB	H	2B	3B	HR	SB	BB	SO	R	RBI
16	.083	36	3	1	0	0	0	1	13	3	2

O'Brien, Eileen

Born: May 24, 1922, Chicago, Illinois. 5'4", 128. BR, TR. Muskegon Lassies, 1946.

Eileen O'Brien played in five games in 1946 before taking over as the Muskegon's chaperone. After baseball she taught in Chicago for 43 years and retired in 1988. Now she lives in Albuquerque, New Mexico.

O'Brien (Cooke), Penny "Peanuts"

Born: Sept. 16, 1919, Edmonton, Alberta, Canada. 5'2", 120, Outfield, 1st Base, BR, TR. Fort Wayne Daisies, 1945.

Penny O'Brien played a season with Fort Wayne before her husband made her quit the league.

O'Brien began playing softball at age 14. "Peanuts" was playing in Saskatoon when she was offered $65 a week to play in the All-American League, which was a lot more than the $18 she was making to drive a taxi.

The league assigned her to expansion club Fort Wayne. The speedster swiped 43 bases on the season and speedily covered the outfield. After the season, her naval officer husband whom she had married in 1944 ordered her home to end her stint in the league. She went on to raise three children: Lucella, Robert and Georgena. She retired in 1985 and still lives in Canada.

BATTING / FIELDING

G	BA	AB	H	2B	3B	HR	SB	BB	SO	R	RBI	PO	A	E	DP	FA
83	.216	282	61	0	0	1	43	16	46	34	23	236	10	14	5	.946

O'Connor, Pat

Kenosha, Wisconsin. Kenosha Comets, 1946.

O'Dowd, Anna Mae "Annie"

Born: April 26, 1929, Chicago, Illinois. 5'9", 175, Catcher, BR, TR. Rockford Peaches, 1949; Chicago Colleens, 1949; Kenosha Comets, 1949; Springfield Sallies, 1950; Kalamazoo Lassies, 1950; Racine Belles, 1951; Battle Creek Belles, 1952.

Anna O'Dowd traveled around the league for four seasons as a backup catcher on seven different teams.

O'Dowd had a very athletic brother who introduced her to baseball when she was growing up. She then played softball in high school. The league held a tryout about a mile from her house and she went. She was a first baseman, but the league said she was more built for catching duties.

"Ann" was signed by Rockford but went on tour with the Chicago Colleens in 1949, traveling the country and learning her new trade. The following season she again was on the traveling team and was one of the best hitters, averaging .313 in 25 games for Springfield. She then joined the Kalamazoo Lassies for the remainder of the season.

After the 1952 season, she decided it was time to go on to other things. "I quit early because I thought 'Where am I going with this?'" she explained. She did spend another year playing professional softball for the Bloomer Girls in Chicago. "I found that was harder," she admitted.

O'Dowd worked at several occupations before retiring in 1992. She now plays golf and goes to league reunions from her home in Marietta, Georgia.

BATTING												FIELDING				
G	BA	AB	H	2B	3B	HR	SB	BB	SO	R	RBI	PO	A	E	DP	FA
70	.183	175	32	3	0	0	15	38	15	13	15	167	54	16	5	.933

Ogden, Joanne

Born: April 23, 1933, Johnson City, New York. 5'2", 124, 2nd Base, TR, BR. South Bend Blue Sox, 1953.

BATTING												FIELDING				
G	BA	AB	H	2B	3B	HR	SB	BB	SO	R	RBI	PO	A	E	DP	FA
42	.253	87	22	2	0	0	6	4	9	11	5	56	34	13	2	.874

O'Hara, Janice

Born: Nov. 30, 1918, Beardstown, Illinois. 5'6", 122, Utility fielder, Pitcher, BR, TR. Kenosha Comets, 1943–49.

One of the original players of the league, Janice O'Hara played many different positions during her seven seasons.

O'Hara started playing softball in Springfield, Illinois, when she was a teenager. League scout Ed Stump interviewed her and sent her to Wrigley Field for the first league tryout. O'Hara made the cut and was assigned to Kenosha.

The Comets started her at first base and she hit a respectable .187 on the season in helping the team win the pennant. In her sophomore year, the Comets turned her into a utility player. She played mostly at first base and in the outfield, but she also filled in at second and third. She also hit the only homer of her career in 1944.

When the league went to overhand pitching in 1947, she was converted into a pitcher. She turned in a 6–8 record in 21 appearances on the year. She had a fastball, curve and a knuckleball, which she loved to throw. The following season she went 4–6 in 20 appearances.

After baseball, she worked as an accountant for 31 years and retired in 1982. She now loves to garden and attend league reunions.

BATTING

G	BA	AB	H	2B	3B	HR	SB	BB	SO	R	RBI
309	.167	936	156	11	8	1	94	99	96	100	83

PITCHING										FIELDING				
W–L	PCT	ERA	G	IP	H	R	ER	BB	SO	PO	A	E	DP	FA
13–17	.433	3.56	55	296	256	169	117	140	81	1541	309	86	34	.956

Olinger, Marilyn

Born: June 7, 1928, Sunbury, Ohio. 5'6", 140, Shortstop, BR, TR. Chicago Colleens, 1948; Grand Rapids Chicks, 1948–53.

A broken ankle ended the six year All-American career of Marilyn Olinger, who was a starting shortstop.

Olinger lived across the street from a playground, but the older kids wouldn't let her play ball with them, so she would steal their equipment. They finally relented and let her play. At age 14, she played organized softball in Columbus, Ohio. She was playing in a state tournament when she was noticed by a league scout and given an invitation to spring training, which was in Opa-locka, Florida.

During spring training, she was assigned to Grand Rapids, but the league sent her to play for the new Chicago Colleens for half a season. She returned to the Chicks to help them win a pennant in her first season.

Marilyn Olinger

The shortstop steadily improved behind the plate and hit a career-high .267 in 1951. With 13 games left in the 1953 season, she broke her ankle. The Chicks ended up winning the championship playoffs that season without her. She decided not to come back the next season. "It got to be like work after awhile and the league was struggling. You could see the handwriting on the wall," she explained.

Olinger went to work for National Cash Register. A couple of years later she returned to playing amateur softball. In 1973, NCR cut back its work force and she was let go. She worked in security for the next 19 years before retiring in 1992. She went to the league's reunion in South Bend in 1993.

BATTING												FIELDING				
G	BA	AB	H	2B	3B	HR	SB	BB	SO	R	RBI	PO	A	E	DP	FA
599	.220	2175	479	34	7	4	197	255	334	334	115	1070	1608	319	125	.894

Oravets, Pauline

Warren, Ohio. Pitcher. Rockford Peaches, 1943.

Pauline Oravets was one of the original players of the league, but she didn't get much of a chance to play in her only season.

Ortman (Klupping), Dorothy

Maywood, Illinois. Died: Date Unknown. Pitcher, TR, BR. Racine Belles, 1944.

Dorothy Ortman was a mediocre pitcher for Racine in 1944.

PITCHING										BATTING		
W–L	PCT	ERA	G	IP	H	R	ER	BB	SO	BA	AB	H
6–8	.429	3.36	15	99	94	53	37	47	5	.058	34	2

Overleese, Joanne "Jo"

Born: Oct. 3, 1923, San Diego, California. 2nd Base, BR, TR. Muskegon Lassies, 1946; Peoria Redwings, 1946.

Joanne Overleese is one of the few doctors to have played in the league.

"Jo" started playing softball at age 9. She advanced to semi-pro softball in California while she was going to college. In the winter of 1946, she tried out for the All-American League and went to Pasagoula, Mississippi, for spring training. She played for one season with Muskegon and Peoria.

After baseball, she attended the Medical College of Pennsylvania and became a general surgeon in Philadelphia for 25 years. She retired from practice in 1977 and went into the emergency department for another 10 years. She still has an office in New Jersey and performs minor surgery.

BATTING											FIELDING				
G	BA	AB	H	2B	3B	HR	SB	BB	SO	R	RBI	PO	A	E	DP	FA
54	.178	174	31	4	1	0	6	25	21	13	15	120	96	15	16	.935

Paire (Davis), Lavonne "Pepper"

Born: May 29, 1924, Los Angeles, California. 5'4", 138, Catcher, Shortstop, 3rd Base, Pitcher, BR, TR. Minneapolis Millerettes, 1944; Fort Wayne Daisies, 1945; Racine Belles, 1946–47; Grand Rapids Chicks, 1948–52; Fort Wayne Daisies, 1952–53.

Lavonne Paire was a versatile player who was used at several positions during her decade in the league. She was a part of five championship teams.

"Pepper" hit .241 for Minneapolis in her first season and the Millerettes won the pennant.

When she went to Racine in 1946, the Belles won the pennant. Then in 1948 she was moved to Grand Rapids, who won the pennant her first season there. A clutch hitter, she led the league in 1950 with 71 RBI. The following season she hit a career-high .264. She spent the last two seasons of her career at Fort Wayne, who won the pennant both years.

Her 355 assists at third base was the second best single-season total in league history. Now retired, she signs autographs at card shows and attends league reunions.

BATTING

G	BA	AB	H	2B	3B	HR	SB	BB	SO	R	RBI
926	.225	3164	713	79	15	2	79	308	117	251	400

PITCHING / FIELDING

W–L	PCT	ERA	G	IP	H	R	ER	BB	SO		PO	A	E	DP	FA
1–0	1.000	1.29	7	21	17	4	3	7	2		2564	1501	239	101	.945

Palermo, Toni

Forest Park, Illinois. Shortstop, BR, TR. Chicago Colleens/Springfield Sallies, 1949–50.

Toni Palermo played two seasons with the league's barnstorming teams, but she never played in the regular league.

BATTING

G	BA	AB	H	2B	3B	HR	SB	BB	SO	R	RBI
33	.205	117	24	0	0	0	14	39	13	30	8

Palesch, Shirley Ellen "Butch"

Born: Nov. 23, 1929, Chicago, Illinois. 5'4", 140, Outfield, BR, TR. Racine Belles, 1949; Rockford Peaches, 1950; Grand Rapids Chicks, 1950.

Shirley Palesch spent two seasons in the league with little success at the plate. Before joining the league, she was a pitcher with a 21–4 record for the Wausau Lumber Jeans. She now lives in Wausau, Wisconsin.

BATTING / FIELDING

G	BA	AB	H	2B	3B	HR	SB	BB	SO	R	RBI		PO	A	E	DP	FA
18	.036	56	2	0	0	0	0	1	4	0	2		4	2	1	0	.857

Panos, Vicki

Born: March 20, 1920, Edmonton, Alberta, Canada. Died: Date Unknown. 5'3", 120, Outfield, BL, TR. South Bend Blue Sox, 1944; Milwaukee Millerettes, 1944.

Vicki Panos played one season with the league and helped Milwaukee win the pennant and championship.

BATTING												FIELDING				
G	BA	AB	H	2B	3B	HR	SB	BB	SO	R	RBI	PO	A	E	DP	FA
114	.263	403	106	1	0	0	141	66	25	84	31	203	19	5	5	.978

Parks (Young), Barbara

Born: Feb. 7, 1933, Brookline, Massachusetts. 5'7", 123, Shortstop, 2nd Base. Springfield Sallies, 1950; Kenosha Comets, 1950–51.

Barbara Parks played on the traveling Springfield Sallies and hit .212 in 40 games before she was called up by Kenosha to play two seasons in the league.

BATTING												FIELDING				
G	BA	AB	H	2B	3B	HR	SB	BB	SO	R	RBI	PO	A	E	DP	FA
26	.083	72	6	0	0	0	1	4	13	4	2	35	30	13	3	.833

Susan Parsons

Parsons (Zipay), Susan

Born: April 1, 1934, Medford, Massachusetts. 5'3", 115, Pitcher, Utility Infielder, TR, BR. Rockford Peaches, 1952–54.

Now a member of the players association Board of Directors, Sue Parsons was a utility player and relief pitcher the last three seasons of the league.

Parsons began playing sandlot baseball at age 5 with her four brothers. Then she played softball with the Catholic youth organization. She admits that a lack of training hindered her career, even though she had natural athletic ability.

Parsons tried out for the league with a chaperone in 1952. Her mother didn't want her 18-year-old daughter going to the league, but Parsons nevertheless took a train from Massachusetts to South Bend for spring training. When the regular season began, she was surprised to see all the people in the stands. "I had no idea of a league like this," she said. For three seasons she played with the Peaches in a back-up roll. Parsons was a utility infielder and pitcher.

After the league ended, Parsons raised a family of three children. At age 35, she took up tennis and became a ranked player in New England. She now runs a small tennis court and calls it a "labor of love."

She joined the AAGPBL Players Association Board of Directors in 1994 when the association was in negotiations with companies for their logo. Board members call her "Zippy," after her married name of Zipay. She now has five grandchildren.

PITCHING

W–L	PCT	ERA	G	IP	H	R	ER	BB	SO
0–2	.000	5.78	18	53	58	45	34	68	7

BATTING

G	BA	AB	H	2B	3B	HR	SB	BB	SO	R	RBI
53	.066	106	7	2	0	0	0	3	23	6	1

FIELDING

PO	A	E	DP	FA
18	39	6	4	.905

Payne, Barbara "Bobbie"

Born: Sept. 18, 1932, Shreveport, Louisiana. 5'7", 118, Utility Infielder, Pitcher, BR, TR. Springfield Sallies, 1949; Muskegon/Kalamazoo Lassies, 1950–51; Battle Creek Belles, 1951; Rockford Peaches, 1951.

Barbara Payne, who played for three seasons in the league, was the only player from Louisiana.

At age 11, Payne was the youngest girl on the Shreveport Garmet softball team. She was playing for Elite Cleaners when the league's traveling team stopped in Shreveport for some exhibition games. They held a tryout and signed her up. She played the next night in town before going on a whirlwind tour of 22 states with the Springfield Sallies.

The following year, she was allowed to graduate from high school a month early so that she could go to spring training in Missouri. She was known as a "pepper pot," because she would go after any ball. "One time I got caught right in the mouth with a hot grounder in Kalamazoo," she recalled. She played mainly at shortstop, but she filled in at other infield positions.

"Bobbie" felt bad about being traded in 1951 to Rockford and decided to call it quits after the season ended. She became a radiology technician. She spent the next 40 years performing her trade and retired in 1992 from the government. After baseball, she took up golfing and has a number of local titles to her credit. She attended the league reunion in Chicago.

BATTING

G	BA	AB	H	2B	3B	HR	SB	BB	SO	R	RBI
194	.182	593	108	12	6	0	17	62	92	57	49

PITCHING

G	IP
1	2

FIELDING

PO	A	E	DP	FA
347	424	115	43	.870

Pearson (Tesseine), Dolly "Buttons"

Born: Sept. 6, 1932, Pittsburgh. 5'5", 125, Outfield, Shortstop, Pitcher, BR, TR. Muskegon Lassies, 1948; Peoria Redwings, 1949; Racine Comets, 1950; Battle Creek Belles, 1951; Kalamazoo Lassies, 1951–52; South Bend Blue Sox, 1953; Grand Rapids Chicks, 1954.

Dolly Pearson had one of the more unusual nicknames — "Buttons." The outfielder-shortstop spent seven seasons in the league with seven teams.

She began her playing days as a youngster on the sandlots in Pittsburgh with the boys. Then at 14 she joined an organized softball league and played second base. She went to a league tryout in South Bend and was invited to spring training the next season. She earned her nickname on the train ride to Florida. "I was trying all the buttons on the train and they started calling me buttons," she explained.

Her first team in the league was Muskegon. On the last day of her rookie year, she celebrated her 16th birthday to everybody's surprise. Everyone thought she was already 16. You had to be 16 to work after 8 P.M. in Michigan, so she had played illegally all year.

The following season she was sent to Peoria and played only about a third of the team's games at various positions. Then it was on to Racine the next season. Buttons started in center field and hit a respectable .235.

At Battle Creek the next year, Pearson was put at shortstop, the position she would play the rest of her career. Her best season was her last with Grand Rapids. When the ball was reduced to major league size, Buttons found she could easily hit it over the fence. She knocked it out of the park 18 times that season.

Although she played with seven different teams, she never once played with a pennant contender or championship winner.

After the league folded, she married Edward Tesseine, who she had met while she was still playing. The couple raised four children: Jean, Sam, Ron and Ed. Dolly, who now has four grandchildren, retired in 1994 after working for several years at Central Michigan University. She attended the South Bend reunion in 1993. She was disappointed when her first baseball card was issued by Larry Fritsch Cards in 1995. The card contained the photo of another player, Dottie Naum. The company has since issued her a new card.

Dolly "Buttons" Pearson

BATTING

G	BA	AB	H	2B	3B	HR	SB	BB	SO	R	RBI
541	.216	1760	381	36	14	18	70	279	183	195	197

PITCHING

FIELDING

W–L	PCT	ERA	G	IP	H	R	ER	BB	SO		PO	A	E	DP	FA
0–2	.000	9.02	5	11	14	14	11	11	1		971	1121	201	99	9.12

Pechulis, Katherine

Urbardge, Washington. Utility, TR, BR. Grand Rapids Chicks, 1948.

Peppas, June

Born: June 16, 1929, Kansas City, Missouri. 5'5", 145, Outfield, 1st Base, Pitcher, BL, TL. Fort Wayne Daisies, 1948–49; Racine Belles, 1949–50; Battle Creek Belles, 1951; Kalamazoo Lassies, 1951–54.

June Peppas was a versatile performer who helped Kalamazoo win the last championship of the league.

Peppas was age 12 when she began playing softball in Fort Wayne. When she grew older she played for the Zollner Pistons and her manager was a scout for the AAGPBL. She was also scouted for a Chicago softball league, but she liked the All-American League. "I wanted to play baseball," she explained. "I liked the idea that you had to think before every play."

Besides playing first base, Peppas pitched every fifth game and played the outfield when needed. She injured her right knee in 1948 and eventually ended up with an artificial knee.

Perhaps her best performance came in the waning moments of the league in the 1954 playoffs. She earned two pitching victories to give Kalamazoo the crown over the Fort Wayne Daisies, the pennant winner.

June Peppas

After baseball, she obtained a degree from Western Michigan University and went into the printing field. She owned her own printing business for 15 years and taught printing for another 15. One of the founders of the player's association, she produced a newsletter that helped communicate with the players after years of absence.

BATTING

G	BA	AB	H	2B	3B	HR	SB	BB	SO	R	RBI
601	.273	2146	586	51	14	23	70	211	178	253	221

PITCHING										FIELDING				
W–L	PCT	ERA	G	IP	H	R	ER	BB	SO	PO	A	E	DP	FA
18–31	.367	3.94	63	370	340	222	162	242	118	5064	269	152	213	.972

Perez (Jinright), Migdalia "Mickey"

Havana, Cuba. Died: Date Unknown. Pitcher. Chicago Colleens, 1948; Springfield Sallies, 1949–50; Battle Creek Belles, 1951–2; Rockford Peaches, 1952–54.

One of the few Cuban players in the league, Mickey Perez was a mediocre pitcher for five seasons but still managed to throw a no-hitter.

The league held spring training in Havana in 1947, encouraging Perez and other Cuban players to come to the United States to play. After struggling to a 10–17 record, she was assigned to the Springfield Sallies, one of the traveling teams, for more seasoning. In 1950 she went 10–8 for the barnstorming Sallies, a team that folded after the season.

Perez was drafted by Battle Creek and went 13–16 in 1951. She led the league in complete games (26), innings pitched (237) and hits allowed (241). After being traded to Rockford, she threw a no-hitter against Grand Rapids on August 10, 1953.

Her best record was 11–11 for Rockford in 1954. She got married during her time in the league and also played under the name Jinright.

PITCHING									BATTING			FIELDING			
W–L	PCT	ERA	G	IP	H	R	ER	BB	SO	BA	AB	H	PO	A	E	FA
57–70	.449	2.73	155	1069	1076	506	324	122	116	.117	367	43	41	323	19	.950

Perkins, Joy

South Bend Blue Sox, 1953.

Joy Perkins played in less than ten games for South Bend in 1953.

Perlick (Keating), Edythe "Edie"

Born: Dec. 12, 1922, Chicago, Illinois. 5'3", 128, Outfield, BR, TR. Racine Belles, 1943–50.

A three time All-Star, Edythe Perlick was one of the first four girls signed to a contract before the first season to help promote the league.

Perlick grew up on the northwest side of Chicago and learned to play baseball in the empty lots. She advanced to the organized leagues and played for the famous champion Rockolas. When the league was first forming, it needed some players for publicity purposes, so Perlick and three others were signed to contracts without having to try out. Their publicity pictures helped scouts with their recruiting efforts.

"Edie" was allocated to Racine and patrolled left field. She hit .268 — one of the highest averages in the league — in her rookie season and helped the Belles win the pennant and championship. She also led the league in RBI (63) and was named to the league's first All-Star team. She continued to play well the next two seasons but the league did not name All-Stars.

In 1946, the clean-up hitter knocked out four homers to again help the Belles win the pennant and championship. The following year she was again picked for the All-Star team after hitting .239 and leading the league in at-bats (436). "I never paid much attention to batting averages and statistics," she explained.

Perlick had another all-star year in 1943 and Racine captured another pennant. She played two more seasons before jumping to the rival Chicago National League for a couple more years. Her 18 home runs rank as one of the highest totals in league history.

Perlick got married in 1953, and had a daughter, Susan. She went to work for A.B. Dick for nearly eight years after her

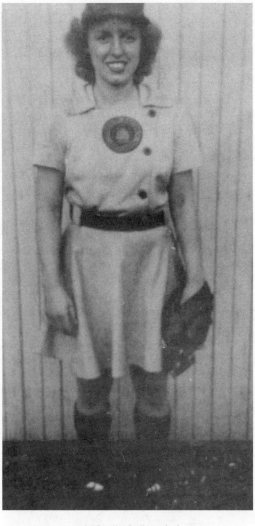

Edythe "Edie" Perlick

playing days. She then moved to Florida and worked for Harris Computer Systems until retirement in 1993. She now enjoys retirement in Pompano Beach.

			BATTING										FIELDING				
G	BA	AB	H	2B	3B	HR	SB	BB	SO	R	RBI		PO	A	E	DP	FA
851	.240	3177	445	62	46	18	392	481	241	138	392		1435	75	80	17	.950

Peters, Marjorie "Pete"

Born: Sept. 11, 1918, West Allis, Wisconsin. 5'2", 112, Pitcher, BR, TR. Rockford Peaches, 1943–44.

One of the original players of the league, Marjorie Peters' two-year career was highlighted by a pitching appearance in the first league game.

"Little Mac" began playing softball at age 7 in the parks. The athlete of her family, she was a speed skater, tennis star and bike racer in her youth. When war broke out, she went to work at a defense plant. She tried out for the league at Borcherd Field in Milwaukee and was invited to Wrigley Field. She made the league and was assigned to Rockford.

In the first game of the new league on May 30, 1943, "Pete" pitched against South Bend. The game went 13 innings and the Peaches lost 4–3. She went 12–19 on the season. The next year's league records show she went 1–5 in nine appearances, but she claims the records are incorrect and that she had many more appearances.

After the season ended, her boyfriend came home from the Army and the two were married. She decided not to go back to the league. Her marriage to Donald Beane lasted until 1948. She played amateur softball for a few years after that. She raised minks before working at Singer Controls. She retired in 1993. She limps now because of two hip replacements.

Marjorie "Pete" Peters

PITCHING										BATTING			FIELDING			
W–L	PCT	ERA	G	IP	H	R	ER	BB	SO	BA	AB	H	PO	A	E	FA
13–24	.351	3.15	48	340	347	203	119	70	35	.209	148	31	21	53	4	.949

Peterson (Fox), Betty Jean "Pete"

Born: Nov. 21, 1933, Wyanet, Illinois. 5'2", 125, Catcher, Infielder, BR, TR. Rockford Peaches, 1952; Kalamazoo Lassies, 1953; Muskegon Belles, 1953.

Betty Jean Peterson played in less than ten games during her two seasons in the league.

Peterson grew up in a rural community and played softball in grade school before playing with town teams in high school. She went to a tryout in Rockford and the Peaches signed her, but the club sent her to play in a farm league in De Kalb for more seasoning in 1952.

Betty Jean "Pete" Peterson

The following year she was picked up by Kalamazoo, but loaned to Muskegon. She was used as a pinch hitter, pinch runner, first base coach and to warm up pitchers. While she was catching, she caught a ball on the end of her index finger and it jammed the knuckle back, cutting it. That incident ended her season early.

In 1954 the league was in trouble, so she decided not to go back since she had a good job and a boyfriend. She married Roger Peterson in 1956 and had three daughters: Debbie, Diana and Danaille. They owned a farm and she kept busy with the children and chores. Roger was in the Navy during World War II, so the retired couple enjoy going to both his and her reunions.

Petras, Ernestine "Tenny"

Born: Oct. 22, 1924, Coaldale, Pennsylvania. 5'5", 125, Shortstop, 3rd Base, BR, TR. Milwaukee Chicks, 1944; Grand Rapids Chicks, 1945–48; Chicago Colleens, 1948; Kenosha Comets, 1949–51; Battle Creek Belles, 1952.

Ernestine Petras was one of the best fielding shortstops in league history, yet she was never named as an All-Star. Her light hitting probably prevented her selection. "Tenny" had the best fielding percentage at her position in five of her nine seasons in the league. She led all shortstops in 1945 (.918), 1946 (.951), 1947 (.942) and 1950 (.957). Her .957 average in 1950 was the third best for a single season in league history. In 1952 she was the best fielding third baseman (.965) while at Battle Creek. She now calls Barnegat, New Jersey, home.

BATTING													FIELDING				
G	BA	AB	H	2B	3B	HR	SB	BB	SO	R	RBI		PO	A	E	DP	FA
834	.198	2790	552	55	16	0	420	342	249	359	196		1791	2411	249	203	.944

Petryna (Allen), Doreen Betty

Born: Nov. 26, 1930, Liberty, Saskatchewan, Canada. 5'4", 140, 3rd Base, BR, TR. Grand Rapids Chicks, 1948. Fort Wayne Daisies, 1949.

A Canadian import, Doreen Petryna was a member of the pennant winning Grand Rapids Chicks in 1948.

Petryna started softball at age 10 in Regina, Saskatchewan. She was 18 when she was picked to play in the league. Her most memorable moment in the league came in 1949 with Fort Wayne: she made 12 assists from third base in one game.

After the 1948 season, she married Roger Allen. After baseball, the couple raised three children. They also played co-ed slow-pitch softball and won two championships in De Kalb, Illinois. Betty taught mentally handicapped students for 20 years and retired in 1995. The couple now like to golf and travel.

BATTING													FIELDING				
G	BA	AB	H	2B	3B	HR	SB	BB	SO	R	RBI		PO	A	E	DP	FA
122	.139	361	50	4	0	0	12	36	42	21	20		178	302	49	12	.907

Pieper, Marjorie "Peeps"

Born: Aug. 2, 1922, Clinton, Michigan. 5'7", 140, Utility Fielder, Pitcher, BR, TR. Fort Wayne Daisies, 1946–47; Kenosha Comets, 1948; Chicago Colleens, 1948; Fort Wayne Daisies, 1949; Racine Belles, 1949; Kenosha Comets, 1950; Peoria Redwings, 1950–51; Battle Creek Belles, 1951–52.

Marjorie Pieper was a versatile infielder who played for seven teams during her seven-year career.

She grew up in Michigan and played more basketball than softball. After high school, she attended the University of Michigan. In 1945, she played softball with the Michigan state champions and was noticed by a league scout. She tried out for the league and was assigned to the Fort Wayne Daisies. She hit a respectable .173 and played shortstop in her rookie season.

She then fell victim to the expansion draft and she played on seven different teams in seven years.

After the league, she taught physical education at the high school and college level. Now retired, she lives in Citrus Hills, Florida, and plays golf and watches sports.

Marjorie "Peeps" Pieper

BATTING

G	BA	AB	H	2B	3B	HR	SB	BB	SO	R	RBI
718	.213	2414	513	76	30	17	181	286	191	256	254

PITCHING

W–L	PCT	ERA	G	IP	H	R	ER	BB	SO
1–2	.333	6.75	8	33	25	33	21	28	14

FIELDING

PO	A	E	DP	FA
1526	714	200	59	.920

Pirok, Pauline

Born: Oct. 18, 1926, Chicago, Illinois. 5'2", 132, Shortstop, 3rd Base, Pitcher, BR, TR. Kenosha Comets, 1943–45; South Bend Blue Sox, 1945–48.

One of the original players of the league, Pauline Pirok was an infielder for six seasons. She helped Kenosha win the pennant in 1943. After baseball, she was a physical education teacher. She now lives in Orland Park, Illinois.

BATTING

G	BA	AB	H	2B	3B	HR	SB	BB	SO	R	RBI
559	.208	1976	411	32	14	0	223	188	105	243	138

PITCHING		FIELDING				
G	IP	PO	A	E	DP	FA
3	8	1006	1533	243	83	.913

Piskula, Grace

Born: Feb. 26, 1926, Milwaukee, Wisconsin.
5'7", 123, Outfield, BR, TR.
Rockford Peaches, 1944.

Grace Piskula was a mid-season replacement player with Rockford in 1944.

Piskula started playing softball at age 14. "Skip," her nickname in Milwaukee, played in the women's leagues in West Allis, a suburb of Milwaukee, when the Rockford Peaches signed her to a contract in mid-season due to injuries on the team. She played in less than 10 games the rest of the season. The following season she went to the Chicago Chicks of the National League to earn more money than in baseball, because she worked during the day and played at night. "My mother said I lived to play ball," she explained.

After earning a master's degree from New York University, she taught physical education for almost 40 years and retired in 1985. Now she lives in Racine, plays golf and goes to league reunions.

Grace Piskula

Podolski, Bertha

Pitcher. Fort Wayne Daisies, 1946.

PITCHING							FIELDING		
W–L	PCT	G	IP	H	R	BB	SO	BA	AB	H
1–1	.500	2	17	12	5	13	1	.222	9	2

Pollitt (Deschaine), Alice "Al" "Rock"

Born: July 19, 1929, Lansing, Michigan. 5'3", 150, Shortstop, 3rd Base, 2nd Base, BR, TR. Rockford Peaches, 1947–53.

Alice Pollitt was a valuable infielder and hitter for Rockford for seven seasons. She helped the Peaches win three championships. She now lives in Levering, Michigan.

BATTING												FIELDING				
G	BA	AB	H	2B	3B	HR	SB	BB	SO	R	RBI	PO	A	E	DP	FA
606	.255	2177	555	41	35	8	181	139	184	250	214	955	1252	200	98	.917

Pratt, Mary "Prattie"

Born: Nov. 30, 1918, Bridgeport, Connecticut. 5'1", 125, Pitcher, TL, BL. Rockford Peaches, 1943–44; Kenosha Comets, 1944–45; Rockford Peaches, 1946–47.

Mary Pratt's roller coaster career was highlighted by a no-hitter during one outstanding season in the league.

Pratt played with the boys at a nearby playground when she was growing up. After high school, she attended Boston University. During her junior year, she tried out for a softball team that played in the Boston Garden. Pratt thought she could play shortstop, but she was told that left-handers didn't play short. She was converted into a pitcher. She played with the Boston Olympets for two seasons. Meanwhile, she obtained her degree and began teaching physical education.

In 1943, she received an invitation to play in the All-American League, but she had to wait until school let out before joining the league. She was assigned to Rockford and chalked up a 5–11 record her first season.

Mary "Prattie" Pratt

The following season she was given an early release by her school so she could attend spring training near Chicago. A month into the season, she was sent to Kenosha, who had lost two pitchers to injuries. Motivated by manager Marty McManus, "Prattie" turned in her career-best season. Her 21–15 record included a no-hitter against Minneapolis on June 14.

In 1946, her school wouldn't release her for spring training, so she quit school. Kenosha didn't give her much run support during the season and she turned in a 1–16 record. Her slide continued the next season with Rockford when she went 1–7. The following season she was 0–2 before calling it quits. The league was converting to overhand pitching, and her diminutive stature didn't allow her to pitch overhand that way.

Pratt continued to teach and eventually earn a master's degree from the University of Massachusetts. She became an associate professor at Salem State University. She retired from teaching in 1986 after 48 years in the profession. She now plays tennis and goes to league reunions. She also writes a newsletter for former players on the East Coast. In 1995, she was inducted into the Boston Garden Hall of Fame. She remains active in many activities to promote women's sports.

PITCHING											BATTING			FIELDING			
W–L	PCT	ERA	G	IP	H	R	ER	BB	SO		BA	AB	H	PO	A	E	FA
28–51	.354	3.53	110	709	530	396	278	240	55		.151	219	33	59	250	20	.939

Price, LaVerne "Ferne"

Terre Haute, Indiana. Pitcher. Milwaukee Chicks, 1944.

BATTING

G	BA	AB	H
4	.000	2	0

Pryer (Mayer), Charlene "Shorty"

Born: Sept. 24, 1921, Watsonville, California. 5'1", 105, 2nd Base, Outfielder, BR, TR. Muskegon Lassies, 1946–50; South Bend Blue Sox, 1950–52.

Charlene Pryer was an All-Star second baseman who led the league in stolen bases for two seasons. After a suspension in late 1952, Pryer decided to leave baseball.

Pryer was inspired to play baseball because her father was a minor league player who almost broke into the majors but suffered a broken elbow in spring training with the Chicago White Sox. She was 12 years old when she first joined an organized fast-pitch league.

A few years later she was chosen for an All-Star team and was seen by the AAGPBL's Bill Allington. However, she joined the Marine Corps instead of the league. After World War II, the "buck" sergeant became a professional singer in Reno, Nevada. She didn't like Reno and tried out for the AAGPBL. She was drafted by the league and assigned to Muskegon.

Pryer's short stature quickly earned her the nickname "Shorty." She roamed the outfield for the Lassies and hit a respectable .202 in her first season, despite a leg injury.

The leadoff hitter worried opponents with her bunting. Once on base, she'd worry pitchers

Charlene "Shorty" Pryer

with her stealing. The healthy centerfielder improved her batting average to .249 the following season and led the league in singles and fielding percentage among outfielders. In the off-season, she sang her heart out on the radio.

In 1949 her season was cut when she broke both sides of her right ankle. "It had rained and the clay ground became very hard. I went to slide and my spikes got caught up in it. I heard both bones break," she recalled. She was in a cast six months.

In 1950, she was dealt to South Bend, where she played second base and the outfield. Her crowding of the plate resulted in her being hit by the most pitches during the 1950 season.

Pryer had her career year in 1951 as she helped the Blue Sox win their first-ever pennant and league playoff championship. She led the league in steals with 129, an average of more than one per game. She also recorded the most hits (133) and the most runs (106). She was also picked for the All-Star team.

The 1952 season saw tensions mount between her and manager Karl Winsch, who would bench her on occasion. "I had been an All-Star and he treated me poorly," she explained. The personality conflict came to a head late in the season when Winsch suspended her. Five other members of the team backed Pryer and walked off the team in her support. The team won the league championship without her and the other five players. She was reinstated, but she decided to quit the league. For years after baseball, she had a numb spot on her leg from all the bruises she took from stealing.

Pryer became a truant officer and teacher's aid for 24 years in Medford, Oregon, where she now resides in retirement. She married twice and has two children, Lynn and Ronn.

BATTING													FIELDING				
G	BA	AB	H	2B	3B	HR	SB	BB	SO	R	RBI		PO	A	E	DP	FA
704	.255	2634	672	44	12	3	510	281	214	463	152		1588	675	118	82	.951

Redman, Magdalen "Mamie"

Born: July 2, 1930, Waupun, Wisconsin. 5'5", 150, Catcher, Utility Infielder, BR, TR. Kenosha Comets, 1948–49; Grand Rapids Chicks, 1950–54.

"Mamie" Redman played every position except pitcher during her seven seasons in the league.

She didn't start playing softball until age 17 in Oconomowoc, Wisconsin. The following year she joined the league. She was initially used as a catcher and had the best fielding average among catchers in 1949 (.978) and 1953 (.975). She later played other positions as fill-ins for other players.

Redman typically played about half of the games in a season. She helped Grand Rapids win a championship in 1953. Her best season as a hitter came in 1954 when she hit .249 and had a career high 20 RBI.

After baseball, she became a high school mathematics teacher.

BATTING												FIELDING				
G	BA	AB	H	2B	3B	HR	SB	BB	SO	R	RBI	PO	A	E	DP	FA
369	.172	918	158	15	2	2	10	162	101	90	63	1017	288	40	19	.970

Reeser, Sara Louise

Born: Feb. 11, 1925, Columbus, Ohio. 5'4", 130, 1st Base, BL, TL. Muskegon Lassies, 1946–48; Kalamazoo Lassies, 1949–50.

Sara Reeser was the best fielding first baseman in 1947 with a .990 average, third best in league history for a single season.

Reeser was a latecomer and didn't start playing softball until age 16 in her hometown's industrial softball league. She was 21 and married before she joined the league in 1946. She helped Muskegon win a pennant in 1947 with her fielding, .231 batting average and 36 stolen bases.

BATTING												FIELDING				
G	BA	AB	H	2B	3B	HR	SB	BB	SO	R	RBI	PO	A	E	DP	FA
342	.218	1177	256	14	6	1	112	149	97	134	88	355	100	58	108	.984

Rehrer (Carteaux), Rita "Spud"

Born: June 30, 1927, Fort Wayne, Indiana. 5'2", 130, Catcher. Peoria Redwings, 1946.

BATTING			
G	BA	AB	H
1	.000	3	0

Reid, Dorice "Dorrie"

Born: Feb. 26, 1929, Superior, Wisconsin. 5'4", 140, Outfield, BR, TR. Chicago Colleens, 1948; Grand Rapids Chicks, 1949–51.

Dorice Reid was a light-hitting outfielder for four years in the league with Chicago and Grand Rapids. She had good speed and swiped 69 bases. She now lives in Vista, California.

BATTING														FIELDING				
G	BA	AB	H	2B	3B	HR	SB	BB	SO	R	RBI			PO	A	E	DP	FA
323	.166	1026	170	11	5	0	69	130	145	108	60			506	38	42	4	.928

Reynolds, Mary "Windy"

Born: April 27, 1921, Gastonia, North Carolina. Died: Date Unknown. Pitcher, 3rd Base, Outfield, TR, BR. Peoria Redwings, 1946–50.

Once selected to the All-Star team, Mary Reynolds was team captain for the Peoria Redwings for several years.

She grew up with five brothers and three sisters in North Carolina. When World War II arrived, Reynolds was a sheet metal worker.

"Windy"—a nickname she earned for her constant chatter on the field—played third base when she wasn't on the mound. Her career best .245 batting average and good fielding at third earned her a spot on the All-Star team in 1947.

Her best year on the mound came in 1948 when she went 9–6 with a 2.27 ERA. She was the best fielding pitcher in 1950 as she committed no errors.

PITCHING

W–L	PCT	ERA	G	IP	H	R	ER	BB	SO
30–38	.441	2.63	79	557	454	226	163	162	194

BATTING														FIELDING				
G	BA	AB	H	2B	3B	HR	SB	BB	SO	R	RBI			PO	A	E	DP	FA
483	.223	1491	332	30	18	1	30	216	143	143	151			505	604	70	31	.941

Richard, Ruth "Richie"

Born: Sept. 20, 1928, Argus, Pennsylvania. 5'4", 134, Catcher, Outfield, Pitcher, BL, TR. Grand Rapids Chicks, 1947; Rockford Peaches, 1948–54.

An All-Star six years in a row, Ruth Richard was one of the best hitting catchers of all-time in the All-American League.

Richard first learned how to catch when she played softball in grammar and high school while growing up in Argus (near Philadelphia). She went to a league tryout in Allentown and was picked to go to Cuba for spring training in 1947. Afterwards, she was assigned to Grand Rapids, where she primarily played right field. The Chicks tried her at pitcher as well because she had such a strong arm, and she made three relief appearances.

In 1948, "Richie" was traded to Rockford and put behind the plate to be a starting receiver. She struggled somewhat for the next two seasons with the bat, but she shined defensively. She helped the Peaches win championships in both seasons. "We had a very good infield and pitching," she explained. She recalled catching two no-hitters during the 1949 playoffs. She also was named to her first All-Star team in 1949.

Richard began hitting for average and with power in 1950. She hit a career high six doubles on the season and averaged .251. The year was spoiled when, on the last day of the season, she broke her ankle and couldn't play in the playoffs. Rockford won the championship again without their best receiver. She was again named an All-Star.

Over the next four years Richard continued to improve on her hitting and was named to the All-Star team each season. When the ball was reduced to major league size in 1954, she pounded out a career high seven homers.

After the league folded, she joined Bill Allington's All-American barnstorming team for four years. "That was quite interesting," she said. The team traveled all over the United States and Canada.

Richard settled down to a regular job in a factory when Allington's team folded. She also played amateur softball for a few more seasons. She worked for Ametek for 26 years and retired in 1993. She now loves to golf, travel and go to league reunions.

BATTING

G	BA	AB	H	2B	3B	HR	SB	BB	SO	R	RBI
725	.241	2518	608	67	20	15	72	142	109	237	287

PITCHING

G	IP
3	7

FIELDING

PO	A	E	DP	FA
2668	605	134	41	.961

Ricketts, Joyce "Rick"

Born: April 25, 1933, Oquawka, Illinois. Died: May 8, 1992. Outfield, BL, TL. Grand Rapids Chicks, 1953–54.

An All-Star for both of the years she played, Joyce Ricketts was one of the best hitters in the league. She helped the Chicks win the league championship in 1953. She clobbered 15 home runs in 1954 after the ball was reduced to major league size.

BATTING

G	BA	AB	H	2B	3B	HR	SB	BB	SO	R	RBI
207	.300	707	212	33	9	20	14	109	39	111	143

FIELDING

PO	A	E	DP	FA
253	46	16	8	.949

Ries (Zillmer), Ruth "Boots"

Born: March 20, 1933, Naperville, Illinois. 5'6", 130, Pitcher, TR, BR. Rockford Peaches, 1951–52.

Ruth Ries saw very little action in two seasons in the All-American League.

Ruth "Boots" Ries

She earned the nickname "Boots" from her large family of eight children because she used to walk around in her father's boots. She first started playing softball in the first grade. A high school teacher who was a scout for the Brooklyn Dodgers told her about the league. She received an invitation to spring training in Peoria in 1951. She was drafted by Rockford as a pitcher.

Ries pitched batting practice only in 1951 to give her more experience. Then in 1952 she finally saw some game action as a reliever, but she proved to be ineffective. "I had a good arm, but I needed more experience," she explained.

After the season ended, she went home and was never called back. "We thought it folded the year we left," she said. Two years later it did.

In 1955, she married Lawrence Zillmer and they had five children: Edward, Thomas, Susan, Ronald and Donald. They now have four grandchildren and live in Walworth, Wisconsin. She attended the 50th reunion of the league in South Bend.

PITCHING

W–L	PCT	ERA	G	IP	H	R	ER	BB	SO
0–1	.000	25.00	3	4	7	14	11	9	1

Rini, Mary

Born: March 5, 1925, Detroit, Michigan. 5'6", 145, Pitcher, TR, BR. Kenosha Comets, 1945; Muskegon Lassies, 1946.

Mary Rini was an undistinguished pitcher for two seasons in the league. In 1945 she committed six balks, which tied her for the league lead. She now lives in Mt. Clemens, Michigan.

PITCHING										BATTING			FIELDING			
W–L	PCT	ERA	G	IP	H	R	ER	BB	SO	BA	AB	H	PO	A	E	FA
2–12	.143	3.62	23	112	103	76	45	48	15	.000	41	0	8	35	7	.860

Risinger, Earlene "Beans"

Born: March 20, 1927, Hess, Oklahoma. 6'2", 137, Pitcher, TR, BR. Springfield Sallies, 1948; Grand Rapids Chicks, 1949–54.

One of the tallest players in the league, Earlene Risinger was an average pitcher who helped Grand Rapids win a championship in 1953.

The rural Oklahoma girl worked in cotton fields to put shoes on her feet and clothes on her back. Her father taught her to throw overhand from the beginning. She played sandlot baseball and basketball. In high school, she coached first base on the boys baseball team because a girl couldn't play on the team.

After graduation she had no money and no future. When she read about the league in the newspaper, she sent a post card. After a tryout in Oklahoma City, she borrowed money from the bank to go to Rockford, but she became homesick and got only as far as Chicago before returning home. The following year she went to Springfield and joined the Sallies as a pitcher.

In her first season, she compiled a 3–8 record. In January 1949, she joined the South American tour, where Johnny Rawlings taught her the finer points of pitching. She learned to throw a curveball and changeup to go along with her blazing fastball.

Her best season came in 1953 when she went 15–10 and led Grand Rapids to the playoffs. In the final inning of the final game of the championship, the Chicks led by a run with the bases loaded and "Beans" on the mound. She ran the count to 3–2 before striking out Doris Sams, one of the best hitters in the league, to clinch the championship for the team.

After league folded in 1954, Risinger went to work as an X-ray technician. Besides the National Baseball Hall of Fame distinction, Beans was elected to the Jackson Company (Ok.) Athletic Hall of Fame.

Earlene "Beans" Risinger

PITCHING											BATTING			FIELDING			
W–L	PCT	ERA	G	IP	H	R	ER	BB	SO		BA	AB	H	PO	A	E	FA
73–80	.477	2.51	187	1347	1073	524	379	599	578		.172	466	80	89	405	35	.934

Rohrer, Kay

Born: June 29, 1922, Los Angeles, California. Died: March 17, 1962. 5'7", 139, Catcher, Shortstop. Rockford Peaches, 1945.

Kay Rohrer was a member of the championship Rockford Peaches in 1945.

She appeared in several Hollywood movies before joining the league. She was a star in the league as well as the ninth best hitter in her only season. Her father, William "Daddy" Rohrer, was a minor league catcher who managed the Fort Wayne Daisies in 1946.

BATTING												FIELDING				
G	BA	AB	H	2B	3B	HR	SB	BB	SO	R	RBI	PO	A	E	DP	FA
100	.239	327	78	8	1	2	26	33	9	34	26	396	106	21	10	.960

Romatowski, Jenny "Romey"

Born: Sept. 13, 1927, Wyandotte, Michigan. 5'4", 145, Catcher, 3rd Base, Outfield, BR, TR. South Bend Blue Sox, 1946; Rockford Peaches, 1947; Racine Belles, 1948; Chicago Colleens, 1948; Peoria Redwings, 1949; South Bend Blue Sox, 1950; Kalamazoo Lassies, 1951–54.

An All-Star in her last season, Jenny Romatowski saw action with seven teams in her nine seasons in the league.

"Romey" started playing softball in her hometown at age 12 before going to the Keller Girls Club in Detroit, where she played left field, shortstop and catcher. A league scout signed her to a contract in 1946. She began playing as a utility infielder for South Bend.

Manager Bonnie Baker then converted her to a catcher. "I had a fast getaway," she said. During the off-season, she attended Michigan State Normal and graduated with a degree in physical education.

Romatowski saved the best for last, hitting .258 and knocking out six homers in 1954. She was selected for the All-Star team. She also helped the Lassies win a championship.

After the league folded, she joined the U.S. Field Hockey team for three national tournaments. Her hockey efforts led her to be named to the Michigan Hall of Fame. Her town of Wyandotte also named her to its hall of fame. She taught school for 31 years and retired in 1983. She took up racing and adopting out greyhounds from her home in Palm Harbor, Florida. She has been to several league reunions.

				BATTING										FIELDING				
G	BA	AB	H	2B	3B	HR	SB	BB	SO	R	RBI		PO	A	E	DP	FA
535	.204	1639	334	21	3	6	31	97	114	115	128		1656	439	87	48	.960

Martha Rommelaere

Rommelaere (Manning), Martha

**Born: Aug. 30, 1922, Deloraine, Manitoba, Canada.
5'4", 120, Outfield, BR, TR.
Chicago Colleens/Springfield Sallies, 1950;
Kenosha Comets, 1950.**

Martha Rommelaere's budding career in the league was cut short due to a back injury.

The Canadian played sandlot ball as a child. She was a track star in high school and could outrun any girl in Saskatchewan. "I could run like a deer," she said. She didn't begin playing softball until she was age 22 with the Moose Jaw Royals. She was missed by scouts from the league during her first years in softball. Then she won the most valuable player award for Edmonton and won an all-expense-paid trip to the league.

Rommelaere was assigned to the traveling teams and hit .243 in 38 games, earning her a promotion to the Kenosha Comets halfway through the season. She had been an infielder in Canada, but she was converted to the outfield because of her speed.

She hurt her back playing and had a lot of trouble with it during her playing days. "It was the sitting on the bus that killed me," she explained. After the 1950 season, she married John Manning and decided to quit baseball because of her back, which took five surgeries to correct. The couple raised three children: Raymond, Lorelee and William. She worked as a seamstress until retirement in 1983.

BATTING												FIELDING					
G	BA	AB	H	2B	3B	HR	SB	BB	SO	R	RBI	G	PO	A	E	DP	FA
30	.188	80	15	0	0	0	8	10	12	7	7	27	19	1	3	1	.870

Roth, Eilaine "I"

Born: Jan. 17, 1929, Michigan City, Michigan. 5'2", 115, Outfield, BR, TR. Peoria Redwings, 1948–49; Kalamazoo Lassies, 1950–51.

Younger than twin sister Elaine by 15 minutes, Eilaine Roth played four years in the league as an outfielder, while her sister was a pitcher for seven years.

Eilaine concentrated on basketball, field hockey and soccer during her school days. She began playing softball during the summers.

The twins were recruited by the league and put on the same team, because it was good for promotions, Eilaine had a good arm and could throw out runners from the outfield. "I remember throwing a ball over the backstop," she recalled.

After two seasons with Peoria, the league broke up the twins, sending "I" to Kalamazoo and "E" to South Bend for a season. The two were reunited in 1951, when "E" was picked up by the Lassies. Eilaine learned how to steal from manager Bonnie Baker. "I stole quite a few," she said.

Eilaine decided to quit baseball after the 1951 season and work for a paper mill for 16 years. She worked at Upjohn until retirement in 1988. She played softball with her sister in Portage for a few years after the league folded in 1954.

When *A League of Their Own* was shot in Cooperstown, Eilaine made an appearance. She also has attended league reunions. Bad knees and a heart problem prevent her from playing any more softball.

BATTING												FIELDING				
G	BA	AB	H	2B	3B	HR	SB	BB	SO	R	RBI	PO	A	E	DP	FA
293	.200	932	186	12	7	0	100	121	57	116	52	356	23	26	5	.936

Roth, Elaine "E"

Born: Jan. 17, 1929, Michigan City, Indiana. 5'2", 123, Pitcher, Outfielder, TR, BR. Peoria Redwings, 1948–49; South Bend Blue Sox, 1950; Kalamazoo Lassies, 1951–54.

The "E" of the twin-sister combination, Elaine Roth was the pitcher in the family and spent seven seasons in the league.

Although not identical to her sister, the two looked very much alike in grade school. In high school, Elaine admitted putting on a few more pounds to look differently than her sister. She also concentrated more on softball than her sister.

Both girls were noticed and recruited by the All-American league, and both were assigned to Peoria. Sometimes the two girls played together in the outfield, but most of the time "E" was on the mound. She was a starting pitcher and turned in an 18–15 performance in her first season, including a one-hitter. "My brother was mad because I didn't get 20 victories," she remembered.

Elaine fell on hard times in her sophomore season, turning in a 4–12 mark. She was shipped to South Bend in 1950 and improved to 7–13. She then joined her sister in Kalamazoo in 1951. She was sent to the bullpen for the remainder of her career and relieved more than she started.

After the league folded in 1954, "E" went to work for Upjohn and played softball in a city league in Portage with her sister. She also took up basketball, volleyball and bowling. She worked 32 years for the pharmaceutical company before retiring. She came back to softball in 1994 to play with a senior team for a couple of seasons. She has also gone to several league reunions.

PITCHING										BATTING			FIELDING			
W–L	PCT	ERA	G	IP	H	R	ER	BB	SO	BA	AB	H	PO	A	E	FA
45–69	.395	2.94	184	1028	944	501	336	260	238	.141	370	52	38	238	29	.905

Rotvig, Barbara

Duluth, Minnesota. Died: December 1964. Pitcher, TR, BR. Kenosha Comets, 1948–51.

Barbara Rotvig's claim to fame was pitching a no-hitter in 1949. However, she was a wild pitcher and had the dubious distinction of hitting the most batters in 1949 (19) and throwing the most wild pitches (16) in 1951.

PITCHING									BATTING			FIELDING			
W–L	PCT	ERA	G	IP	H	R	ER	SO	BA	AB	H	PO	A	E	FA
28–41	.406	2.58	82	551	375	242	158	289	.144	194	28	11	133	17	.895

Rountree, Mary "Square Bush"

Born: June 23, 1922, Miami, Florida. 5'5", 125, Catcher, BR, TR. Peoria Redwings, 1946; Fort Wayne Daisies, 1947–52; Grand Rapids Chicks, 1952.

Mary Rountree was a capable catcher who led the league in fielding percentage one season. She went on to become a doctor, a distinction held by few players.

Rountree received her first baseball uniform when she was 5 years old. She emulated her older brother and became a catcher. As a teenager, she played with two championship teams in Florida in 1938 and 1940 and went to national tournaments both years. Before World War II, she went to work with the State Department in Washington, D.C. In the spring of 1943 she received a call from league publicity director Arthur Meyeroff. She declined the offer to come to the league because she had a good job at the time. After the war, she tried out in Miami for Max Carey and was signed to a contract.

"Square Bush" recalled her very first game against Racine. The game was played on a high school football field in front of a large crowd. When the Belles got a woman on third base, they tried the squeeze play. "I flipped off the mask and tagged the runner coming in. Then I threw to first to double off the hitter," she said.

During the off-season, Rountree pursued a medical degree. She would not show up until a month into the season, which is why she never played a full season. In 1952, she committed only four errors for a .986 fielding percentage — best in the league. Her salary of $125 a week helped her save enough to go on to medical school.

She completed medical school in 1956 and enjoyed a long and productive 32-year career in medicine, which included 17 years of teaching. She retired in 1988 and now lives in Coral Gables, Florida.

Mary "Square Bush" Rountree

				BATTING										FIELDING				
G	BA	AB	H	2B	3B	HR	SB	BB	SO	R	RBI		PO	A	E	DP	FA
422	.206	1211	250	14	6	0	89	166	86	105	107		1644	386	88	40	.959

Roy, Patricia

Born: Oct. 3, 1938, Goshen, Indiana. 5'10", 125, 1st Base, 3rd Base, BR, TR.
Ft. Wayne Daisies, 1954.

Patricia Roy's only season in the league was cut short after an insurance company refused to cover the too-young 15 year old.

Roy grew up in Harland, Indiana (near Fort Wayne), and played pickup games with the boys until she joined a boys' Pony League. After she got three hits in one game and showed up her male counterparts, she was told that girls couldn't play in the league. So, she went to the Junior Girls Baseball League in Fort Wayne, which was sort of a farm club for the league. "We were called the same last

Patricia Roy

names as the league — Daisies, Lassies, Blue Sox. And we wore the hand-me-down uniforms from the league. Some were pretty used," she explained.

In 1954, the Fort Wayne team was short of players and gave the young girl a tryout. Normally the league took older girls, but these were becoming desperate times. Roy was still in high school and had a hard time convincing her parents she was old enough to play in the league. "I still have my contract and it is co-signed by my mother," she said.

The rookie was given plenty of opportunity to play. Her best game was on the road in South Bend when she collected two of her three career hits. A teammate, Shirley Ann Weierman, slid hard into second and broke her ankle. After her injury, the insurance company decided it would not cover any girl in the league under age 18. She and Weierman were released immediately.

Roy went on to Ball State University to get bachelor's and master's degrees. She played for the Valparaiso Queens and traveled all over the Midwest. She taught in East Gary until landing in Indianapolis in 1972 as the assistant commissioner of the Indiana High School Athletic Association.

Although her AAGPBL career lasted only a month, she's very proud of the experience and got goose bumps when she saw the movie about the league, *A League of Their Own.*

			BATTING										FIELDING				
G	BA	AB	H	2B	3B	HR	SB	BB	SO	R	RBI		PO	A	E	DP	FA
14	.079	38	3	0	0	0	0	0	9	0	2		95	2	5	1	.951

Roylance, Juanita

Miami, Florida. Outfield. Muskegon Lassies, 1946.

BATTING

G	BA	AB	H
6	.067	15	1

Ruhnke (Sanvitis), Irene

Born: March 30, 1920, Chicago, Illinois. 5'4", 130, Outfield, Utility Infielder, BR, TR. Rockford Peaches, 1943–44; Minneapolis Millerettes, 1944; Fort Wayne Daisies, 1945–46; Rockford Peaches, 1947.

One of the original players in the league, Irene Ruhnke played several positions during her five seasons in the league. She began as a shortstop-outfielder with Rockford in 1943. Later in her career, she was platooned at second and third base. She now lives in Rockford.

			BATTING										FIELDING				
G	BA	AB	H	2B	3B	HR	SB	BB	SO	R	RBI		PO	A	E	DP	FA
385	.196	1327	260	22	18	2	87	91	80	137	130		524	333	103	27	.893

Ruiz, Gloria "Baby-Face"

Born: June 25, 1928, Havana, Cuba. Outfield, BR, TR. Peoria Redwings, 1948–49.

Gloria Ruiz was one of the Cuban players who was signed after the league held spring training in Cuba in 1947.

		BATTING												FIELDING			
G	BA	AB	H	2B	3B	HR	SB	BB	SO	R	RBI		PO	A	E	DP	FA
52	.095	126	12	0	0	0	10	19	26	8	8		60	3	4	2	.940

Rukavina, Terry

Born: May 14, 1931, Middleton, Ohio. 5'7", 140, Outfield, Utility Infielder. Chicago Colleens/Springfield Sallies, 1950; Kalamazoo Lassies, 1951, '53.

Terry Rukavina was a versatile player for four seasons in the league.

She played on the player development teams in 1950 and hit .273 in 77 games. She then filled in at many different positions with Kalamazoo for two years. After baseball, she played with the Kalamazoo basketball team that won the state championship. She went to work at a steel company for 34 years and retired in 1991.

		BATTING												FIELDING			
G	BA	AB	H	2B	3B	HR	SB	BB	SO	R	RBI		PO	A	E	DP	FA
147	.163	356	58	7	1	1	6	31	72	34	23		215	143	40	11	.900

Rumsey, Janet

Born: Oct. 16, 1931, Moores Hill, Indiana. 5'8", 135, Pitcher, TR, BR. Battle Creek Belles, 1951; South Bend Blue Sox, 1951–54.

Janet Rumsey was an All-Star pitcher who tossed the league's last no-hitter.

Rumsey's father was responsible for getting her into baseball. "I used to play catch with my father. He'd hit fungoes (fly balls) to me," she explained. In school the girls didn't have a softball team, so she played on a boys' team in junior high.

In 1950, the 18 year old saw a movie short on the Fort Wayne Daisies

Janet Rumsey

and wrote the team. She was invited to a tryout, but she didn't make the grade. She didn't give up trying, though, and the following season she gave it another go with the South Bend Blue Sox. She tried out for first base and the outfield. Rumsey was a poor hitter, but manager Karl Winsch saw that she had a good arm and kept her as a pitcher.

The first year she struggled to a 4–8 record, yet the team won the league championship and the playoffs. During the season she was temporarily loaned to Battle Creek. She was more effective the following season and the team again won the playoffs. The team went through a poor season in 1953 and she suffered along with the Blue Sox, posting an 11–19 mark.

By 1954 she had perfected a sidearm curveball, a sinker and a fastball. This arsenal of pitches led to her selection on the league's last All-Star team. On August 24 against Grand Rapids, she had a perfect game going until she walked a batter. "The next hitter got a ball through the infield, but the runner was forced out at second to preserve the no-hitter," she recalled.

The season and the league ended shortly after the game. She went to work for Cummins Engine Company in Columbus, Indiana, where she retired in 1985. She now enjoys golf and tennis.

PITCHING

W–L	PCT	ERA	G	IP	H	R	ER	BB	SO
39–43	.476	2.33	105	703	585	269	182	262	259

BATTING											FIELDING			
G	BA	AB	H	2B	3B	HR	SB	BB	SO	R	PO	A	E	FA
115	.169	243	41	3	0	0	1	20	47	16	60	294	21	.944

Russell, Betty

Born: Oct. 1, 1924, Globe, Arizona. 5'6", 145, Outfield. Racine Belles, 1946.

Betty Russell saw little action in the Racine outfield in 1946. She played for the Arizona Ramblers before coming to the league.

BATTING

G	BA	AB	H	2B	3B	HR	SB	BB	SO	R	RBI
12	.143	28	4	1	0	0	0	0	3	0	1

Russo (Jones), Margaret

Born: Sept. 29, 1931, Milton, New York. 5'4", 130, Shortstop, 3rd Base, BR, TR. Peoria Redwings, 1950–51; Battle Creek Belles, 1952; Muskegon Belles, 1953; Rockford Peaches, 1954.

Margaret Russo was an excellent fielder and a solid hitter in the league for five years. She led the league in fielding percentage at shortstop for two seasons. In 1952, she committed 37 errors, while in 1954 she had just 29 miscues. She converted 43 double plays one season, the second highest single season total in the history of the league.

BATTING												FIELDING				
G	BA	AB	H	2B	3B	HR	SB	BB	SO	R	RBI	PO	A	E	DP	FA
501	.230	1640	377	39	19	15	104	251	147	251	166	911	1424	202	138	.886

Sachette, Toni

Fort Wayne Daisies, 1954.

Toni Sachette played in less than ten games with Fort Wayne in the last year of the league.

Sams, Doris "Sammy"

**Born: Feb. 2, 1927, Knoxville, Tennessee. 5'9", 145, Pitcher, Outfield, TR, BR.
Muskegon Lassies, 1946–49; Kalamazoo Lassies, 1950–53.**

A two time Player of the Year and a five time All-Star, Doris Sams was an all-around athlete who could pitch, hit and field as well as any player.

Sams came from a family of baseball players. Her grandfather was a semi-pro pitcher who taught her how to pitch. Her father was a semi-pro center fielder who taught her how to field. She started playing softball with older girls in 1938 when she was 11. She helped her softball team win the state tournament for the next eight years and in 1941 represented Tennessee in the nationals.

When the league rolled through Knoxville in 1946 she tried out and won a spot on the Muskegon team. Her father was very proud of her. "He always wanted to be a professional," she recalled.

The league was in the process of converting to the sidearm delivery and Sams had learned to throw sidearm from the outfield. "I was a natural sidearm," she said. Her windups included a figure eight, windmill and submarine. In her rookie season she pitched in 25 games and played the outfield, while hitting .274.

The following season Sams baffled hitters with her different deliveries and on August 18 she mystified every hitter on Fort Wayne. "The last girl that came to

Doris "Sammy" Sams

bat hit a liner than ricocheted off my knee. The ball went to the shortstop. She threw to first base for the last out," Sams explained. The perfect game was only the third in league history. She helped the Lassies win the pennant for the first time in their history with an 11–4 record and the best winning percentage (.733) in the league. Her ERA was a 0.98, second lowest on the season, and she was the best fielding pitcher in the league. She also hit a club record .280 and drove in 41 runs. Her all-around play earned her Player of the Year honors and a spot on the All-Star team.

The following season she set a club record for RBI (59) and was 18–10 on the year, but was ignored by the All-Star team. She couldn't be ignored in 1949. She tied Jean Faut for the batting crown with a .279 average, while gaining the most hits (114) in the league on the season. She also compiled a 15–10 record and was the best fielding pitcher (.985) in the league with only two errors. Again she was named Player of the Year and was put on the All-Star team.

"Sammy" started fooling around with a more overhand delivery in 1950 and her pitching become less effective. However, she broke the .300 batting average barrier for the first time and was again selected for the All-Star team.

In 1951 she quit pitching. "I wanted two salaries, so they put me in the outfield," she explained. Able to concentrate more on hitting, she again topped the .300 mark (.306) and was named to her third straight All-Star team. She remembered bouncing off the fence going for a fly ball with the bases loaded. "I didn't know I had caught the ball. The crowd didn't know I had it until I threw it in," she recalled.

Her greater concentration on hitting paid off in 1952. With the ball at 10 inches in circumference, the women could hit it with more authority and Sams knocked 12 of the major league sized balls out of the park to lead the league. Her average rose to .314. She made just eight errors in the outfield and tied Eleanor Callow for the best fielding percentage (.969). The All-Star team selection was never in doubt.

She played in just 46 games in her final season and decided to quit. "It looked as if it (the league) was folding. Those buses were beating me to death," she added.

Sams went to work for a utility company for 25 years and retired in 1979. She now plays golf, rides bikes and attends league reunions.

PITCHING

W–L	PCT	ERA	G	IP	H	R	ER	BB	SO
64–47	.577	2.16	134	1007	719	356	242	408	396

BATTING

G	BA	AB	II	2B	3B	HR	SB	BB	SO	R	RBI
721	.278	2485	690	82	23	22	154	214	194	290	286

FIELDING

PO	A	E	DP	FA
1113	417	63	0	.961

Sands (Ferguson), Sarah Jane "Salty"

Born: July 27, 1935, Orangeville, Pennsylvania. 5'4", 120, Catcher, Outfield, BR, TR. Rockford Peaches, 1953–54.

Sarah Sands was a catcher-outfielder for the last two seasons of the league.

She fell in love with baseball at an early age. A batgirl at age 6, the self-described "tomboy" liked to play catcher. "Catching was my love and I'd warm up the pitcher between innings," she said about her role on the town's team.

Sands heard about the All-American League when she was a senior in high school. She went to Allentown to show a scout her stuff. After five tosses the scout knew he had found a player. "Salty" played part time for the Peaches, filling in behind the plate and in the outfield for two seasons. At the end of the league, she remembered the league completely ran out of money and they never did get paid for the last week of the season. "Those two years of baseball were worth four years of college. It was the greatest experience of my life," she said.

After baseball, she married William Ferguson and they had two children — William II and Tammy. She worked for several years for the military and once got to meet the seven original astronauts. Now a school bus driver, she also went to Cooperstown for the filming of *A League of Their Own.* "It's hard work, but you do a lot of standing around," she said of the movie business.

Sarah Jane "Salty" Sands

BATTING

G	BA	AB	H	2B	3B	HR	SB	BB	SO	R	RBI
136	.210	414	87	5	0	1	9	13	48	37	29

FIELDING

PO	A	E	DP	FA
169	27	14	6	.933

Satterfield, Doris

North Belmont, North Carolina. Died: Date Unknown. Outfield, Pitcher. Grand Rapids Chicks, 1948–53.

Doris Satterfield was an outstanding outfielder with Grand Rapids for six season. In 1953 she was the best fielding outfielder (8 errors, .971 average) and was selected to the All-Star team. She led the league in doubles (22) in 1949 and was third in batting average (.259).

BATTING

G	BA	AB	H	2B	3B	HR	SB	BB	SO	R	RBI
683	.271	2517	682	90	42	9	209	199	121	321	365

PITCHING

G	IP
1	2

FIELDING

PO	A	E	DP	FA
1324	65	42	14	.971

Sawyer, Helen

Catcher, Rockford Peaches, 1943.

Helen Sawyer was one of the original players in the league.

Schachter, Blanche

Born: Sept. 20, 1926, Brooklyn, New York. 5'2", 125, Catcher, BR, TR. Kenosha Comets, 1948.

Blanche Schachter tore cartilage in her right knee, which ended her short career. She had surgery on the knee and returned to teaching. She didn't play softball for another seven years. She became a tennis coach on a high school team that went undefeated for five years. She now conducts exercise classes three days a week in West Springfield, Massachusetts.

BATTING

G	BA	AB	H
9	.040	25	1

Schallern, Ellen

Miami, Florida. Outfield, TR, BR. Fort Wayne Daisies, 1946.

Schatz, Joan

Winnipeg, Manitoba, Canada. Outfield, BR, TR. Chicago Colleens/Springfield Sallies, 1950; Kalamazoo Lassies, 1951–52.

In 1950, Joan Schatz led the barnstorming teams in at-bats (323), hits (104) and home runs (4), while hitting .322 in 77 games. However, when she came to the league the following two seasons, she wasn't given much of a chance to play.

	BATTING											FIELDING				
G	BA	AB	H	2B	3B	HR	SB	BB	SO	R	RBI	PO	A	E	DP	FA
13	.186	43	8	0	0	0	4	2	6	4	0	27	1	1	0	.966

Scheer, Edna "Bunny"

Born: Nov. 4, 1926, Cedarburg, Wisconsin. 5'5", 104, Pitcher, TR, BR. Rockford Peaches, 1950.

Edna Scheer contributed to Rockford's winning of the pennant and championship in

1950 with her 3–1, record, although she had a high ERA. After baseball, she was a partner in a restaurant. She now lives in Jackson, Wisconsin.

		PITCHING								BATTING			FIELDING			
W–L	PCT	ERA	G	IP	H	R	ER	BB	SO	BA	AB	H	PO	A	E	FA
3–1	.750	5.58	18	71	63	52	44	66	21	.286	28	8	2	15	3	.842

Schenck, Audrey

Chicago, Illinois. 3rd Base. Chicago Colleens/Springfield Sallies, 1950.

Audrey Schenck was a member of the traveling teams in 1950 for just two games.

BATTING

G	BA	AB	H	2B	3B	HR	SB	BB	SO	R	RBI
2	.333	6	2	1	0	0	0	0	1	1	1

Schillace (Donahoe), Claire Joan

Born: March 29, 1922, Melrose Park, Illinois. 5'3", 128, Outfield, BR, TL. Racine Belles, 1943–46.

Claire Schillace was the first woman to sign a professional baseball contract with the league. She helped Racine win championships in 1943 and 1946.

Schillace played in the Chicago softball leagues before coming to the All-American League. She became a lead-off hitter and center fielder for Racine. On July 7, 1943, she set a league record by making three sacrifices in a game, which was later tied by two other players.

After her rookie year, she held out for $10 more a week and ended up settling for a $5 raise. During the off-season, she taught school. She married Joseph Donahoe and followed him to foreign countries, where he set up schools in which she taught. She was consulted on *A League of Their Own* and appeared at the end of the film. She now resides in Chevy Chase, Maryland.

					BATTING							FIELDING				
G	BA	AB	H	2B	3B	HR	SB	BB	SO	R	RBI	PO	A	E	DP	FA
417	.202	1391	282	15	14	2	153	226	92	201	113	622	56	43	9	.943

Schmidt, Marilyn

Hollywood, California. Catcher, TR. Rockford Peaches, 1952.

Marilyn Schmidt played in less than ten games with Rockford in 1952.

Schmidt (Weitzman), Violet "Vi"

Born: May 6, 1927, Fort Wayne, Indiana. 5'1", 118, Pitcher, TR, BR. Rockford Peaches, 1946; Fort Wayne Daisies, 1947.

Violet Schmidt was a sidearm pitcher that didn't get much playing time during her one season in the league.

Schmidt began playing sandlot baseball when she was 8 years old. At age 11 her mother died and she was put in an orphanage. She garnered more experience playing softball with a Catholic youth organization league before she and three others talked to the Fort Wayne Daisies manager and received an invitation to a tryout. She wanted to be an outfielder, but manager Bill Allington saw her throw sidearm and converted her into a pitcher.

The Hoosier got more work during a preseason tour of the South than what she received after the season started. "Vi" did recall pitching against South Bend. After the season was over, she married Elmer Weitzman and quit baseball. She went on to raise three children: Barbara, Jo Lynn and Steven. Her husband passed away in 1969.

When the movie *A League of Their Own* was shot in Cooperstown, she was there and ended up in two scenes in the movie. She is now a housekeeper for a church in Mishawaka, Indiana.

BATTING				PITCHING		
G	BA	AB	H	W–L	PCT	G
4	.333	3	1	0–0	.000	4

Schofield, June "Moneybags"

Toronto, Ontario, Canada. Infielder, Pitcher, BR, TR. Springfield Sallies, 1948; Peoria Redwings, 1949; Muskegon Lassies, 1949.

June Schofield had the most RBI in 1948 for the Springfield Sallies. She played another season with two other teams.

BATTING

G	BA	AB	H	2B	3B	HR	SB	BB	SO	R	RBI
234	.232	818	190	19	12	2	38	93	83	49	76

PITCHING

W–L	PCT	ERA	G	IP	H	R	ER	BB	SO
0–1	.000	36.36	1	1	1	4	4	8	1

Schroeder, Dorothy "Dottie"

Born: April 11, 1928, Champaign, Illinois. 5'7", 150, Shortstop, Pitcher, BR, TR. South Bend Blue Sox, 1943–45; Kenosha Comets, 1945–47; Fort Wayne Daisies, 1947–52; Kalamazoo Lassies, 1953–54.

Dorothy Schroeder was the only player to play in all 12 seasons of the league. The three time All-Star set several career marks and was one of the best fielding shortstops in the league.

Schroeder's father played and managed a semi-pro team when Dottie was growing up, so she would mess around with the bats and balls. "When I was a little kid, we used to play rounders," she recalled. At age 11 she played on her first team, a 4H fast-pitch softball team. She joined the Illinois Commercial College team the following year.

In 1943 her dad saw an advertisement in the *Chicago Tribune* about the league. He answered the ad and his 15-year-old daughter received an invitation to try out in St. Louis. Of the 65 girls who tried out that day, she and Lois Florreich made the cut and were sent to Wrigley Field for spring training. She was one of the youngest players in the league. She was assigned to South Bend after spring training as a shortstop, which was the position she had always played.

In her rookie season, she had the best fielding percentage of all short-stops (.924) and hit .188. The following season she was more error prone and was hit by more pitches than any other player. She reached a career high in stolen bases (70). Playing shortstop was rough on her knees and she had to have surgery after the season.

Dorothy "Dottie" Schroeder

The pigtailed shortstop began the 1945 season with the Blue Sox, but she was reassigned to Kenosha by the league. She played there for three seasons before being sent to Fort Wayne. When the league switched to overhand pitching, Dottie's hitting improved to over .200 for the first time. "My average got better and better. I prided myself in push bunting and sacrificing," she explained.

With her help, Fort Wayne became a powerful team and won the pennant in 1952. She considers that team the strongest she ever played for in her career. "We had power and speed," she commented. The team's only shortfall was losing the championship playoffs. She made her first All-Star team in 1952 and was the Daisies' Most Popular Player.

The Daisies traded the veteran the following season to Kalamazoo. She didn't like the trade and was able to get some revenge in a game the next season. Fort Wayne jumped out to score 20 runs in a game threatened by rain. It never did rain, though, and the Lassies chipped away at the lead until winning the game in the ninth. She made the All-Star squad again in 1953 and 1954.

In the 1954 playoffs, her team exacted more revenge against the Daisies. In the final game of the championship, Dottie had a couple of key doubles to lead her team over the Daisies for the final championship of the league.

In her 12 years, she racked up some impressive numbers. She played the most games (1,249), missing just 82 regular season games in 12 seasons. She is also the all-time leader in RBI

(431), at-bats (4,129), walks (696), and strikeouts (566). She ranks second in hits (870) and third in home runs (42). Three times she was the best fielding shortstop in the league.

After the league folded, Dottie joined Bill Allington's barnstorming team and played on the road for four more years. She hung up her cleats for good after that and went to work at Collegiate Cap and Gowns for 35 years. She retired in 1993 and now lives in Champaign, Illinois. She attends league reunions and loves to watch baseball. "Pete Rose is the only player I'd pay to see. He should be in the Hall of Fame," she remarked.

BATTING

G	BA	AB	H	2B	3B	HR	SB	BB	SO	R	RBI
1249	211	4129	870	79	26	42	312	696	566	571	431

PITCHING / FIELDING

W–L	PCT	ERA	G	IP	H	R	ER	BB	SO		PO	A	E	DP	FA
0–2	.000	3.19	3	18	14	11	6	6	7		2579	3376	571	315	.913

Schulze, Shirley

Chicago, Illinois. Outfield, BR, TR. Milwaukee Millerettes, 1944.

BATTING / FIELDING

G	BA	AB	H	2B	3B	HR	SB	BB	SO	R	RBI		PO	A	E	DP	FA
15	.182	44	8	0	0	0	7	6	4	5	2		14	2	2	1	.889

Schweigerdt, Gloria "Tippy"

Born: June 10, 1934, Chicago, Illinois. 5'4", 120, Pitcher, BR, TR. Chicago Colleens, 1950; Grand Rapids Chicks, 1951; Battle Creek Belles, 1951–52.

Only 15 when she joined the league, Gloria Schweigerdt pitched for three seasons.

Her brother got her involved in sandlot ball when she was 7, she recalled. At age 15 she went to a league tryout at Thillens Stadium in Skokie. The league assigned her to the traveling Chicago Colleens for more seasoning. She traveled all over the country and compiled an 8–7 record. Her biggest thrill was pitching a no-hitter in Yankee Stadium. "No other woman had ever pitched off that mound before me," she said.

The following season the fastball-curveball pitcher was assigned to Grand Rapids. The rookie remembered winning one game against the best pitcher in the league — Jean Faut of South Bend. "Tippy" was traded to Battle Creek during the season. In all, she appeared in 14 games and was 3–4 on the season. Then in 1952 she compiled a 10–10 ledger with the Chicks.

Schweigerdt saw the end to the league coming in 1952, so she left for marriage and to raise a family. She raised two children, Gordon and Gloria, before divorcing her husband. She was a meat cutter after her baseball days and retired in 1996. She attended the 50th league reunion in South Bend in 1993. She now lives in Buffalo Grove, a suburb of Chicago.

Gloria "Tippy" Schweigerdt (on right)

PITCHING										FIELDING			
W–L	PCT	ERA	G	IP	H	R	ER	BB	SO	PO	A	E	FA
13–14	.481	2.88	42	256	230	114	82	95	80	12	71	6	.913

Scott, Patricia A. "Pat"

Born: July 14, 1929, Covington, Kentucky. 5'7", 155, Outfielder, Pitcher, TR, BR.
Racine Belles, 1948; Springfield Sallies, 1948; Ft. Wayne Daisies, 1951–53.

Pat Scott was one of the best overhand pitchers during her four years in the league.

Scott began playing baseball when she was 8. "I used to throw a ball against the barn. We had a ballpark on our farm, like (the movie) *Field of Dreams*," she explained. She played more baseball in Burlington, Kentucky, than the traditional softball that most girls played in the forties. During her high school years, she played fast-pitch softball in Cincinnati.

One day she was reading the morning newspaper and saw an advertisement for a tryout at Wrigley Field. She went to Chicago and was picked for the league in 1947.

Patricia A. "Pat" Scott

The following season, the pitcher tossed an 11-inning game and helped her team to victory by stroking two singles, a double and a home run. During the season, her mother became ill and she had to return home. It seemed her playing days were over.

Then in 1951, league president Max Carey was desperate for pitching and located Scott in Springfield, Ohio. He talked her parents into letting her return to the league. She pitched for Fort Wayne the next three seasons.

Her manager was Jimmie Foxx, a Hall of Famer. Scott confirmed that Foxx had a drinking problem, but he never let it affect his performance on the field and was a gentleman around the ladies. "I never saw him miss a game and never cuss," she said.

Pat considers her most exciting victory as a one-run, pennant-winning game against Rockford in 1952. The pitcher was a good hitter as well. "I was a place hitter and a good bunter," she boasted.

In 1954, she couldn't pass up an agricultural exchange program to attend college in Europe. Scott attained a degree in zoology at the University of Kentucky. For the next 32 years she was a medical technologist in Cincinnati.

The former player likes to help children with baseball and still plays some softball. Oil painting has become her hobby now that she's retired in Walton, Kentucky.

PITCHING

W–L	PCT	ERA	G	IP	H	R	ER	BB	SO
48–26	.649	2.46	84	630	377	232	172	174	187

BATTING												FIELDING			
G	BA	AB	H	2B	3B	HR	SB	BB	SO	R	RBI	PO	A	E	FA
91	.218	261	57	10	1	0	0	8	13	30	21	41	209	6	.977

Shadic (Campbell), Lillian "Pete"

Born: June 14, 1929, Chatham, New York. 5'5", 145, Outfield, BR, TR. Springfield Sallies, 1949.

Lillian "Pete" Shadic played one season barnstorming with the league.

Shadic played basketball and softball in high school before answering an advertisement about the league. She went to a tryout in New Jersey and was assigned to Springfield to get more experience. While no statistics were kept, she recalled hitting two home runs once in a game. The mother of seven lives in Craryville, New York.

Shafranis, Geraldine

Chicago, Illinois. Outfielder. South Bend Blue Sox, 1943.

Geraldine Shafranis was one of the original players of the league.

Shastal (Kustra), Mary

Winnipeg, Manitoba, Canada. Milwaukee Chicks, 1944.

Shero (Witiuk), Doris "Baser"

Born: May 22, 1929, Winnipeg, Manitoba, Canada. 5'2", 115, Outfield, BR, TR. Racine Belles, 1950; Battle Creek Belles, 1951.

An outfielder with a colorful nickname, Doris Shero played two seasons with the Belles.

The youngest of eight children lived adjacent to a school and began playing softball as a teenager. She then advanced to organized ball and played with CUAC in Winnipeg. She received a tryout at spring training in 1950 at West Baden, Indiana. She was assigned to Racine. Sophie Kurys nicknamed her "Baser" because she covered the outfield with ease and stole bases, but she hit only .093. After limited action the following season, she quit baseball.

She married former Chicago Blackhawks hockey player Steve Witiuk. The two started a family and an electrical contracting business. Both grew rapidly. They raised four children: Debbie, Tracy, Patty and Steve. The business went from nothing to 24 workers at its height. In 1991, they sold the business to their daughters and retired. When the movie *A League of Their Own* was released in 1992, Dora (her actual first name) threw out the first pitch at a Seattle Mariners game the night before the premiere. Now retired and living in Spokane, Washington, the two have seven grandchildren. Dora's brother, Fred Shero, was once hockey coach of the Philadelphia Flyers.

BATTING												FIELDING				
G	BA	AB	H	2B	3B	HR	SB	BB	SO	R	RBI	PO	A	E	DP	FA
97	.094	234	22	0	0	0	16	25	32	19	13	89	7	9	2	.914

Shinen, Dorothy

Los Angeles, California. Outfield. Kenosha Comets, 1945.

Dorothy Shinen was a part-time outfielder for one season in Kenosha along with her sister.

BATTING													FIELDING					
G	BA	AB	H	2B	3B	HR	SB	BB	SO	R	RBI		G	PO	A	E	DP	FA
36	.145	83	12	1	0	0	5	12	9	4	5		25	19	2	1	0	.955

Shinen (Volkov), Kay

Born: Dec. 9, 1921, Los Angeles, California. 5'5", 125, 3rd Base, BR, TR. Kenosha Comets, 1945.

Kay Shinen played third base, while her sister Dorothy played outfield during her only season in the league.

Shinen began playing softball at age 14 and went on a goodwill tour of Far East countries when she was 16. She barnstormed with Joe Louis' Brown Bombers before joining the All-Americans for a season with Kenosha. She played third and hit with some authority — one of the longest home runs in Kenosha history was hit by her.

After baseball, she married William Volkov in 1952 and raised two sons, Tim and Bill. She also worked as a legal secretary. In 1995, she was working as a litigation secretary for an automobile club in Southern California, where she lives. She now has two granddaughters.

BATTING													FIELDING					
G	BA	AB	H	2B	3B	HR	SB	BB	SO	R	RBI		G	PO	A	E	DP	FA
98	.168	333	56	3	4	1	18	25	14	23	20		90	167	271	49	11	.899

Shively, Twila "Twi"

Born: March 20, 1922, Decatur, Illinois. 5'6", 128, 1st Base, Outfield, BR, TR. Grand Rapids Chicks, 1945–47; Chicago Colleens, 1948; Peoria Redwings, 1948–50.

Twila Shively was a good fielder who displayed an average bat over her six seasons in the league.

She began playing softball when she was 8 years old. She moved up in the softball ranks in Chicago. "I was playing in an amateur softball league in Chicago when a scout came along and offered me a tryout," Shively recalled. She and another girl were picked from the 45 who participated in the workout. She went from a $16-a-week job at Hydrox to $75 a week for the AAGPBL.

Twila "Twi" Shively

"Twi" was a starter from the beginning. She remembered one game that had a storybook finish: two outs and the bases loaded in the final inning with her at bat and the game on the line. She came through with a grand slam home run!

Her career took a wrong turn when she broke an ankle sliding. The team doctor was gone and another doctor told her she could walk and be back in the lineup in a week or two. She ended up in a cast and the weeks turned into months.

She quit playing after the 1950 season and went on to Illinois State to obtain a teaching degree. She taught in a high school in South Bend for 30 years and coached softball and volleyball. She now attends league reunions.

BATTING													FIELDING				
G	BA	AB	H	2B	3B	HR	SB	BB	SO	R	RBI		PO	A	E	DP	FA
614	.200	2141	429	42	20	4	255	291	322	274	166		2028	102	67	38	.970

Shollenberger, Fern "Shelly"

Born: May 18, 1923, Hamburg, Pennsylvania.
Died: Dec. 24, 1977. 5'4", 125, 3rd Base, BR, TR.
Kenosha Comets, 1946–51;
Kalamazoo Lassies, 1952–54.

A four time All-Star, Fern Shollenberger was one of the best fielding third basemen in the league's history.

For the first three years of her nine-year career, Kenosha had her playing the infield and the outfield. She was best, though, at third base and finally landed that job permanently in 1948. "Shelly" led third basemen for the next three years in fielding. In 1950 she was selected for her first All-Star team.

In 1954, she hit career bests in batting average (.268), homers (8) and RBI (58).

Fern "Shelly" Shollenberger

BATTING													FIELDING				
G	BA	AB	H	2B	3B	HR	SB	BB	SO	R	RBI		PO	A	E	DP	FA
918	.221	3286	725	61	17	9	167	237	155	350	231		1274	2449	230	147	.942

Siegfried, Delores

2nd Base. Muskegon Lassies, 1947.

Sindelar, Joan "Jo"

Born: Aug. 29, 1931, Chicago, Illinois. 5'7", 125, Outfield, BR, TR. Chicago Colleens, 1949–50; Kalamazoo Lassies, 1951–53.

Joan Sindelar spent five seasons with the league, her first two with the traveling Chicago Colleens. She hit .260 in 72 games while playing for the Colleens in 1950. She joined the regular league the following season with Kalamazoo. She was a rookie the next two years with the Lassies because she played in less than 50 games. She earned a starting role in 1953 and hit a career high .224. She now lives in Phoenix, Arizona.

BATTING												FIELDING				
G	BA	AB	H	2B	3B	HR	SB	BB	SO	R	RBI	PO	A	E	DP	FA
126	.201	319	64	8	1	2	4	44	64	35	16	134	10	8	0	.948

Skokan, Josephine

Pitcher, Rockford Peaches, 1943.

Josephine Skokan was one of the original players in the league.

Sloan, Frances "Sliver"

Miami, Florida. Died: June 24, 1986. Pitcher. Grand Rapids Chicks, 1946.

BATTING			
G	BA	AB	H
3	.000	0	0

Smith, Charlotte

Born: 1919, Chattanooga, Tennessee. 5'6", 130, 1st Base, Shortstop, Outfield, BR, TR. Racine Belles, 1943–44.

Charlotte Smith was one of the original players of the league. Her father was a minor league pitcher. Number 4 helped Racine win the pennant and championship in 1945.

BATTING												FIELDING				
G	BA	AB	H	2B	3B	HR	SB	BB	SO	R	RBI	PO	A	E	DP	FA
130	.241	353	85	2	2	0	93	39	18	57	33	107	94	35	7	.852

Smith (McCulloch), Colleen "Smitty"

Vancouver, British Columbia, Canada. 5'6", 120, 3rd Base, BR, TR. Grand Rapids Chicks, 1949.

Colleen Smith's claim to fame was knocking in the winning run in an extra-inning game. "Smitty" played third base with Grand Rapids in 1949.

		BATTING												FIELDING				
G	BA	AB	H	2B	3B	HR	SB	BB	SO	R	RBI		PO	A	E	DP	FA
40	.184	98	18	1	0	0	3	7	11	7	4		45	81	11	8	.920

Smith, Hazel

Born: February 16, 1930, Chicago, Illinois. 5'5", 135, Catcher, TR, BR. Battle Creek Belles, 1951.

Smith, Helen

Rockford Peaches, 1946.

	BATTING		
G	BA	AB	H
2	.500	6	3

Smith, Helen "Gig"

Born: Jan. 5, 1922, Richmond, Virginia. 5'6", 133, Outfield, BR, TR. Kenosha Comets, 1947; Grand Rapids Chicks, 1948.

Helen Smith saw limited action in the outfield with two teams in two seasons in the league. She never once made an error in 29 games.

Before joining the league, she played with the U.S. Army, where she served as a technical sergeant in Intelligence. After her baseball days, she graduated from the Pratt Art Institute and Virginia Commonwealth University to obtain a bachelor's degree. She taught art for 31 years in Richmond, Virginia. She was inducted into the Softball Fastpitch Hall of Fame in 1975.

		BATTING												FIELDING				
G	BA	AB	H	2B	3B	HR	SB	BB	SO	R	RBI		PO	A	E	DP	FA
29	.212	66	14	2	0	0	2	6	6	8	2		13	3	0	0	1.000

Smith, Jean

**Born: May 9, 1928, Ann Arbor, Michigan.
5'6", 128, Outfield, Pitcher, TR, BR.
Kenosha Comets, 1948; Fort Wayne Daisies,
1948–49; Peoria Redwings, 1950–51;
Grand Rapids Chicks, 1952–54.**

Jean Smith began as an outfielder in the league and later doubled as a relief pitcher during her seven years in the league.

Smith started playing softball at age 12. At 15 she began playing for the Dad's Root Beer Team. "They lied about my age. You were supposed to be 16 to play in the league," she explained. She helped the team win some state tournaments.

In 1947 she went to a league tryout in Grand Rapids and received an invitation to spring training the next season in Opa-locka, Florida. After spring training, she was assigned to Kenosha and played in the outfield. Before the season was over she was transferred to Fort Wayne. In 1950 she ended up with Peoria and was also used as a relief pitcher. She had a fastball and a curve. "I was a thrower and not a pitcher," she admitted.

Jean Smith

After the league folded in 1954, she came home for a year before joining on with Bill Allington's All-Stars, a barnstorming team of fellow players. She played with the team until it folded a few years later.

Smith settled down in Harbor Springs, Michigan, where she worked as a secretary and bookkeeper until retirement in 1992. She attended the Chicago reunion of the league.

PITCHING

W–L	PCT	ERA	G	IP	H	R	ER	BB	SO
10–10	.500	3.61	39	172	137	92	69	129	45

BATTING

G	BA	AB	H	2B	3B	HR	SB	BB	SO	R	RBI
567	.215	1853	396	67	18	13	194	333	188	320	174

FIELDING

PO	A	E	DP	FA
1129	144	58	15	.957

Smith, Shirley

**Born: Jan. 24, 1923, Toronto, California. 5'3", 132, Outfield, 2nd Base, BR, TR.
Peoria Redwings, 1947.**

Shirley Smith played a season with Peoria in 1947.

BATTING													FIELDING				
G	BA	AB	H	2B	3B	HR	SB	BB	SO	R	RBI		PO	A	E	DP	FA
61	.152	171	26	1	0	0	8	21	19	14	6		79	60	9	5	.939

Sopkovic, Kay

Born: June 23, 1924, Youngstown, Ohio. 5'5", Utility, BR, TR. South Bend Blue Sox, 1945.

Kay Sopkovic played one season for South Bend in 1945. She now lives in Phoenix, Arizona.

BATTING											
G	BA	AB	H	2B	3B	HR	SB	BB	SO	R	RBI
12	.067	15	1	0	0	0	0	0	1	0	1

Sowers, Barbara

Born: May 4, 1932, Livonia, Michigan. 5'8", 148, Outfield, BR, TR. Muskegon Belles, 1953; Grand Rapids Chicks, 1954.

Barbara Sowers was a starting outfielder in her two seasons with two teams in the league. She hit a respectable .284 in 1954 with Grand Rapids. After baseball she graduated from Eastern Michigan University with bachelor's and master's degrees and worked as a counselor until retirement. She now lives in Port Charlotte, Florida.

BATTING													FIELDING				
G	BA	AB	H	2B	3B	HR	SB	BB	SO	R	RBI		PO	A	E	DP	FA
140	.248	363	90	11	2	4	12	78	54	51	49		202	10	21	1	.910

Stahley, Adele "Rustie"

Born: June 10, 1928. 5'4", 150, Utility, TR, BR. Fort Wayne Daisies, 1947.

Starck, Mae

Pitcher. Rockford Peaches, 1947.

Steck (Weiss), Elma "El"

Born: May 3, 1923, Columbus, Ohio. 5'4", 120, Outfielder, BL, TR. Peoria Redwings, 1948; Rockford Peaches, 1948–49; Chicago Colleens/Springfield Sallies, 1949.

Primarily a reserve outfielder, Elma Steck was one of the oldest rookies at age 25 when she joined the league.

Steck started playing softball in the ninth grade. During World War II, she was a WAVE in the Navy and finished a bachelor's degree at Ohio State University. She was attending the University of California when she tried out for the league in Los Angeles. She was assigned to Peoria, but she couldn't report until late June after her semester ended. The Redwings used her sparingly in the outfield. She got a starting nod one game late in the season, but the next day she was shipped to Rockford.

The following season "El" again reported late to the league. She played some with the Peaches before she was assigned to the traveling teams to tour the South. "I think they were grooming me to be a chaperone," she said. She decided to quit baseball after the following season.

A couple of years later she married Ken Weiss, a catcher for Des Moines, a Chicago Cubs farm team. The two had a lot in common, although he never made it to the majors. The couple raised a family of four: Dan, Mike, Lynne and Cindy. She also earned two doctorates and taught for three decades, retiring from Phoenix College in 1980. She then taught part-time until retiring for good in 1993. She now has six grandchildren, plays golf and goes to league reunions.

Joyce M. "Lucky" Steele

BATTING

G	BA	AB	H	2B	3B	HR	SB	BB	SO	R	ER
17	.061	33	2	0	0	0	1	3	7	1	1

Steele, Joyce M. "Lucky"

Born: Dec. 25, 1935, Wyalusing, Pennsylvania. 5'7", 125, 1st Base, Outfield, BB, TL. Kalamazoo Lassies, 1953.

Joyce Steele learned not to cry during her one season in the league.

Steele's first experience with baseball came when she was 8 years old. She played on a Little League boys team until an opposing manager complained and she was sent home. "I was crushed," she recalled. But the high school coach would let her practice with the boy's baseball team, so her skills improved.

The Pennsylvania native read about tryouts

for the league in Battle Creek, Michigan. Her parents cashed in their war bonds so she could go. It was worth it, as she made the cut and the team.

In her very first game, "Lucky" was sitting in the dugout when someone hit a foul ball and smacked her square in the head. She shook it off, though. "You don't cry in baseball," she explained.

After a season with the league, she left to get more playing time in a softball league. She went to work for Fairway Spring Company for 22 years before owning her own bar and now the Lovelton Hotel, a nine-room inn, in the Poconos.

BATTING

G	BA
9	.279

Stefani, Margaret

Born: Dec. 19, 1917, Croweburg, Kansas. Died: Date Unknown. 5'2", 130, Utility Infielder, BR, TR. South Bend Blue Sox, 1943–47; Rockford Peaches, 1948.

One of the original players in the league, Margaret Stefani was an excellent hitter and was selected to the first All-Star team.

Stefani hit the most triples (11) in the league and was the best fielding second baseman with only 31 errors in her first season. The following year she led the league in sacrifices (20).

She set a career record by not striking out in 57 consecutive games during her last season in the league. She also helped the Peaches win the championship in 1948. She became a chaperone for South Bend in 1949.

BATTING												FIELDING				
G	BA	AB	H	2B	3B	HR	SB	BB	SO	R	RBI	PO	A	E	DP	FA
642	.227	2158	489	41	37	8	301	366	65	317	256	1921	1295	190	138	.944

Stephens, Ruby

Born: Oct. 2, 1924, Clearwater, Florida. 5'4", 115, Pitcher, TR, BR. Racine Belles, 1946; South Bend Blue Sox, 1947; Springfield Sallies, 1948; Kenosha Comets, 1948–51.

Ruby Stephens was one of the better overhand pitchers in the league. She was playing for the 25th Century Men's Club when she was signed to a contract to play in the league. After a slow start in which she tied the record for the most balks (6) in a season and recorded a 9–15 record in 1947 she went 20–11 for two teams the next season. Her best game was one of her last as she threw a no-hitter against Kalamazoo on July 12, 1951.

PITCHING										BATTING			FIELDING			
W–L	PCT	ERA	G	IP	H	R	ER	BB	SO	BA	AB	H	PO	A	E	FA
62–53	.539	2.35	150	961	727	380	242	338	305	.163	325	53	29	211	20	.923

Stevenson, Emily

Born: July 26, 1925, Champaign, Illinois. 5'7", 160, Outfield, Catcher, BR, TR. Milwaukee Chicks, 1944.

Emily Stevenson helped Milwaukee win a pennant and championship in 1944 — her only season in the league.

G	BA	AB	H	2B	3B	HR	SB	BB	SO	R	RBI		PO	A	E	DP	FA
BATTING													FIELDING				
32	.162	74	12	0	0	0	0	12	8	0	5		27	11	2	3	.950

Stevenson, Rosemary "Stevie"

Born: June 2, 1936, Stalwart, Michigan. 5'7", 137, Outfield, BL, TR. Grand Rapids Chicks, 1954.

By the time Rosemary Stevenson made it to the AAGPBL, it was in its last year. She made the most of it, though.

Stevenson first began playing baseball after finishing her chores. Her father was a ball player, and she would chase foul balls for a nickel. Her father tried to get her into boy's baseball, but they said she wasn't strong enough. She began playing fast-pitch softball when she was 11.

Getting into the AAGPBL was a quirk of fate for the young girl. "I was reading in the back of the rule book about the league and decided to write them," she said. The Fort Wayne Daisies gave the 17 year old a tryout two weeks before her high school graduation at Battle Creek, Michigan, in 1954. After three days of grueling workouts, the Daisies chose 6 girls out of the 106 who participated, and she was one of them.

Stevenson remembered her first game was played on a Saturday night. "I was on my own at 17!" she exclaimed. The Michigan native's biggest thrill was a homer off of June Peppas and catching a ball hit by Joanne Weaver with two out and the bases loaded. "I went up on that fence and got it."

After baseball, she worked for Michigan Bell for 34 years and retired in 1989. But retirement wasn't for her. She completed a degree at Aquinas College and now teaches at Muskegon Catholic Central. She was inducted into the Upper Peninsula of Michigan Hall of Fame in 1990.

When *A League of Their Own* was filmed in Cooperstown, she was on hand to sign autographs and play in the Old Timers Game featured at the end of the film. "Never in a hundred years did we think we would ever get in the Hall of Fame." But they did.

G	BA	AB	H	2B	3B	HR	SB	BB	SO	R	RBI		PO	A	E	DP	FA
BATTING													FIELDING				
32	.233	82	19	3	0	3	3	4	27	15	7		18	2	3	0	.870

Stocker (Bottazzi), Jeanette "Jan"

Born: Dec. 13, 1926, Allentown, Pennsylvania. 5'5", 140, Catcher, BR, TR. Kenosha Comets, 1946.

Jeanette Stocker played four months before being sent to South Bend, but she decided to quit rather than report. After baseball, she got married and had one son. She now has two grandchildren.

BATTING

G	BA	AB	H
3	.000	3	0

Stoll, Jane "Jeep"

Born: Aug. 8, 1928, West Point, Pennsylvania. 5'2", 135, Outfield, BR, TR. Peoria Redwings, 1946; Grand Rapids Chicks, 1947; Springfield Sallies, 1948; South Bend Blue Sox, 1949–52; Kalamazoo Lassies, 1953–54.

Jane Stoll was a fine defensive outfielder who played on three championship teams during her nine seasons in the league.

Stoll's father began teaching her baseball when she was 8. He was a semi-pro player and an umpire. As a teenager, she played in industrial softball leagues. "They used to think I worked there," she said.

Her high school coach wrote the league about her talents and she received a tryout in Chicago. She was assigned to Peoria as a rookie, played in 58 games and hit .140. The league shifted her to Grand Rapids the following season and she helped the team win the pennant.

"Jeep"—a nickname acquired because of her height and ruggedness—became a regular in 1948 at Springfield. In the off-season she played with the Americans, an exhibition team of the league that traveled to Central and South America. "It was beautiful down there," she recalled.

Jane "Jeep" Stoll

In 1949 she was assigned to South Bend and brought her average up to .232. She hit .268 in 1951, helping the team win the pennant and playoffs. The following season she broke the .300 mark but didn't finish the season with the team. Stoll was one of five players who walked off the team in supporting Shorty Pryer, who had been suspended by the manager.

Stoll asked to be traded and was dealt to Kalamazoo in 1953 to finish out her career. She had a knee operation during the final season and played in only 34 games, but the Lassies still won the 1954 playoffs.

After baseball, she owned a dog grooming shop in Chicago before going to Arizona to work for AT&T. She retired in Phoenix in 1993.

BATTING												FIELDING				
G	BA	AB	H	2B	3B	HR	SB	BB	SO	R	RBI	PO	A	E	DP	FA
774	.247	2636	651	88	15	5	216	367	189	319	312	1289	119	55	25	.963

Stolze, Dorothy "Dottie"

Born: May 1, 1923, Tacoma, Washington. 5'4", 129, Outfield, Utility Infielder, BR, TR. Muskegon Lassies, 1946–49; Racine Belles, 1949; Peoria Redwings, 1950–51; Grand Rapids Chicks, 1952.

Dorothy Stolze played all the infield positions during her seven-year career, but she was best at second base in 1950.

"Dottie" played ten years of amateur softball before joining the league. She became a starter at second in her rookie year at Muskegon. Then in 1948 she set the team record for hits with 113. In the off-season, she attended San Francisco State College and majored in physical education.

She was the best fielding second baseman in 1950 with Peoria as she committed just 21 errors and had a .956 fielding percentage. She recorded a career-best .243 average that season.

BATTING												FIELDING				
G	BA	AB	H	2B	3B	HR	SB	BB	SO	R	RBI	PO	A	E	DP	FA
705	.219	2649	579	36	13	1	300	208	125	309	192	1761	924	168	111	.941

Stone (Richards), Lucille "Lou"

Born: Dec. 25, 1925, Boston, Massachusetts. 5'4", 130, Shortstop, BR, TR. Racine Belles, 1945.

Lucille Stone was christened to fill in the gap for Racine at shortstop, but she never lived up to the expectations. She worked in the shipyards before joining the league in 1945. She now lives in Florida.

BATTING												FIELDING				
G	BA	AB	H	2B	3B	HR	SB	BB	SO	R	RBI	PO	A	E	DP	FA
19	.040	50	2	0	0	0	0	7	12	1	2	20	37	16	1	.781

Stovroff, Shirley "Shirt"

Born: March 18, 1931, Madison, Illinois.
Died: Dec. 16, 1994. 5'6", 120, Catcher,
Outfield, BR, TR. Springfield Sallies, 1948;
South Bend Blue Sox, 1948–52.

Shirley Stovroff was one of the best
fielding catchers in the league during her five-
year career. After helping South Bend win a
pennant championship in 1951 with a career-
best .266 average and 54 RBI, she left the
league with a week left in the 1952 season to
support roommate Shorty Pryer, who had
been suspended for a week.

Shirley "Shirt" Stovroff

	BATTING												FIELDING				
G	BA	AB	H	2B	3B	HR	SB	BB	SO	R	RBI		PO	A	E	DP	FA
455	.216	1306	282	39	3	1	56	231	170	138	143		1745	388	82	27	.963

Studnicka (Brazauskas), Mary Lou "ML"

Born: July 19, 1931, Chicago, Illinois.
5'5", 162, Pitcher, TR, BR.
Racine Belles, 1950;
Grand Rapids Chicks, 1951–53.

Mary Lou Studnicka was an
excellent pitcher over four seasons in
the league.

Studnicka began playing baseball
with the boys in the empty lots of
Chicago when she was 9. She got
involved in "kitten" ball at age 11. She
progressed up to one of the four teams
in Chicago that emulated the All-American League and provided players. She
was an overhand pitcher and was paid
$2 a game.

Mary Lou "ML" Studnicka

She received an invitation to spring training in Cuba in 1947, but her mother wouldn't allow her to miss school to attend. She had to wait until she was 18 before she was invited to play with Racine. She would take a train to Racine on the weekends to play, but the Belles never put her in a game in 1950.

The following year she was taken by Grand Rapids and given a chance to play. She won 12 games in a row and ended the season at 15–5.

"ML" pitched two more years for the Chicks and lost more games than she won, although her ERA was about the same. Grand Rapids couldn't give her enough run support. She recalled winning a game by a 9–8 score to illustrate the point.

In 1954 she decided she had had enough after being dealt to Fort Wayne. "I was getting a little tired of it. I didn't want to go to Fort Wayne. There were a few girls there I didn't like," she explained. She also was suffering from an injured ankle and had had two hernia operations during her playing days.

After marrying Adam Brazauskas in 1956, she delivered three girls: Pauline, Lora and Elizabeth. In between daughters, she played softball up until she was 42 and worked for the Chicago Police Department in the identification section. Her husband died in 1970 and she remarried Paul Caden a couple of years later. The two have 10 grandchildren and one great granddaughter. She worked 28 years with the police before retiring. She now umpires softball games in Hot Springs Village, Arkansas.

PITCHING

W–L	PCT	ERA	G	IP	H	R	ER	BB	SO
38–30	.559	2.49	78	525	447	232	145	226	196

BATTING												FIELDING			
G	BA	AB	H	2B	3B	HR	SB	BB	SO	R	RBI	PO	A	E	FA
87	.180	189	34	0	0	0	1	9	25	10	15	36	142	12	.937

Stuhr (Thompson), Beverly

Born: May 5, 1932, Rock Island, Illinois. 5'1", 115, Outfield, BL, TR. Peoria Redwings, 1949; Racine Belles, 1950.

Beverly Stuhr joined the league while she was still in high school. She began playing softball at age 9. After baseball, she settled down in Rockford, Illinois.

BATTING												FIELDING				
G	BA	AB	H	2B	3B	HR	SB	BB	SO	R	RBI	PO	A	E	DP	FA
27	.146	48	7	0	0	0	0	6	13	4	1	18	2	3	0	.870

Surkowski (Deyotte), Ann

Born: Feb. 22, 1923, Moose Jaw, Saskatchewan, Canada. 5'3", 120, Outfield. South Bend Blue Sox, 1945.

Ann Surkowski joined older sister Lena on the South Bend team for one season in 1945.

BATTING												FIELDING					
G	BA	AB	H	2B	3B	HR	SB	BB	SO	R	RBI	G	PO	A	E	DP	FA
21	.103	39	4	0	0	0	4	3	7	5	1	18	11	2	3	1	.867

Sutherland, Shirley

Rockford, Illinois. Catcher, BR, TR. Chicago Colleens/Springfield Sallies, 1950; Battle Creek Belles, 1951; Grand Rapids Chicks, 1951.

Shirley Sutherland played with the player development teams in 1950 before joining the league for the 1951 season.

BATTING											
G	BA	AB	H	2B	3B	HR	SB	BB	SO	R	RBI
39	.121	141	17	4	0	1	8	14	19	18	14

Swamp, Rella

Appleton, Wisconsin. Infielder. Rockford Peaches, 1943.

Rella Swamp was one of the original players of the league.

Swanagon, Mary Lou "Swannie"

Born: Jan. 30, 1927, Sikeston, Missouri. 5'5", 130, Shortstop, TR, BR. Grand Rapids Chicks, 1946.

Taylor, Eunice "Tuffy"

Born: Feb. 12, 1934, Kenosha, Wisconsin. 5'4", 140, Catcher, BR, TR. Chicago Colleens, 1950; Kenosha Comets, 1951.

Eunice Taylor was 16 when she joined the All-American League with the Chicago Colleens. She hit .175 with one home run in 47 games while barnstorming with the Colleens. She recalled that Yogi Berra was the umpire of their exhibition game in Yankee Stadium. After baseball, she was a partner in a pet supply business and raised parrots. She now lives in Fort Lauderdale, Florida.

BATTING												FIELDING				
G	BA	AB	H	2B	3B	HR	SB	BB	SO	R	RBI	PO	A	E	DP	FA
38	.193	114	22	1	1	0	1	4	11	5	10	80	18	9	0	.916

Taylor, Mary

Long Beach, California. Outfield, 1st Base, BR, TR. Fort Wayne Daisies, 1953; Kalamazoo Lassies, 1954.

Mary Taylor was an outfielder-first baseman the last two years of the league.

G	BA	AB	H	2B	3B	HR	SB	BB	SO	R	RBI		PO	A	E	DP	FA
					BATTING										FIELDING		
79	.251	247	62	4	0	4	10	23	38	42	28		176	5	13	6	.933

Teillet (Schick), Yolande "Yo"

Born: Sept. 28, 1927, St. Vital, Manitoba, Canada. 5', 125, Catcher, Outfield, BR, TR. Fort Wayne Daisies, 1945; Grand Rapids Chicks, 1946.

Yolande Teillet was a catcher-outfielder for two seasons in the league. Her career was hampered by injury and cut short by an illness in the family.

She first played organized softball when she was 13. She learned to catch in her first league, which proved to be a valuable asset as the league was always looking for good receivers. She received an invitation to Wrigley Field in 1945 for spring training and was assigned to Fort Wayne. The rookie saw limited action. One time when she was catching, she let the ball get through to hit the umpire in the stomach. "It was hilarious to see the snuff flying all over the place," she recalled.

Then in 1946 "Yo" went to Grand Rapids. Her season was cut short when her thumb got crushed in a practical joke that went awry. The following year her father became ill and she decided not to return to the league.

She played with a local softball team, the St. Vital Tigerettes, in 1948 before she married William Schick. They created their own baseball team of nine children: Robert, John, Donna, William Jr., Carolyn, Claire, Theresa, Richard and Anthony. Now retired in Fort Gary in Winnipeg, Manitoba, she bowls and performs volunteer work. She now has 18 grandchildren. She attended the 1993 reunion of the players in South Bend.

BATTING

G	BA	AB	H	R	RBI
17	.227	22	5	2	3

Terkowski, Georgia

Passaic, New York. Rockford Peaches, 1952–53.

BATTING

G	BA	AB	H	2B	3B	HR	SB	BB	SO	R	RBI
17	.171	35	6	1	1	0	?	1	13	6	93

Terry, Betty

California. Peoria Redwings, 1946.

BATTING

G	BA	AB	H
8	.158	19	3

Tetro (Atkinson), Barbara

Grand Rapids, Michigan. Utility, Pitcher. Grand Rapids Chicks, 1948.

Barbara Tetro relieved in one game during her season in the league.

BATTING

G	BA	AB	H
1	.000	0	0

Tetzlaff, Doris "Tetz"

Born: Jan. 1, 1921, Watertown, Wisconsin. 5'5", 155, Outfield, Utility Infielder, BR, TR. Milwaukee Chicks, 1945–47; Grand Rapids Chicks, 1945–47; Chicago Colleens, 1948; Fort Wayne Daisies, 1948; Muskegon Lassies, 1949; Fort Wayne Daisies, 1950–53.

Doris Tetzlaff was one of the best fielding third basemen during her decade in the league. Tetzlaff was 11 when she first began playing softball. She also was an avid speedskater and tennis player during her college years at La Cross State University. She then joined the league in 1944. The speedster stole a career high 101 bases her rookie year and scored 62 times to help Milwaukee win the pennant.

The following season she led the league in walks (88) and the franchise moved to Grand Rapids. When expansion came in 1948, she was moved to Chicago, then Fort Wayne. She led the league in strikeouts (74). She spent the next season with Muskegon before she was sent back to Fort Wayne. She didn't play much thereafter.

After baseball, she taught physical education until retiring in 1981. She once captured the Wisconsin state senior women's speedskating title and the Iowa state championship. Since her retirement she took up golf and has recorded six holes in one. She now resides in Dayton, Ohio.

BATTING												FIELDING				
G	BA	AB	H	2B	3B	HR	SB	BB	SO	R	RBI	PO	A	E	DP	FA
625	.190	2056	391	29	15	4	284	399	262	267	161	964	1643	281	98	.903

Tezak (Papesh), Virginia May Rita

Born: May 22, 1928, Joliet, Illinois. 5'6", 145, Outfield, 1st Base, Pitcher. Racine Belles, 1948.

Virginia Tezak played a few games with Racine in 1948. She was all-around athlete in high school, playing basketball, baseball and tennis. She also won a speed skating trophy before joining the league for one season.

BATTING

G	BA	AB	H
4	.000	7	0

Thomas, Mava Lee "Tommy"

Born: Sept. 1, 1929, Ocala, Florida. 5'2", 145, 3rd Base, Catcher. Ft. Wayne Daisies, 1951.

Mava Lee Thomas may be the only AAGPBL player whose father played in the major leagues. Her father, Herb Thomas, played for the Boston Braves and New York Giants for three seasons in the 1920s.

In the fourth grade, Thomas became interested in softball and found she was a natural. "Tommy," a nickname she picked up from her dad, attended 27 schools while growing up in Florida because her father was a coach and scout for the Giants.

She heard about the AAGPBL when she was playing for the VFW in Ocala. "I called my dad and he said he knew Max Carey," she explained. Her father could have pulled a few strings for her, but she wanted to earn her own way into the league. The switch-hitter did just that, joining the Fort Wayne Daisies for the 1951 season.

Tommy remembered one freezing, miserable game in Racine. "That was the coldest game I ever played and it was July!" she recalled. There was another game that was rained out, so she went with some of the other women to play basketball at the YWCA. They all were fined.

After the season was over, Thomas went into the Navy and played softball. She got married in 1953, but the marriage lasted only two years.

In the 1950s she played exhibition games for the Hagerstown Mollies. She also finished a degree at the University of Florida and went to work for the government as a recreational instructor.

On January 6, 1995, the former player retired in Ocala after working for 35 years in recreation. She looks back on the league differently than some of the former players. "They seem to be bitter, like baseball was everything," she explained.

She's proud to be the only player with a major league father. She talked him into playing an old-timers game when he was 87. "He had spike scars on his arm from Ty Cobb," she said.

Thompson, Annabelle

Edmonton, Alberta, Canada. Pitcher, TR, BR. Racine Belles, 1943.

One of the original players of the league, Annabelle Thompson was a mediocre pitcher for the championship Racine Belles in 1943.

PITCHING										BATTING			FIELDING			
W–L	PCT	ERA	G	IP	H	R	ER	BB	SO	BA	AB	H	PO	A	E	FA
11–15	.423	3.51	32	223	237	159	86	64	28	.153	85	13	11	78	10	.900

Thompson, Barbara

Born: Feb. 24, 1934, Rockford, Illinois. 5'3", 135, Outfield, BR, TL. Rockford Peaches, 1951–52.

Barbara Thompson played the outfield in 18 games with Rockford over two seasons. She was a registered nurse after her baseball career. She still lives in her hometown of Rockford.

BATTING												FIELDING				
G	BA	AB	H	2B	3B	HR	SB	BB	SO	R	RBI	PO	A	E	DP	FA
18	.204	49	10	0	0	0	4	10	11	6	3	13	5	1	2	.947

Thompson (Griffin), Viola "Tommy"

Viola "Tommy" Thompson

Born: Jan. 2, 1922, Greenville, South Carolina. 5'5", 120, Pitcher, TL, BL. Milwaukee Chicks, 1944; Grand Rapids Chicks, 1945; South Bend Blue Sox, 1946–47.

Viola Thompson's pitching career fell victim to the switch to sidearm and overhand pitching.

She began playing softball in the third grade. After high school, she played for the textile teams. "I was playing with a men's softball team in the morning and a women's team at night," she explained. A scout from the league recruited her and teammate Lib Mahon for the league.

Thompson was assigned to Milwaukee, which was run by Max Carey, a Major League Hall of Famer. "He was one of the best teachers of the game," she commented. "Tommy" learned fast and was 15–12 her first season in helping the Chicks win the pennant and championship.

Milwaukee became Grand Rapids in 1945 and Thompson fell on

hard times with an 11–19 mark. However, she rebounded the following season with South Bend and went 15–6. She was a control pitcher and had a natural curve.

She appeared in only one game in 1947 as the league moved entirely to sidearm pitching. Her sister, Fredda Acker, joined her on the team as an overhand pitcher in 1947. She transferred over to the National League in Chicago for the next few years before getting married in 1954 to Claude Griffin. The couple had two daughters, Claudia and Carol. Viola went to work as a supervisor in a textile plant and retired in 1982. The couple now live in Belton, South Carolina, and attend league reunions. "He's really proud of me for being one of the girls in the All-American League," she said. At last count she had four grandchildren.

PITCHING

W–L	PCT	ERA	G	IP	H	R	ER	BB	SO
41–37	.526	2.51	99	685	621	315	191	236	99

BATTING													FIELDING				
G	BA	AB	H	2B	3B	HR	SB	BB	SO	R	RBI		PO	A	E	DP	FA
99	.095	211	20	0	0	0	2	39	41	11	12		29	184	30	?	.876

Tipton, Gloria

Dayton, Ohio. Pitcher, TL, BL. Kenosha Comets, 1946.

Gloria Tipton was in the WACS during World War II before joining the league for one season.

Tognatti, Alice

Outfield. Fort Wayne Daisies, 1946.

BATTING													FIELDING				
G	BA	AB	H	2B	3B	HR	SB	BB	SO	R	RBI		PO	A	E	DP	FA
21	.067	45	3	0	0	0	2	5	24	2	1		21	1	1	0	.957

Torrison, Lorraine "Peggy"

Minneapolis, Minnesota. Died: Date Unknown. 3rd Base, BR, TR. Minneapolis, 1944.

Lorraine Torrison left the team after the second road trip because she was homesick.

BATTING													FIELDING				
G	BA	AB	H	2B	3B	HR	SB	BB	SO	R	RBI		PO	A	E	DP	FA
16	.167	54	9	0	1	0	1	9	8	7	5		22	22	7	1	.863

Travis (Visich), Gene "Dolph"

Born: Oct. 18, 1926, Mt. Vernon, New York. 5'5", 140, 1st Base, Outfield, BL, TB. Rockford Peaches, 1948.

Gene Travis played less than ten games with the championship Rockford Peaches in 1948.

Travis began her playing days in the streets at age 7 and played softball throughout her youth. She saw an article about the league and wrote Branch Rickey. She received an invitation to try out, but she didn't make the cut in 1945. She was told to hone her skills and come back in a couple of years. She played with the Brooklyn Celtics for the next two years. She tried out again in 1947 in Peru, Illinois, and made the cut this time. "I persevered until I made it," she explained.

"Dolph" went to Opa-locka, Florida, in 1948 for spring training. The rookie was assigned to the Peaches. She was ambidextrous, so she threw left handed at first base and

Gene "Dolph" Travis

right handed in the outfield. "I studied books on how to play first," she said. She didn't get much of a chance to play during the season.

Her brother died after the season and she was left to care for her mother, so she returned her contract unsigned. She married Edward Visich in 1952 and had six children: Stephen, Katheryn, Edward, Andrea, Robert and Peter. She became an executive secretary when she wasn't caring for her children. Now retired in Westwood, New Jersey, the grandmother of three goes to league reunions. She was named the Female Athlete of the Year in 1993 by a local March of Dimes.

Trezza, Betty "Moe"

Born: Aug. 4, 1925, Brooklyn, New York. 5'3", 125, Shortstop, 3rd Base, Outfield, BR, TR. Minneapolis Millerettes, 1944; Fort Wayne Daisies, 1945; South Bend Blue Sox, 1945; Racine Belles, 1946–50.

With a nickname that had nothing to do with her or her name, Betty Trezza was a versatile player who possessed good speed, a sure glove and a rifle arm.

The youngest of 12 children started playing street ball in Brooklyn at age 6. She joined organized softball leagues in her teen years. While playing in a regional tournament in Central

Racine Belles Dugout in 1947 — Betty Trezza (center).

Park in 1944, a scout approached her about playing in the All-American League. "I was surprised he picked me," she said.

She was assigned to Minneapolis, a new team in 1944, and played shortstop. She didn't have a nickname, so she called herself "Moe." She miscued just 20 times during the season to end up with the best fielding percentage among shortstops. However, she hit just .108. The franchise moved to Fort Wayne and she played there until the last month of the season. She was then sent to South Bend.

The league assigned her to Racine in 1946. Trezza's hitting improved to .175 on the season and she helped the Belles win a pennant. During the sixth game of the championships, she knocked in the winning run in the 16th inning to give the Belles the crown.

In 1947 she filled in at center field and stole a career-high 66 bases. Trezza tied a league record for double plays assisted from the outfield. She went back to shortstop in 1948 and helped the Belles win another pennant.

Trezza finally eclipsed the .200 mark in 1950 when she hit .231. She decided to quit baseball and jump to the Chicago softball league in 1951 for three seasons.

After her playing days, she ended up in keypunching as a supervisor for Pfizer Inc. She retired in 1991 and now attends league reunions.

BATTING												FIELDING				
G	BA	AB	H	2B	3B	HR	SB	BB	SO	R	RBI	PO	A	E	DP	FA
717	.173	2566	444	29	28	6	363	285	241	331	191	1531	1533	258	101	.922

Tronnier, Ellen

**Born: June 28, 1927, Cudahy, Wisconsin.
5'6", 135, Outfield, BR, TR.
South Bend Blue Sox, 1943.**

Ellen Tronnier

One of the original players of the league, Ellen Tronnier was one of the youngest players to join the league at age 15.

Tronnier began playing softball at age 12 with the Appleton Bluejays. She then joined the All-American League. No records on her performance are available, but she said she played in more than ten games. She didn't return the following season because she would miss too much school, so she decided to play softball at home, which lasted some 30 years. Tronnier earned a bachelor's degree at La Crosse University and taught for 33 years in Milwaukee public schools. She retired in 1983 and loves to hunt and fish now. She also goes to league reunions.

The Wisconsin Amateur Softball Association inducted her into its hall of fame in 1990.

Tucker, Elizabeth "Betty"

Born: Jan. 28, 1924, Detroit, Michigan. 5'4", 123, Pitcher, TR, BR. Peoria Redwings, 1946; Fort Wayne Daisies, 1947; Rockford Peaches, 1947; Grand Rapids Chicks, 1947; Chicago Colleens, 1948; Peoria Redwings, 1949.

Elizabeth Tucker struggled through the league's transition from softball to baseball on expansion teams that didn't give her much run support. What resulted was one of the poorest winning percentages in the league. "It was kind of demoralizing," she explained.

Tucker grew up playing stickball and kickball with the boys in the streets of Detroit. At age 12 she started playing organized softball. She became a pitcher with Hudson Motor Company during the war years. After World War II she couldn't find a job she liked, so she joined the All-American League to make a living.

"Betty" was assigned to Peoria, an expansion club, in 1946. The new, disorganized club turned in a poor performance, which reflected on her 1–12 record as well. The following year the league was converting to sidearm pitching and she tried the new style. She wasn't effective and went 0–12 with three different teams. "It was very discouraging for me. Nobody really showed me how to pitch," she said.

But the league went to overhand pitching in 1948 and she handled that transition much better. She had been a catcher in her softball days and was accustomed to throwing overhand. She went to another expansion team, the Chicago Colleens. She performed much better and went 11–17 on the season. Because of her good speed, she was used as a pinch runner.

The following season Tucker landed in Peoria again and went 4–8. She decided then that she had had enough with losing seasons in the league so she jumped over to the Chicago softball league to play and work full-time during the day. She played there until the league folded, which was about the same time as the All-American League.

After her playing days, she stayed in Chicago and worked at A.B. Dick Company until 1968. She then moved to Arizona and worked at the Tuscon General Hospital as a debt collector. Retired since 1986, she now travels frequently and goes to league reunions.

PITCHING

W–L	PCT	ERA	G	IP	H	R	ER	BB	SO
16–49	.246	3.00	187	573	463	305	191	247	153

BATTING | FIELDING

G	BA	AB	H	2B	3B	HR	SB	BB	SO	R	RBI	PO	A	E	FA
187	.186	199	37	2	3	0	20	48	51	42	18	17	126	19	.883

Tysver (Chiancola), Joan

Born: 1931, Glouchester, Massachusetts. Died: Dec. 20, 1992. Pitcher. Grand Rapids Chicks, 1950; Rockford Peaches, 1951.

PITCHING

W–L	PCT	ERA	G	IP	H	R	ER	BB	SO
0–3	.000	9.46	10	40	51	52	42	48	7

Vanderlip (Ozburn), Dollie "Lippy"

Born: June 4, 1937, Charlotte, North Carolina. 5'8", 140, Pitcher, TR, BR. Fort Wayne Daisies, 1952–53; South Bend Blue Sox, 1954.

At 14, Dollie Vanderlip may have been the youngest player to sign a contract with the league. She turned in an average performance on the mound in three seasons.

She first tried out for the league at age 13 and signed the following year with Fort Wayne. She turned 15 the day after she arrived with the Daisies. "Lippy" pitched in relief for two seasons with the pennant-winning Fort Wayne Daisies. Her best season came in 1954 when she went 11–4 as a starter for South Bend.

After the league folded, she joined Bill Allington's All-Americans and met her future husband. They married in 1958 and had two children. She went on to college and finished with three degrees. She attended Appalachian State University, the University of Iowa and the University of La Crosse. She now lives in La Crosse, Wisconsin.

PITCHING | BATTING | FIELDING

W–L	PCT	ERA	G	IP	H	R	ER	BB	SO	BA	AB	H	PO	A	E	FA
13–12	.520	2.80	43	209	187	104	65	132	64	.130	69	9	16	96	9	.926

Ventura (Manina), Virginia "Jean"

Born: Nov. 30, 1935, Garfield, New Jersey. 5'9", 165, 1st Base, BR, TR. Rockford Peaches, 1951, '53.

Virginia Ventura played very little in two seasons for Rockford.

After seeing little playing time in 1951, she jumped to the rival Chicago National League in 1952. She returned to Rockford in 1953 and received a little more playing time. However, she was ineffective at the plate. After her playing days, she married and had two sons and a daughter.

She helped organize a girls' softball league in her hometown. She also owned her own real estate company. She now lives in Lodi, New Jersey.

BATTING

G	BA	AB	H	2B	3B	HR	SB	BB	SO	R	RBI
11	.074	27	2	0	0	0	0	2	8	1	0

Villa (Cryan), Margaret

Born: Dec. 21, 1924, Montabello, California. 5'2", 115, Catcher, Outfield, 3rd Base, 2nd Base, BR, TR. Kenosha Comets, 1946–50.

Margaret Villa's claim to fame during her five years in the league came in one game during her first season. On June 9, 1946, she set three league records: most RBI (9) in a game, most total bases (11) in a game and most advanced bases (23) in a game. She now lives in La Mirada, California.

BATTING / FIELDING

G	BA	AB	H	2B	3B	HR	SB	BB	SO	R	RBI	PO	A	E	DP	FA
537	.209	1832	382	32	21	5	200	302	151	249	168	1407	800	131	88	.944

Vincent (Mooney), Georgette "Jette"

Born: July 5, 1928, Fall River, Massachusetts. Died: Date Unknown. 5'3", 130, Pitcher, TR, BR. Racine Belles, 1947–48; South Bend Blue Sox, 1949–52, '54.

Georgette Vincent was an average pitcher who played on two championship teams during her seven seasons in the league.

After receiving little playing time with Racine, she was assigned to South Bend. She had her best season in 1951 and helped the Blue

Georgette "Jette" Vincent

Sox win the pennant and championship with a 13–9 record. Vincent was 8–8 the next season as South Bend added another championship. She also played at second base in the championship when the team was down to 12 players due to a strike.

After missing the 1953 season and getting married, Vincent played the last season in the league under the name Mooney.

PITCHING

W–L	PCT	ERA	G	IP	H	R	ER	BB	SO
38–34	.527	2.88	97	600	457	276	192	374	294

BATTING

G	BA	AB	H	2B	3B	HR	SB	BB	SO	R	RBI
152	.153	294	45	3	3	0	21	36	33	35	22

FIELDING

PO	A	E	FA
50	184	17	.932

Violetta (Kunkel), Karen

Negaunee, Michigan. Utility, TR, BR. Grand Rapids Chicks, 1953.

Karen Violetta played less than ten games with Grand Rapids in 1953. After baseball, she was the director of Great Lakes Sports and Olympic Academy in Marquette, Michigan. She served as the executive secretary of the players association in 1987 and was a technical director representative for *A League of Their Own*. She now lives in Brooksville, Florida.

Vonderau, Kathryn "Katie"

Born: Sept. 26, 1927, Fort Wayne, Indiana. 5'7", 155, Catcher, BR, TR. Fort Wayne Daisies, 1946; Muskegon Lassies, 1947; Chicago Colleens, 1948; Peoria Redwings, 1948–49; Muskegon Lassies, 1949; Fort Wayne Daisies, 1950–52; Muskegon Belles, 1953.

Kathryn Vonderau was a good defensive catcher with a quick throwing arm who played for eight seasons in the league.

She played first base and caught on the Bob Inn softball team in Fort Wayne before joining the league in 1946. She was initially assigned to her hometown, but then the league started shuffling her around to fill in where she was needed. She suffered a knee injury in 1948 with Peoria, which somewhat limited her playing time. She returned to Fort Wayne in 1950

Kathryn "Katie" Vonderau

and helped the Daisies win a pennant in 1952. She was then sent to Muskegon in 1953, her last year in the league.

"Katie" shared the catching duties most of her career. Her best year as a hitter came in 1951 when she hit .221 and drove in a career high 32 RBI.

After baseball, she had a long and distinguished teaching career at all academic levels. Her academic honors include bachelor's and master's degrees from Indiana University and a doctorate from the University of Iowa. Her last teaching assignment, at the University of Wisconsin, was to teach students how to become physical education teachers. She retired in 1988.

Now living in Albuquerque, New Mexico, she is a member of the players association board of directors. She loves to play golf and attend league reunions.

				BATTING									FIELDING				
G	BA	AB	H	2B	3B	HR	SB	BB	SO	R	RBI		PO	A	E	DP	FA
642	.189	2038	385	42	9	1	46	129	184	147	169		2444	563	178	66	.944

Voyce, Inez "Lefty" "Hook"

**Born: Aug. 16, 1924, Rathbun, Iowa.
5'6", 148, 1st Base, Pitcher, BL, TL.
South Bend Blue Sox, 1946;
Grand Rapids Chicks, 1947–53.**

Although she was one of the best fielding first basemen and power hitters in the league, Inez Voyce wasn't picked as an All-Star during any of her eight seasons in the league.

Voyce was 5 when she began playing ball with the boys in the fields of Iowa. She didn't play organized softball, though, until her junior year in high school. She was a WAVE in the Navy when she first heard about the All-American League from a coworker. She was given a tryout in Los Angeles and was assigned to play with South Bend.

After a season with the Sox, she was sent to Grand Rapids to out her career. She helped the Chicks win a pennant and two championships during her playing days. "Lefty" was the

Inez "Lefty" "Hook" Voyce

best fielding first baseman in three of the seasons she played. Another player nicknamed her "Hook," but she didn't like it. In 1949 she was temporarily turned into a pitcher. "They didn't have anyone else," she explained. She was 1–1 in four appearances.

In 1949 Voyce led the league in homers (3) and total bases (316). Her .257 average was fourth best in the league. Her most productive long-ball season came in 1952 when she knocked out 10 homers. In that same season she was fined $10 and suspended for 10 days for hitting umpire Al Stover during a game. Surprisingly, she was overlooked for the All-Star team each year, despite her numbers.

After closing out her eight-year career, she was an office worker until retirement in 1990. She now lives in Santa Monica, California, golfs frequently and attends league reunions.

BATTING

G	BA	AB	H	2B	3B	HR	SB	BB	SO	R	RBI
894	.256	3047	781	81	28	28	168	480	144	386	422

PITCHING										FIELDING				
W–L	PCT	ERA	G	IP	H	R	ER	BB	SO	PO	A	E	DP	FA
1–1	.500	3.43	4	21	20	8	8	5	0	8093	271	156	335	.961

Vukovich, Frances "Be Bop"

Born: Aug. 30, 1930, Smithdale, Pennsylvania. 5'7", 140, Pitcher, TL, BL. Chicago Colleens, 1950; Racine Belles, 1951.

Frances Vukovich played one year with the player development teams before going to the league for another year.

Vukovich hadn't played any organized ball before she answered an ad about a tryout in McKeesport, Pennsylvania. She made the cut and was assigned to the Chicago Colleens as a pitcher because of her good fastball. She went 9–9 with the Chicago Colleens in 20 appearances and batted .284 in 1950.

Her numbers were good enough for her to be drafted by the Racine Belles. "Be Bop" didn't get much of a chance to pitch and was hit hard when she did.

She moved to Chicago after baseball and worked for Illinois Bell. She then moved to Los Angeles and worked for Pacific Bell until retirement in 1988. She now lives in Holland, Michigan, and goes to league reunions when she isn't golfing.

PITCHING

W–L	PCT	ERA	G	IP	H	R	ER	BB	SO
0–3	.000	5.08	5	16	8	18	9	16	3

Waddell (Wyatt), Helen "Sis"

Born: April 24, 1930, Lemayne, Pennsylvania. 5'6", 115, Utility Infield, Outfield, BR, TR. Rockford Peaches, 1950–51; Battle Creek Belles, 1951.

An all-around player, Helen Waddell was a member of the championship Rockford Peaches during her two seasons in the league.

Nicknamed "Sis" by her five brothers, she grew up playing ball with them. In high school she became an all-star basketball player. Since her school had no softball team, she traveled to Harrisburg to join the Roverettes. She received a letter from the league inviting her to a tryout

in Allentown. She made the cut and was invited to spring training in West Baden, Indiana. She was then assigned to Rockford. In her rookie year she played "whenever someone got hurt." The Peaches won the pennant and the championship that season.

The following season the regular second baseman retired and she took over the position. With about a month left in the season, she was loaned to Grand Rapids. After the season, she married Neil Wyatt and left the league to work in a factory. The couple raised two boys: Neil II and Scott. She now has two granddaughters — one she affectionately calls "Peaches." She retired from working at a bank in 1995.

Helen "Sis" Waddell

BATTING												FIELDING				
G	BA	AB	H	2B	3B	HR	SB	BB	SO	R	RBI	PO	A	E	DP	FA
123	.137	366	46	5	0	0	9	41	73	36	29	147	166	67	21	.824

Wagner, Audrey

Born: Dec. 27, 1927, Bensenville, Illinois. Died: Date unknown. 5'7", 145, Outfield, Pitcher, BR, TR. Kenosha Comets, 1943–49.

Player of the Year and twice an All-Star, Audrey Wagner was one of the best hitters in the league's history.

Wagner, one of the original players in the league, was assigned to Kenosha and helped the Comets win a pennant in their first season by hitting .230 with 43 RBI.

Her average dropped below .200 the next two seasons, but she led the league in triples (9) in 1945. The league switched to sidearm pitching the next season and Wagner's average jumped up to .281, one of the best in the league. She also led the league in homers (9) and doubles (15).

Wagner hit over .300 the next season and led the league in four categories: hits (119), doubles (25), homers (7) and RBI (53). With numbers that could hardly be ignored, she was picked for her first All-Star team.

As good as her numbers were in 1947, she topped them the next year. She hit .312, which was best in the league, and led the league in hits (130). She also drove in 56 runs. Her outstanding performance earned her Player of the Year honors and another spot on the All-Star team.

Wagner's performance dropped off considerably in 1949, her final season in the league. Her season highs for doubles and triples ended up being the third best in league history. And her 55 career triples are second best in league history.

She used the money she had earned in the league to go to medical school and become a doctor.

BATTING

G	BA	AB	H	2B	3B	HR	SB	BB	SO	R	RBI
694	.254	2464	627	77	55	29	246	258	225	289	297

PITCHING										FIELDING				
W–L	PCT	ERA	G	IP	H	R	ER	BB	SO	PO	A	E	DP	FA
1–2	.333	3.66	7	35	36	23	11	7	5	914	90	52	15	.951

Wagoner, Betty "Waggy"

Born: July 15, 1930, Lebanon, Missouri. 5'2", 110, Outfield, Pitcher, TL, BL. Muskegon Lassies, 1948–49; South Bend Blue Sox, 1949–54.

Named to the 1950 All-Star team, Betty Wagoner was an excellent outfielder and part-time pitcher who helped South Bend win two championships during her seven year career.

Wagoner became interested in baseball while watching her father, Irwin, play town ball in the small Missouri town of Lebanon. She played softball for the YWCA in her teen years. After reading about the league in *Life* magazine, Wagoner made it her goal to one day play for the AAGPBL.

She later wrote the league and was invited to a tryout. She was drafted as an outfielder.

In her first season, which was split between Muskegon and South Bend, she played 82 games without an error and hit a solid .278. The following season she led the league in walks (87), again playing for both teams.

In 1950 she became one of the leading hitters in the league and earned a spot on the All-Star team. She hit .296 with a career-best 115 hits and 11 doubles during the season. "Waggy," as she was affectionately called by her teammates, also began pitching in 1950, but was met with little success as she posted an 0–3 record.

Betty "Waggy" Wagoner

She helped South Bend win the pennant and championship with a .272 average in 1951. Her 5–2 record and .295 average the following season again helped the Blue sox win a second consecutive championship with only 12 players. "Everybody put in 110 percent on the 1952 team," she explained.

The team and her pitching record went downhill in 1953. She struggled to a 4–13 record. She recalled one game in which she gave up 15 hits but only two runs. She accomplished this because she had learned a good move to first base and had picked off a couple of runners.

In the last year of the league she hit a career best .320 in 48 games, while going 4–4 on the mound.

After baseball she joined some fellow players on the South Bend Rockettes, a women's basketball team. She played until 1960 on the team, while working at Bendix. In 1986 she retired; she now lives in South Bend.

PITCHING

W–L	PCT	ERA	G	IP	H	R	ER	BB	SO
13–22	.371	3.68	42	287	284	169	117	193	118

BATTING

G	BA	AB	H	2B	3B	HR	SB	BB	SO	R	RBI
666	.271	2248	609	54	14	0	221	403	145	367	191

FIELDING

PO	A	E	DP	FA
1043	142	47	30	.962

Walker, Martha

Pitcher, Racine Belles, 1943.

Martha Walker played in less than ten games in 1943 and holds the league record for giving up the most walks (21) and runs (19) in a game against South Bend on June 19, 1943.

Walmesley, Thelma

Born: April 13, 1918, Sudbury, Ontario, Canada. 5'5", 122. BR, TR. Racine Belles, 1946.

Thelma Walmesley saw little action during one season in the league with Racine. She played for the Quebec Champions in Montreal before joining the league.

BATTING

G	BA	AB	H
6	.000	16	0

Walulik (Kiely), Helen "Hensky"

Born: May 3, 1929, Plainfield, New Jersey. 5'8", 121, Outfield, 2nd Base, Pitcher, BR, TR. Muskegon Lassies, 1948; Fort Wayne Daisies, 1948; Chicago Colleens/ Springfield Sallies, 1949; Kalamazoo Lassies, 1950.

Helen Walulik was a pitcher-infielder for two years in the league and spent one with the player development tour.

The highlight of her career was when she hit her only home run, an inside-the-park dinger for Fort Wayne against Kenosha. She received a box of chocolates and dozen red roses for her feat.

After her baseball days, Walulik married her high school sweetheart in 1953. They had three children: Karen, Jill and Bob. She worked for Johnson & Johnson Company for 22 years as a quality assurance technician before retiring in 1992.

BATTING

G	BA	AB	H	2B	3B	HR	SB	BB	SO	R	RBI
67	.153	131	20	1	0	1	5	2	13	11	10

PITCHING										FIELDING				
W–L	PCT	ERA	G	IP	H	R	ER	BB	SO	PO	A	E	DP	FA
3–8	.273	3.28	32	148	127	82	54	88	46	48	44	9	3	.911

Wanless (Decker), Betty

Born: Aug. 28, 1928, Springfield, Illinois. Died: December 20, 1995. 5'5", 134, 3rd Base, BR, TR. Grand Rapids Chicks, 1953; South Bend Blue Sox, 1954.

Betty Wanless reportedly hit the longest home run — 425 feet — ever recorded at Grand Rapids Park. Wanless had some power and knocked out 18 homers during her two years in the league.

BATTING												FIELDING				
G	BA	AB	H	2B	3B	HR	SB	BB	SO	R	RBI	PO	A	E	DP	FA
171	.262	627	164	23	3	18	74	56	71	124	82	207	360	69	22	.892

Warfel, Betty

Born: May 15, 1926, Enola, Pennsylvania. Died: Sept. 23, 1990. 5'8", 135, Pitcher, Utility Infielder, TR, BR. Rockford, 1948–49.

Berry Warfel was a versatile player with Rockford for two seasons in the league. After baseball, she worked for Westinghouse for 33 years. She also enjoyed bowling.

PITCHING										BATTING			FIELDING			
W–L	PCT	ERA	G	IP	H	R	ER	BB	SO	BA	AB	H	PO	A	E	FA
6–5	.545	2.63	20	96	57	36	28	48	18	.143	251	36	80	124	26	.887

Warren, Nancy "Hank"

Born: June 13, 1921, Springfield, Ohio. 5'5", 130, Pitcher, TR, BR. Muskegon Lassies, 1946–48; Chicago Colleens, 1948; Peoria Redwings, 1949–51; Fort Wayne Daisies, 1951–52; Muskegon Belles, 1953; Kalamazoo Lassies, 1954.

Once an All-Star, Nancy Warren pitched for nine years in the league and ended up with over 100 victories during her career.

Warren played baseball with her four brothers in their backyard at an early age. At 14 she joined her first organized fast-pitch softball team. She was playing for Fink and Heine Packers at the national tournament when she was noticed by league scouts. The All-Ohio shortstop was given a tryout the next spring in Pascagoula, Mississippi, and was assigned to Muskegon as a shortstop. However, the Lassies already had an All-Star shortstop, so she sat on the bench. Halfway through the season she demanded to be played or traded. She got her opportunity to play and pitch, but she broke an ankle in the process to end her season.

In her sophomore year, she was 17–11 with a 1.13 ERA for Muskegon. "Hank"—a nickname she picked up as a youth—was doing just as well in 1948, but was sent to Chicago to help the new franchise. "Every time they wanted to bolster a team, they'd transfer you," she explained. "I felt I was the one who benefitted from the trade." Chicago folded at the end of the season and she was sent to Peoria. The Redwings became her favorite team, but her record wasn't as good with them. She led the league in losses (16), runs (92) and earned runs (64) in 1949.

In 1951 she was sent to Fort Wayne. The Daisies had a good team and they gave her plenty of run support, leading to her best ever record of 17–6. She helped lead the team to its first pennant. Her 1952 performance led to her selection to the All-Star team the next season. However, she was traded to a lousy Muskegon team and she experienced her worst season in 1953 with a 6–17 record. In the final year of the league, she was the best fielding pitcher and did not commit an error all year.

After baseball, Warren went to work for North Central Airlines in Peoria. She ended up working 25 years with the airline industry, retiring in 1980. After baseball, her softball team won the Michigan state championship in 1956. She now lives in Port Charlotte, Florida, and goes to league reunions.

PITCHING										BATTING			FIELDING				
W–L	PCT	ERA	G	IP	H	R	ER	BB	SO	BA	AB	H	PO	A	E	DP	FA
114–93	.527	2.41	105	1428	1134	580	382	422	626	.155	669	104	115	605	47	3	.939

Warwick (McAuley), Mildred "Millie"

Born: Oct. 28, 1922, Regina, Sasketchewan, Canada. 5'2", 115, 3rd Base, BR, TR. Rockford Peaches, 1943–44.

One of the better hitters early in league history, Mildred Warwick set a league hitting streak record during her short career.

Growing up with five brothers, including a twin, Warwick could hardly avoid not playing softball when she was a child in a big field near her home. At age 12 she began playing softball in school. She was playing for the Regina Army-Navy Bombers when a scout from the league saw

Mildred "Millie" Warwick

her and invited her to Wrigley Field. "I was so nervous when I went to training camp, I didn't think I'd ever make it," she recalled.

But she did and was assigned to Rockford. At the beginning of the season, she showed right away that she could hit consistently. From June 20 to 27 she hit safely in 13 consecutive games to establish a league record that stood until it was tied in 1945 by Lib Mahon. It may have been an all-time record, but the league quit keeping records after the 1948 season. She also set another league record of 10 assists in one game by a third baseman.

Warwick played another season before getting married in March 1945. She decided to leave baseball and settle down with her new husband, professional hockey player Ken McAuley, a goalie with the New York Rangers. "The league was not a good league for married women," she explained.

She continued to play fast-pitch softball in Canada and played for Edmonton, which won the Canadian title in 1951. She worked for the Department of Energy for 27 years and retired in 1988. She was inducted into the Saskatchewan Hall of Fame in 1986 with her four brothers. She also was admitted into the Alberta Baseball Hall of Fame in 1991. Her husband passed away in 1992. She now goes to league reunions and lives in Edmonton.

				BATTING									FIELDING				
G	BA	AB	H	2B	3B	HR	SB	BB	SO	R	RBI		PO	A	E	DP	FA
189	.236	696	164	9	9	2	103	54	24	107	67		361	553	112	24	.891

Watson (Stanton), Marion

Born: July 2, 1923, Chatham, Ontario, Canada. 5'10", 185, Pitcher, TL, BR. Peoria Redwings, 1946; Muskegon Lassies, 1947.

A broken leg cut short the career of Marion Watson, one of the tallest pitchers in the league.

Watson didn't start playing softball until she entered public school at age 14. She played in city leagues and in 1939 led the Maple City Laundry team to the Ontario championship. A scout from the AAGPBL saw her and invited her to a tryout.

Because she had never played baseball, her first season in the league with Peoria was spent learning about the game. She had not worn spikes or a glove before coming to the league. She saw limited action in eight games her first season.

In 1947, the league went to Cuba for spring training. Several days after signing her contract, she slid into home and broke her right leg in two places. The league flew her home to Canada so her doctor could set the leg. "I got paid for the whole season," she recalled.

Watson's thoughts of going back to the league the next season were dashed by another accident. "I was riding a motorcycle and broke the other leg, and it was in a cast for two years," she explained.

She married Edgar Stanton in 1948 and settled down to raise three children: Nancy, Beth and Barbara. The league was inducted into the National Baseball Hall of Fame in 1988, yet she didn't hear about it for a long time afterwards.

PITCHING		BATTING				
G		BA	AB	H	R	RBI
8		.000	11	0	0	0

Wawryshyn (Moroz), Evelyn "Evie"

Born: Nov. 11, 1924, Tyndall, Manitoba, Canada. 5'3", 130, 2nd Base, BR, TR. Kenosha Comets, 1946; Muskegon Lassies, 1946–47; Springfield Sallies, 1948; Fort Wayne Daisies, 1949–51.

Once an All-Star, Evelyn Wawryshyn was an excellent hitter and fielder for six seasons.

Wawryshyn first played softball in elementary school on a boy's team with her brother. She then advanced to amateur ball with the Canadian Ukranian Athletic Club of Winnipeg. She was spotted by the league, but she refused an invitation. "It didn't seem real," she explained. After going to Winnipeg Normal School, she began teaching. When she received a second invitation from the league, she figured it was for real and decided to go. In her first season, she was a utility player for two teams and hit a respectable .217.

In the off-season "Evie" was a teacher, so she'd miss spring training. She was assigned to the expansion Springfield Sallies in 1948 and led the team in hitting. Two years later with Fort Wayne, she was named to the All-Star team.

After her baseball career, she married John Litwin in 1952. They had two children, Linda and Gregory, before he died of a heart attack two years later. She remarried Henry Moroz in 1960 and they had four children: Dawn, Sheryl, Penny and Tommy. At last count she had 10 grandchildren. She retired in 1986 and has attended two league reunions. She was inducted into Manitoba's Baseball Hall of Fame in 1992.

BATTING													FIELDING				
G	BA	AB	H	2B	3B	HR	SB	BB	SO	R	RBI		PO	A	E	DP	FA
544	.266	1943	275	37	16	1	273	177	175	275	193		1156	948	131	119	.941

Weaver, Jean

Born: Aug. 28, 1933, Metropolis, Illinois. 5'8", 138, 3rd Base, Outfield, Pitcher, BR, TR. Fort Wayne Daisies, 1951–53.

The middle Weaver sister on Fort Wayne, Jean's career took a turn for the worse after she cut off her big toe in a farming accident.

Jean started playing softball at age 13 with the Kennedy Kids before joining Magnavox with her sisters. When the Weaver sisters were drafted in 1950 by Fort Wayne, manager Max Carey didn't have room for Jean. Before the 1951 season began, Jean recalled an exhibition game they played in Bluefield, West Virginia. "All three of us hit a homer that night," she said.

In her rookie season she played both third base and in the outfield and hit a respectable

Jean Weaver

.247. Then in the off-season she had the accident that had an adverse effect on her career. "I couldn't dig in at the plate anymore," she explained. Her batting average dropped to .225 and she was tried out on the mound, but not with much success—0–2 record 12.90 ERA. The Daisies won their first pennant that season.

She could have been classified as the comeback player of the year in 1953 as she became strictly a pitcher and had the best winning percentage on the season (.875) with a 7–1 mark in helping the Daisies win another pennant.

The following season she was traded to Battle Creek. She decided not to report to the team. "I knew the league was going to fold," she explained. She went to Chicago and got a job with Motorola, where she worked for 30 years before retiring and moving back to her hometown in Metropolis.

BATTING

G	BA	AB	H	2B	3B	HR	SB	BB	SO	R	RBI
172	.246	520	128	15	6	2	41	25	62	71	55

PITCHING

W–L	PCT	ERA	G	IP	H	R	ER	BB	SO
7–3	.700	3.99	25	106	84	74	47	100	51

FIELDING

PO	A	E	DP	FA
187	251	43	15	.911

Weaver, Joanne "The Little"

Metropolis, Illinois. 5'11", 142, Outfield, Pitcher, BR, TR. Fort Wayne Daisies, 1950–54.

Joanne Weaver is the last professional baseball player to hit over .400. Selected as Player of the Year in 1954, Weaver was on three All-Star teams and set several single season and career records.

Weaver was the youngest of three sisters who all played on the Magnavox softball team. When the league's touring teams stopped in Missouri in 1950, all three of the Weaver sisters went to a tryout and were drafted by the league and assigned to Fort Wayne. Joanne was 14, so she didn't get much playing time in her first season.

In 1951, she suffered an ankle injury early in the season which limited

Joanne "The Little" Weaver

her play to 48 games on the year. She hit .276, which was the third best average on the team behind her big sister, Betty, and Evie Wawryshyn.

The following season she turned 16 and became of age in the league. She led the league in hitting with a .344 average and helped Fort Wayne win its first pennant. "I was blessed with coordination and I could run real well," she explained. Her average earned her a spot on the All-Star team. Her fielding was the only skill lacking.

Weaver's fielding improved considerably the following season to a .952 average. Her hitting stayed about the same, which was good enough to win another batting title. Fort Wayne won another pennant, and she made the All-Star team again.

About halfway through the 1954 season, the league reduced the size of the ball from 10 inches to major league size. As a result, Weaver and others started hitting the ball over the fence. By the end of the season, she had sent 29 balls out of the yard, more than any other player had hit in a season. She also hit .429, which remains the highest professional baseball batting average this century. Only two other players in baseball history have hit for a higher average. She led the league in total bases (254), runs scored (109), hits (143) and stolen bases (79). Her RBI and hits totals are the second best single season marks in league history. Again she landed on the All-Star team and the league selected her as Player of the Year. Fort Wayne again won the pennant with her help.

Weaver is very modest about her accomplishments and considers meeting golf legend Mildred "Babe" Didrikson-Zaharias as her greatest thrill while in the league. The league ended too early for her. "I was just getting wound up," she commented.

She joined Bill Allington's All-American team and barnstormed for several years. The team did some crazy promotions and once she raced against a horse and lost by a nose.

She went back home to finish high school before going back to Fort Wayne and working for Essex for 30 years. She retired in 1987 and returned to Illinois. She now enjoys living on a farm.

BATTING

G	BA	AB	H	2B	3B	HR	SB	BB	SO	R	RBI
329	.359	1220	438	52	17	29	79	32	24	109	87

PITCHING		FIELDING				
G	IP	PO	A	E	DP	FA
3	4	552	40	43	10	.932

Weddle (Hines), Mary "Giggles"

Born: April 26, 1934, Woodsfield, Ohio. 5'3", 118, 3rd Base, Outfield, Pitcher, TR, BR. Ft. Wayne Daisies, 1954.

A jack-of-all-trades player, Mary Weddle could play any position on the field. She joined the league in the last year of its existence and once threw a one-hitter.

Weddle came from a very large family of ten brothers and four sisters that had its own team, the Weddle Auctioneers. "We were poor and didn't have anything else to do," she explained. Her father was a semi-pro pitcher.

Weddle was a shortstop for a boys team in junior high, but they wouldn't allow her to play baseball with the boys in high school, so she played with a VFW softball team. "I threw a

Mary "Giggles" Weddle

baseball 248 feet at a track meet and I don't think that's ever been broken," she said about her throwing ability.

In 1953, she played softball for the Phoenix Queens for $150 a month. Her abilities in Phoenix were seen by the AAGPBL and she was offered $185 a month to play. She reported to Fort Wayne without ever going to spring training. "I wasn't there five minutes and a reporter wanted me for an interview," she said.

During her year in the league, she played at third base shortstop and in the outfield. She was even called in to relieve the starter at times. "The manager said to throw the ball hard." Weddle had no problem complying with that request.

Weddle got married the year after the league ended. She and husband Lewis have three children and five grandchildren. She still plays softball today. She hadn't heard about the league being inducted in the National Baseball Hall of Fame until 1993. "It's a lot for us old folks to take," she remarked.

PITCHING

W–L	PCT	ERA	G	IP	H	R	ER	BB	SO
3–1	.750	3.83	15	47	23	30	20	60	21

BATTING

G	BA	AB	H	2B	3B	HR	SB	BB	SO	R	RBI
76	.216	241	52	6	2	2	5	38	37	38	21

FIELDING

PO	A	E	DP	FA
53	87	21	1	.130

Weeks, Rossey

Born: Sept. 7, 1924, Jacksonville, Florida. 5'7", 155, Catcher, BR, TR. Racine Belles, 1947; Rockford Peaches, 1947.

An injury cut short the playing career of Rossey Weeks, who played less than a season in the league as a backup catcher.

Weeks was a little girl when she swiped a stick from her brothers and sisters to learn how to play stick ball. She earned the nickname "Slugger" from her family. She joined a church league and the coach called her "Flash" because she was so quick. She lived up to the nickname while running track and field in her school days.

When she heard about the league, she went to Miami for a tryout. Max Carey liked what he saw and signed her to a contract. She went to Havana, Cuba, for spring training and was assigned to Racine. Not long after the season began, she was reassigned to Rockford to fill in for an injured player. Near the end of the season, she was injured catching the ball with her ungloved hand. "I split my hand wide open," she said. The broken middle finger ended her short career in the league.

Weeks went on to play amateur softball for many years in Florida. She became an office worker with the Jacksonville Naval Air Station and retired in 1989. She still lives in Jacksonville.

BATTING

G	BA	AB	H
7	.059	17	1

Rossey Weeks

Marie "Blackie" Wegman

Wegman, Marie "Blackie"

Born: April 30, 1925, Cincinnati, Ohio. 5'7", 130, 3rd Base, 2nd Base, Outfield, Pitcher, BR, TR. Rockford Peaches, 1947; Fort Wayne Daisies, 1948; Muskegon Lassies, 1949; Grand Rapids Chicks, 1950.

Marie Wegman was an excellent defensive infielder who was moved around the league during her four-year tenure.

Wegman has a photo of herself playing baseball with her father at age 3. She played scrub games with the neighborhood boys and didn't play organized softball until she was 14. Because softball was not offered at school for girls, she joined an industrial league and was on a traveling team. She was in a drugstore when an AAGPBL scout asked if she knew about the league. She replied, "No." He talked her into trying out and the next thing she knew she was on a plane headed for spring training in Cuba.

During her first season with the league she got homesick, although she loved baseball. She played primarily at third base.

"Blackie," as she was called, was moved from team to team each season to make the teams even. She considers herself more of a defensive player. "I had problem with curveballs," she admitted.

After four years in the league she had to return home to help out her family. She now regrets her father, who died in 1945, wasn't able to see her play professionally. Because of her playing, she gained a second family in Racine and has stayed in contact with them ever since. "Many fans owned shops by the park and used to save ration stamps so players could have candy bars and cigarettes," she recalled.

Wegman retired in 1988 after working as a treasurer of a credit union. She still lives in Cincinnati.

BATTING

G	BA	AB	H	2B	3B	HR	SB	BB	SO	R	RBI
291	.180	834	150	14	3	1	51	102	124	60	47

PITCHING | | | | | | | | | FIELDING

W–L	PCT	ERA	G	IP	H	R	ER	BB	SO		PO	A	E	DP	FA
0–0	.000	6.56	3	11	13	11	8	9	5		349	527	92	32	.905

Weierman, Shirley Ann

Born: June 27, 1938, Lima, Ohio. 5'6", 120, 3rd Base, BR, TR. Fort Wayne Daisies, 1953–54.

Shirley Weierman didn't get much of a chance to play during the two years she was with the pennant-winning Daisies. She was injured in her last season. Weierman became a dentist after baseball. She now lives in Columbus, Ohio.

BATTING | | | | | | | | | | | FIELDING

G	BA	AB	H	2B	3B	HR	SB	BB	SO	R	RBI		PO	A	E	DP	FA
11	.179	28	5	0	0	0	0	1	12	0	0		13	24	4	2	.902

Wenzell, Margaret "Marge"

Born: May 21, 1925, Detroit, Michigan. 5'4", 118, Utility Fielder, BR, TR. Grand Rapids Chicks, 1945; Muskegon Lassies, 1946; Peoria Redwings, 1947; Fort Wayne Daisies, 1947; Springfield Sallies, 1948; Racine Belles, 1949; Fort Wayne Daisies, 1949; Kalamazoo Lassies, 1950; Battle Creek Belles, 1951–52; South Bend Blue Sox, 1952–53.

Good field, weak stick was how you could describe the versatile Marge Wenzell, who played for nine different teams during her nine years in the league.

Wenzell's father, Edward, was a semi-pro player and her two brothers played baseball, so she naturally learned the game. She joined an industrial softball league when she was 14. Other players from her league entered the AAGPBL when it first began, so she tried out for the league in 1945 and was allocated to Grand Rapids.

The following season she was moved to Muskegon and suffered a dislocated shoulder to end her season after just eight games. The defensive player staged a comeback in 1947 but she struggled at the plate.

In 1948 she rebounded to play full time. During the season she hit the only home run of her career — one that she'll never forget. Springfield was in South Bend and she hit a line drive between the outfielders. "I was circling the bases and they waved me home. I slid into home on my belly for an inside-the-park home run," she explained. The best part of the hit was that it was the winning run and her parents were in attendance. Her father later became a scout for the AAGPBL.

Wenzell's greatest thrill came when her South Bend Blue Sox won the playoffs with only 12 players. The downhill movement of the league in talent led her to quit after the 1953 season and work for General Motors for a couple of years. She then moved to California and worked for an electric company, retiring in 1985. Today she lives in Cathedral City.

Marge Wenzell

BATTING												FIELDING				
G	BA	AB	H	2B	3B	HR	SB	BB	SO	R	RBI	PO	A	E	DP	FA
557	.188	1677	316	30	21	1	147	256	170	179	128	805	584	148	68	.904

Westerman (Austin), Helen "Pee Wee"

Born: Sept. 10, 1926, Springfield, Illinois. 5'7", 118 Catcher, BR, TR. Kenosha Comets, 1943; Rockford Peaches, 1944.

Helen Westerman was one of the original players of the league and spent one full season and part of another with the AAGPBL.

Helen "Pee Wee" Westerman

Westerman began practicing baseball with a men's team at age 14. She picked up the nickname "Pee Wee" from her male counterparts. The following year she played with a girl's softball league as a catcher. One of her teammates, Elise Harney, was scouted by the AAGPBL. Harney told the scout that she needed Westerman, so the league invited her as well to tryouts at Wrigley Field.

Westerman and Harney both made the cut and were assigned to Kenosha. She would receive $55 a week from the league. In February 1943, they returned to Chicago for spring training. "We practiced in an ice skating rink, because it was too cold outside," recalled the receiver.

During the 1943 season, Westerman hit .183 and was the best fielding catcher in the league, as she caught the most games and had the most putouts. The following season she was given a raise to $75 a week and assigned to the Rockford Peaches, but her mother became ill and she quit the league to care for her.

Following the league, she played semi-pro softball with the Chicago Cardinals and Chicago Bluebirds for a couple of seasons. She became a restaurant manager for a decade and worked in an auto parts factory for 27 years, retiring in 1989.

BATTING													FIELDING				
G	BA	AB	H	2B	3B	HR	SB	BB	SO	R	RBI		PO	A	E	DP	FA
82	.183	263	48	3	1	0	20	15	14	36	21		395	60	21	8	.956

Whalen, Dorothy "Dot"

Born: June 22, 1923, Brooklyn, New York. 5'6", 140, Catcher, BR, TR. Springfield Sallies, 1948.

A "Punch-and-Judy" hitter, Dorothy Whalen was a back-up receiver for one season in the league.

Whalen was an all-around athlete as a youngster, but she didn't start playing softball until she was 17 years old. She joined the Marine Corps during World War II. After the war, she was playing women's professional basketball when she tried out for the league in Madison Square Garden. She was assigned to Springfield, a new franchise in 1948. "Dot" played part-time during the season as a catcher. "I was so amazed at how good girls were. I didn't have enough training," she said.

The following season she joined the Chicago Bloomer Girls. Her claim to fame was hitting a fielder's choice that won the world championship for the team. She played in the league until the mid–1950s when that league folded. She took up being a handball player for the next 27 years. The insurance broker then took up golf at age 60 and had a 12-handicap; however, a genetic eye disorder has left her nearly blind, so she has trouble getting around. She attended league reunions before her eyesight became too bad.

	BATTING												FIELDING				
G	BA	AB	H	2B	3B	HR	SB	BB	SO	R	RBI		PO	A	E	DP	FA
49	.153	111	17	2	0	0	11	14	13	9	5		187	28	24	1	.900

Whiteman, Vera

Battle Creek, Michigan. 2nd Base. Grand Rapids Chicks, 1946.

	BATTING												FIELDING				
G	BA	AB	H	2B	3B	HR	SB	BB	SO	R	RBI		PO	A	E	DP	FA
16	.133	45	6	0	0	0	3	6	9	6	2		12	12	1	2	.960

Whiting, Betty Jane

Born: July 21, 1925, La Salle, Michigan. Died: Date Unknown. 5'6", 147, 1st Base, Outfield, Catcher, BR. Milwaukee Millerettes, 1944; Grand Rapids Chicks, 1945–46; Fort Wayne Daisies, 1947; Chicago Colleens, 1948; South Bend Blue Sox, 1948–50; Kalamazoo Lassies, 1950–51; Battle Creek Belles, 1951–52.

Betty Jane Whiting was a good fielding first baseman who played for nine seasons on seven different teams in the league.

Whiting twice led the league in being hit by pitches. Her best fielding season came in 1946 when she committed only 13 errors and led the league in fielding percentage (.989) at first base. She helped South Bend win the pennant in 1948 after playing part of the year with the Chicago Colleens. Her best year at the plate came in her last year in the league when she hit .231.

	BATTING												FIELDING				
G	BA	AB	H	2B	3B	HR	SB	BB	SO	R	RBI		PO	A	E	DP	FA
943	.190	2947	561	64	17	3	198	422	303	311	232		8266	294	161	303	.982

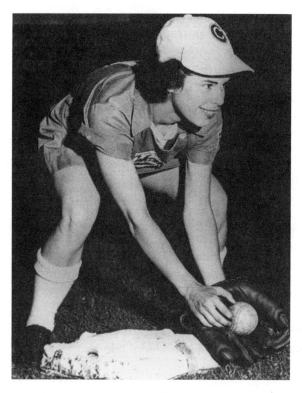

Norma Whitney

Whitney (Dearfield), Norma

Born: May 29, 1928, McKeesport, Pennsylvania. 5'2", 115, 2nd Base, BR, TR. Chicago Colleens, 1949; South Bend Blue Sox, 1950.

An injury limited the career of Norma Whitney to less than two years in the league.

Whitney got a late start in softball. She didn't start playing until age 14 with a town team that played other towns. She saw an ad in the newspaper for a tryout in her town and answered it. She and another of the 150 girls that tried out made the cut and were sent to South Bend for another tryout. After making the cut again, she was assigned to the Chicago Colleens for further development. The team went to 33 states in 1949. "It was tiring at times. We played every day and traveled all night," she explained. She hit .214 on the season.

The following season she was assigned to South Bend and her play was limited, since she was a rookie. Then she suffered a detached retina and spent 33 days in the hospital. It ended her playing career.

Whitney married Duane Dearfield in 1952. They had four children: Karen, Duane, Diane and Tim. The grandmother of ten retired in 1990. She now goes to league reunions.

Wicken (Berthiaume), Elizabeth "Wiggles" Ann

Born: May 26, 1927, Regina, Saskatchewan, Canada. 5'2", 115, Outfield, BL, TL. Grand Rapids Chicks, 1946–47; Muskegon Lassies, 1947.

Elizabeth Wicken was a good defensive outfielder for two years in the league. She now resides in Williams Lake, British Columbia.

BATTING												FIELDING				
G	BA	AB	H	2B	3B	HR	SB	BB	SO	R	RBI	PO	A	E	DP	FA
117	.182	407	74	12	5	0	26	51	47	32	34	132	17	7	0	.955

Wigiser, Margaret "Wiggy"

Born: Dec. 17, 1924, Brooklyn, New York. 5'6", 160, Outfield, BR, TR. Minneapolis Millerettes, 1944; Rockford Peaches, 1944–46.

Margaret Wigiser was a solid hitter and good fielder for three seasons in the league, including one year with the championship Rockford Peaches.

At age 13 she took up playing softball in the neighborhood. She was going to school at Hunter College when she tried out for the league in New Jersey with hundreds of others. She made the cut and was assigned to Minneapolis. The Millerettes failed to draw much of a crowd, so the league put the team on the road. "Wiggy" enjoyed meeting all the different players and fans in the Midwest. "It was a wonderful learning experience," she said. One night she hit a home run and was traded the next day to Rockford. In 1945 she hit a career-high .250 and helped the Peaches win the pennant and championship. The team couldn't repeat as champs the following season.

Wigiser finished up her degree and turned her attention to teaching in New York City high schools. She advanced to become the director of women's sports and brought about organized sports to more than 10,000 women. She retired in 1989 and settled down in Hobe Sound, Florida, where she golfs frequently.

		BATTING											FIELDING				
G	BA	AB	H	2B	3B	HR	SB	BB	SO	R	RBI		PO	A	E	DP	FA
203	.227	700	159	10	8	4	65	63	45	80	88		271	29	24	5	.926

Wildfong (Measner), Hazel

Born: June 2, 1925, Holdfast, Saskatchewan, Canada. Died: 1984. 5'5", 135. Rockford, 1946.

	BATTING		
G	BA	AB	H
1	.000	1	0

Wiley (Sears), Janet "Pee Wee"

Born: Oct. 12, 1933, South Bend, Indiana. 5'4", 112, 1st Base, Pitcher, BR, TR. Chicago Colleens, 1950; South Bend Blue Sox, 1950–52; Rockford Peaches, 1953.

Injuries and a suspension curtailed Janet Wiley's performance and cut back her playing career.

"Pee Wee" picked up the nickname during her sandlot days when she was a youngster. Then she got an inside track on the AAGPBL when she became a bat girl for the South Bend Blue Sox in 1945. When she was 16, she received a letter from the league for a tryout. She was then picked to play for her hometown team.

In 1950, she was assigned to the barnstorming Chicago Colleens and hit .289 before coming to South Bend to play in the league midway through the season. Known more for her

Janet "Pee Wee" Wiley

defensive skills, she alternated with Dottie Mueller at first base. "She was a better batter than I was," she explained. Wiley hit a paltry .134 her first year. The following season she improved to .221 and became a regular for the Sox at first base with Mueller pitching. The Sox won the pennant and the championship that year for the first time in their history.

In 1952 she suffered a knee injury early in the season and was used sparingly when she had a run in with manager Karl Winsch. She was standing up for fellow player Shorty Pryer, but Winsch felt she was insubordinate and suspended her for 30 days. She decided she would not go back to the team. "I was so angry, I wouldn't play for him anyway," she explained. She was granted an all-out release from her contract by the league office. In 1953 she was signed by Rockford and used sparingly because of knee problems.

After her playing days, she got married and fostered six children. Her experience in the league helped her as a mother. "It helped me to encourage our girls to be whatever they wanted to be and the boys to respect them for it," she explained. She also coached junior high softball. She now lives in South Bend and attends league reunions.

BATTING

G	BA	AB	H	2B	3B	HR	SB	BB	SO	R	RBI
147	.195	380	74	5	2	0	7	31	69	31	25

PITCHING		FIELDING				
G	IP	PO	A	E	DP	FA
1	1	1086	48	34	41	.971

Williams (Heverly), Ruth

Born: Feb. 12, 1926, Nescopeck, Pennsylvania. 5'4", 130, Pitcher, TR, BR. Racine Belles, 1946; Fort Wayne Daisies, 1946; South Bend Blue Sox, 1947–50; Peoria Redwings, 1950; Kalamazoo Lassies, 1950–53.

Ruth Williams was a starting and relief pitcher for five teams in her eight year career.

She began playing softball at age 12 with a church league. When she was a sophomore at East Stroudsburg University, she played for the New York Traders, a fast-pitch team. They paid her travel expenses and meal money for her to play on the weekends. Her father saw an advertisement for the All-American League in the *Philadelphia Inquirer*. Williams was invited to a tryout in Allentown of some 400 women. The scout told her afterwards, "You'll hear from us in a few days." She figured she hadn't made it, but then three days later received train fare to Chicago.

Williams was assigned to Racine, but was transferred ten days later to Fort Wayne and rode the bench most of the season. She was traded to South Bend the next year. Meanwhile, she finished her degree and began teaching at Ambler High School in Pennsylvania.

At the beginning of the season Sox manager Chester Grant asked her if she could pitch. She said she could even though she didn't. "I would do anything to play," she said. She began pitching and was remarkably good in her first season with a 12–8 mark and a 1.70 ERA. Her performance slacked off to a 10–10 mark the following season.

She considers 1949 as her best season because she helped her team finish in a regular season tie for first place with Rockford. Since she was still teaching in Pennsylvania, the team flew her in for the Memorial Day weekend to pitch. She won two games and flew back to finish out the school year. She started and relieved that season. "It took me only ten pitches to warm up," she explained. She threw a lot of junk pitches at the hitter: changeups, drop balls and curves. They worked and she ended the season with a 10–6 mark.

Williams made a stop in Peoria in 1950 before she landed on the Kalamazoo squad. She didn't get much run support from the lowly Lassies and had losing records the remaining four years of her career. During her pitching career she recorded eight two-hitters. She had a no-hitter going into the ninth inning of one game before disaster struck. Two errors and two hits later, the thrill was gone.

She married Leonard Heverly at the end of the 1953 season and left the league behind. The teacher continued her work in Ambler and the couple adopted a son, Michael. In 1980, tragedy struck. Her husband was killed by a drunk driver. She retired soon after the incident. Williams was going to league reunions until she suffered a heart attack in 1995, which has slowed her life down considerably.

PITCHING										BATTING			FIELDING			
W–L	PCT	ERA	G	IP	H	R	ER	BB	SO	BA	AB	H	PO	A	E	FA
65–69	.485	2.19	162	1114	879	403	271	395	315	.132	333	44	64	356	24	.946

Wilson, Dolores "Dodie"

Born: Dec. 17, 1928, Stockton, California. Outfield, BR, TL. Peoria Redwings, 1947; Chicago Colleens, 1948.

Dolores Wilson was an outfielder for two seasons in the league.

BATTING												FIELDING				
G	BA	AB	H	2B	3B	HR	SB	BB	SO	R	RBI	PO	A	E	DP	FA
79	.217	230	50	1	1	0	16	21	22	17	23	44	7	8	0	.864

Wilson, Verna

Rochester, New York. Rockford Peaches, 1946.

Verna Wilson played in only one game with Rockford in 1946.

BATTING

G	BA	AB	H
1	.000	1	0

Wiltse (Collins), Dorothy "Dottie"

Born: Sept. 23, 1923, Inglewood, California. 5'7", 125, Pitcher, TR, BR. Minneapolis Millerettes, 1944; Fort Wayne Daisies, 1945–50.

Dottie Wiltse was the strikeout queen during the early underhand fast-pitch days of the AAGPBL. She led the league in several categories for a couple of seasons.

"I pitched my first game in 1936 at age 11. We won the Southern California championship," she recalled. Wiltse was one of five chosen by her manager, Bill Allington, to go to the AAGPBL in 1944. "We basically brought him into the league in mid-nineteen forty-four," she said. Allington became a manager.

In Wiltse's first season, she made an immediate impact with her fastball. She struck out a league high 205 batters that season and hit 44. "I brushed them back," she explained.

The following season she was moved to Fort Wayne and had her career year. The untiring hurler tied three other starters in pitching the most games on the season (46). She also had the most strikeouts (293), most hit batters (20), most shutouts (17) and tied for the highest winning percentage (.744).

More importantly to her was a doubleheader she pitched on August 28, 1945. She won both games and met the man she would someday marry, Harvey Collins.

The league moved from underhand to sidearm and then to overhand pitching, while Wiltse moved to Collins. The new wife made the conversion successfully, unlike some other underhand pitchers. The highlight of

Dorothy "Dottie" Wiltse

the 1947 season was her becoming the best fielding pitcher — she made only three errors on the season and had the highest fielding percentage (.965).

In 1948 she became pregnant with her son, Dan. She played half the season and then took off the rest of the year to deliver her son.

After two more seasons in the league, she turned her attention to raising a family. She delivered a daughter, Patty. Now a great grandmother, she has two grandchildren and one great grandson.

She worked for General Electric for some time in Fort Wayne. She then took up golf like her husband and followed in his footsteps by winning the city golf championship in 1971.

In 1987, the players of the league formed a player's association and she joined the board of directors. She now publishes a newsletter for the association, which numbers more than 300 former players.

Wiltse holds the single season record for strikeouts (294) and hitting the most batters (44).

PITCHING										BATTING			FIELDING			
W–L	PCT	ERA	G	IP	H	R	ER	BB	SO	BA	AB	H	PO	A	E	FA
117–76	.606	1.81	223	1576	896	470	317	612	1004	.123	523	66	115	327	32	.933

Wind, Dorothy

Born: 1926, Chicago, Illinois. 5'6", 128, Shortstop, BR, TR. Racine Belles, 1943–44.

Dorothy Wind, one of original players of the league, set the league record with six base hits in a single game on June 28, 1943. She helped Racine win the pennant and championship in 1943. Wind also played volleyball and basketball before becoming a pro baseball player. She attended college in the off-season.

BATTING											FIELDING				
G	BA	AB	H	2B	3B	HR	SB	BB	SO	R	RBI	PO	A	E	DP	FA
144	.250	529	132	8	11	2	64	35	22	85	63	227	497	103	23	.876

Wingrove (Earl), Elsie "Windy"

Born: Sept. 26, 1923, Zelma, Saskatchewan, Canada. 5'6", 130, Outfield, BR, TR. Fort Wayne Daisies, 1946; Grand Rapids, Chicks, 1946–47.

Elsie Wingrove roamed the outfield for a couple of seasons in the league.

"I played ball ever since I can remember on the farm," Wingrove said about her start in baseball. She played with her four brothers and sisters and father. Then at age 9 she joined the girl's adult team. After high school, she went to business college in Saskatoon and continued to play amateur softball until she was noticed by a league scout and sent to Pascagoula, Mississippi.

Wingrove was assigned to Grand Rapids after spring training, but she was loaned to Fort Wayne for a month during her rookie season. Not known as a power hitter, she always tried hard. "I always had a desire to hit a ball over the wall at Grand Rapids. The closest I came was hitting the wall," she said.

She married immigration officer Russell Earl in 1948, which spelled an end to her playing days. She became a customs broker and raised a family of two boys, Norman and Gary. In 1988, she retired and began going to league reunions with her spouse. She still lives in Canada, but spends winters in Arizona. She now has three grandchildren.

BATTING												FIELDING				
G	BA	AB	H	2B	3B	HR	SB	BB	SO	R	RBI	PO	A	E	DP	FA
119	.181	353	64	7	1	0	19	20	40	30	15	124	16	7	2	.952

Winter, Joanne "Jo"

Born: Nov. 24, 1924, Chicago, Illinois. Died: September 22, 1996. 5'8", 138, Pitcher, TR, BR. Racine Belles, 1943–50.

Twice an All-Star, Joanne Winter ranks as one of the best pitchers in the All-American League. One of the original players of the league, she put her name in the record book in several categories.

Winter recalled chasing baseballs for the boys when she was only 3 years old. She was interested in all sports when she was growing up near Chicago and participated in swimming, volleyball, basketball, soccer, track, tennis and handball. At age 11 she played on her first softball team, the Oak Park Coeds. She then advanced to the Bloomer Girls and the Admiral Music Maids. Her family moved to Phoenix, Arizona, and she joined the Ramblers, but before she could crack the lineup, she received a wire inviting her to play in the All-American League.

The underhand hurler was assigned to Racine and went 11–11 the first season in helping the Belles win a pennant and championship. She struggled the next two seasons with losing records, going 22–45 over the span. Then she went through a delivery transformation with the help of a Mexican hurler. "I went to a sling-shot delivery, a half of a windmill," she explained. "The windmill was hard on my delivery."

The change in delivery and pitches — she learned to throw a rise — baffled batters. She went from being one of the worst pitchers to one of the best. At one stretch during the 1946 campaign, she threw 63 consecutive scoreless innings, which resulted in six shutouts in a row. One game was a 17-inning affair against Peoria. The remarkable feat (the major league record is 59 by Orel Hershiser) resulted in her being named to the All-Star team. She also helped the Belles win another pennant and championship. She considers a 1–0 victory over Rockford for the championship as one of the best games in her career. She had stranded 19 batters on base, yet allowed nobody to score. She ended the season with a 33–10 record, tying her with Connie Wisnewski for the most wins ever in one season. The two shared the pitching title that season.

Following a 22–13 ledger in 1947, Jo led the league in three categories in 1948: wins (25), innings pitched (329) and strikeouts (248). Her 25–12 record pushed Racine to another pennant. She was again named to the All-Star team.

Underhand delivery was banded after the 1948 season, so Jo converted over to a three-quarters delivery with help from Leo Murphy, a former catcher with the Pittsburgh Pirates. She developed back problems from the delivery and had a losing record for the next two years.

Like several underhand pitchers, she abandoned the league for the Chicago National League when she was offered a bigger contract. The Admirals offered her $150 a week and a bonus of $400 if she won at least 25 games in a season. "I was so nervous winning that game (25th)," she recalled. She played several seasons in Chicago before going to Arizona to play for the Phoenix Queens. She pitched her best season ever, going 36–6 in 1957. She finally quit the league because of the owner.

Jo taught tennis before deciding to take up golf. She worked at Motorola at night and hit the greens by day. She won the Arizona state championship and finally got her chance to go on the pro golf tour in 1962. However, her age and lack of experience put her at a disadvantage on the links. "I couldn't compete with the pros," she explained. She took up teaching golf instead and made a living from it.

In her career in the All-American League, she ended up with the third most wins (133), the second most losses (115), the second most innings pitched (2,159) and the second most games pitched (287). She also owns the record for the most games lost in a season (23).

PITCHING											BATTING			FIELDING			
W–L	PCT	ERA	G	IP	H	R	ER	BB	SO		BA	AB	H	PO	A	E	FA
133–115	.536	2.06	287	2159	1470	822	495	759	770		.168	790	135	139	620	48	.941

Wirth, Senaida "Shoo Shoo"

Born: Oct. 4, 1926, Tampa, Florida. Died: Date Unknown. 5', 114, Shortstop, 2nd Base, BR, TR. South Bend Blue Sox, 1946–51.

Senaida Wirth was the only rookie on the 1946 All-Star team.

In her rookie year, Wirth swiped a career high 89 bases and hit .245. She was the best fielding shortstop in 1948, committing 20 errors and having a .964 fielding average. She helped the Blue Sox win pennants in 1949 and 1951 and the league championship in 1951, which was the year of her career best batting average (.274).

BATTING												FIELDING				
G	BA	AB	H	2B	3B	HR	SB	BB	SO	R	RBI	PO	A	E	DP	FA
616	.248	2120	526	26	12	2	359	313	160	360	201	1127	1898	186	124	.942

Wisniewski, Connie
"Iron Woman" "Polish Rifle"

Born: Feb. 18, 1922, Detroit, Michigan. Died: May 4, 1995. 5'8", 147, Pitcher, Outfielder, TR, BL. Milwaukee Chicks, 1944; Grand Rapid Chicks, 1945–52.

A five-time All-Star and once Player of the Year, Connie Wisniewski was one of the best players of the AAGPBL. She set many records during her eight year career and is considered by many as the best underhand pitcher of the league.

Wisniewski grew up playing softball in Detroit and became known as the "Iron Woman" for frequently pitching doubleheaders. In the early 1940s, she led the Hudson Motors to the city championship. A scout from the league grabbed her up as soon as he saw her in 1944. She would probably have been named Rookie Pitcher of the Year if the league would have had such an award. Her winning percentage of .697 was best in the league as she led Milwaukee to the pennant and playoffs.

She earned her nickname "Iron Woman" the following season by pitching a season high 46 games, including both ends of a doubleheader once. Wisniewski also led the league in ERA (0.81), wins (32), innings pitched (391) and winning percentage (.744). Her performance earned her a place on the All-Star team and the league's first Player of the Year award.

Her dominance over league hitters continued the following year when she again led the league in ERA (0.96) and winning percentage (.786). She also had 33 victories, which tied her with Joanne Winter for the league lead. She was again named to the All-Star squad.

In 1947 the league switched to sidearm delivery and the "Polish Rifle," as some players called her, struggled to a 16–14 record and a sore elbow. She began to play in the outfield and her hitting improved to .291.

Overhand pitching the following season meant the end to her pitching days, as she was one of many pitchers who couldn't convert to the true baseball style of pitching. She turned her attention to hitting and became the league's third best hitter with a .289 average. She also showed a power surge and led the league in home runs (7). Again she was an All-Star, but in the outfield this time.

After another All-Star season in 1949 and finishing second in batting average, she jumped to the National Girls Baseball League for one season and more money. However, she didn't like it and returned to the AAGPBL in 1951. She was again an All-Star and hit a career high .326. After a lackluster season in 1952, she decided her career as well as the league were on the downhill slide and she quit.

She went to work for General Motors in Grand Rapids for 28 years and owned a restaurant called The Chicks Dugout. When she retired, she moved to Florida.

PITCHING

W–L	PCT	ERA	G	IP	H	R	ER	BB	SO
107–48	.690	1.48	170	1374	924	336	226	245	266

BATTING												FIELDING				
G	BA	AB	H	2B	3B	HR	SB	BB	SO	R	RBI	PO	A	E	DP	FA
656	.275	2165	595	79	30	7	185	296	166	339	231	563	619	79	11	.937

Wohlwender (Fricker), Marion "Wooly"

Born: March 13, 1922, Cincinnati, Ohio. 5'4", 125, Catcher, BR, TR. Kenosha Comets, 1943.

Marion Wohlwender never played in a regular-season game and spent less than a month in the league.

She learned to play baseball when she was growing up in Cincinnati. "I'm the only one who had a ball," she explained. Her brother taught her how to be a catcher. She started playing organized softball at age 15 with the Dick Brown Rosebuds. She then went to work and play for H.H. Meyers, a meat plant. She was scouted by the league and sent to Wrigley Field for tryouts. She made the cut and was assigned to Kenosha, but she decided the league wasn't for her. "I was just so homesick, I went home," she said.

Wohlwender continued to play softball in Cincinnati. She married George Fricker in

1945 and they raised three children: Marianne, John and Bob. She worked part time at a grocery store and is now retired. Her husband died in 1994. She now performs volunteer work and spends time with her four grandchildren.

She felt guilty that she left the league the way she did, but she didn't like leaving her hometown. "I still don't feel good about it," she said.

Wood, Loita

Lima, Ohio. Pitcher, TR, BR. Fort Wayne Daisies, 1950–51; Kenosha Comets, 1951.

PITCHING										BATTING			FIELDING			
W–L	PCT	ERA	G	IP	H	R	ER	BB	SO	BA	AB	H	PO	A	E	FA
3–16	.158	4.75	24	165	166	116	87	96	37	.139	72	10	3	63	1	.985

Wood, Mary

Lakewood, Ohio. Outfield, BR, TR. Peoria Redwings, 1946; Kenosha Comets, 1947.

BATTING												FIELDING				
G	BA	AB	H	2B	3B	HR	SB	BB	SO	R	RBI	PO	A	E	DP	FA
152	.165	480	79	6	3	0	59	64	77	36	19	270	23	21	5	.933

Wright, Sadie

Battle Creek Belles, 1951.

Wronski (Straka), Sylvia "Roni"

Born: Dec. 2, 1924, Milwaukee, Wisconsin. 5'2", 140, Pitcher, TR, BR. Milwaukee Chicks, 1944; Grand Rapids Chicks, 1945.

Sylvia Wronski saw action only when the regular pitching staff on the Chicks needed a rest between starts and she was called upon to perform admirably.

Wronski came from a large family of eight children and was a "tomboy." She played baseball and football with her brothers. She used to take the arms, legs and heads off her dolls and use the body for a football. She finally started playing organized softball in high school and in a West Allis league. She then went to a league tryout at Boucherd Field and was chosen to pitch on her hometown team.

The fastball pitcher occasionally threw from the side to fool batters. "Roni" did a good job of fooling them, too. During the season she compiled a 4–2 record in helping the Chicks win the pennant and championship. The following season the franchise moved to Grand Rapids. She was cut from the team a month into the season.

Wronski became Straka in 1947 when she got married. She and Edward fostered three children — Donald, Christine and Theresa — before he passed away in 1954. She struggled to raise three children the next few years while working part-time in local factories. In 1990 she retired after 21 years with Briggs and Straton. She now lives in Milwaukee and watches over her six grandchildren and three great-grandchildren.

PITCHING										BATTING			FIELDING			
W–L	PCT	ERA	G	IP	H	R	ER	BB	SO	BA	AB	H	PO	A	E	FA
4–2	.667	3.06	13	53	44	33	18	30	2	.050	20	1	8	23	7	.816

Wuethrich, Lorraine

Milwaukee, Wisconsin. Died: April 27, 1992. Infielder. Rockford Peaches, 1943–44.

Lorraine Wuethrich played in less than ten games in the two seasons she was in the league.

Yahr, Betty

Born: April 22, 1923, Ann Arbor, Michigan. Outfield, BL, TR. Rockford Peaches, 1946.

Betty Yahr, a light-hitting outfielder, was released halfway through her only season in the All-American League.

Yahr was 13 when she first began playing organized softball. She received an invitation to come to spring training in 1946 through a coach she knew at Western Michigan University.

She was allocated to Rockford and played right field. "I scored the winning run in one game," she recalled. Then two months into the season, she was released. She couldn't play softball for another year because of her professional status, but after that she played for the next 20 years. Yahr worked at a printing company for 42 years and retired in 1988 at age 65. She lives in her hometown of Ann Arbor.

BATTING												FIELDING				
G	BA	AB	H	2B	3B	HR	SB	BB	SO	R	RBI	PO	A	E	DP	FA
22	.171	76	13	1	1	0	2	12	12	11	8	31	1	4	0	.889

Young, Janet

Pitcher, Battle Creek Belles, 1951.

PITCHING	
G	IP
2	3

Renae "Ray" Youngberg

Youngberg, Renae "Ray"

**Born: April 3, 1933, Waukegan, Illinois.
5'6", 150, 3rd Base, Pitcher, BR, TR.
Grand Rapids Chicks, 1951–54.**

Renae Youngberg played most of her career in the AAGPBL with tuberculosis, but she never let the disease slow her down.

Youngberg first played baseball in the fifth grade in a two-room schoolhouse in Minnesota. "They let two of us (girls) on the boys team," she said. Throughout her teens she played either baseball or softball.

The 16 year old got a tryout with the AAGPBL in 1949, but she didn't make the team. However, she was good enough to be assigned to a Chicago team that sometimes fed girls to the two touring teams of the league. Two months later, Youngberg joined one of the touring teams in Ardmore, Oklahoma, to replace injured players. She remembered the team having four Cubans. When they went to Texas, one of the players got upset with an umpire over a call and started swearing in Spanish. Unfortunately, the umpire understood Spanish and promptly booted the Cuban out of the game.

"Ray" will never forget when she found out she had TB. It was on a Friday the 13th in 1950. She had a positive skin test and an X-ray confirmed the disease. It didn't stop her from playing, though. "Luckily I had a progressive doctor who felt I could keep playing," she explained. To allow the lung to heal, her doctor collapsed the diseased lung.

In 1951 she tried out in Grand Rapids, Michigan, and she was invited to spring training. She made the team despite her condition. She played like any normal player. "I got plenty of rest and ate properly," she explained. "I was in top shape; it didn't affect me."

The third baseman for Grand Rapids played well her first year. During one game she blocked the base and got spiked for her efforts. The next day she played with the leg stitched up and ended up getting boils under the cut. She also got hit between the eyes on a throw from left field. Nothing could stop her from playing, though.

At the beginning of her second year with the team a fire broke out at Bigelow Field. The stadium was destroyed and along with it their uniforms. The team had to wear some old Peoria uniforms until new uniforms could be made. "We had a heck of a time finding spikes. And we had to buy new gloves," she remembered.

During the 1953 season, Youngberg played a month for the Muskegon team to fill in for an injured player. Near the end of the season she was sent to South Bend to fill in when six players walked off the team. She ended up playing on the championship team.

When the league ended after the 1954 season, Youngberg attended Illinois State and received a degree in physical education. She then taught elementary and junior high physical education for 30 years and retired in 1986. She now lives in Portage, Michigan.

BATTING

G	BA	AB	H	2B	3B	HR	SB	BB	SO	R	RBI
341	.214	1141	244	28	5	8	36	124	79	127	123

PITCHING		FIELDING				
G	IP	PO	A	E	DP	FA
1	4	381	765	97	48	.922

Youngen, Lois

Born: Oct. 23, 1933, Westfield Center, Ohio. 5'3", 115, Catcher, Outfield, BR, TR. Kenosha Comets, 1951; Fort Wayne Daisies, 1951–52; South Bend Blue Sox, 1953–54; Fort Wayne Daisies, 1954.

Lois Youngen was a catcher-outfielder for three different teams during her four year career. She helped Fort Wayne win pennants in 1952 and 1954.

BATTING												FIELDING				
G	BA	AB	H	2B	3B	HR	SB	BB	SO	R	RBI	PO	A	E	DP	FA
116	.255	325	83	8	0	1	3	46	22	39	44	254	37	9	9	.970

Ziegler, Alma "Gabby" "Ziggy"

Born: Jan. 9, 1921, Chicago, Illinois. 5'3", 125, 2nd Base, Shortstop, Pitcher, BR, TR. Milwaukee Chicks, 1944; Grand Rapids Chicks, 1945–54.

The Player of the Year in 1950, Alma Ziegler was an excellent hurler during the overhand era of the game. She played the second most games in league history during her 11 seasons.

Ziegler played baseball with the boys while growing up in Chicago. Her family moved to California and she began playing organized softball in high school. She read about the league in *Life* magazine and went to a tryout in Los Angeles. She went to Chicago for spring training and was assigned to Milwaukee. "Gabby"—who

Alma "Gabby" "Ziggy" Ziegler

earned the nickname for her gift of gab—started at second base and helped the Chicks to a pennant and championship.

The franchise moved to Grand Rapids the following season and she remained on the team as a second baseman and occasional shortstop. In 1947 she led all second basemen in fielding and led the league in walks (62). The Chicks again won the championship.

The team was short of pitchers the following season and she was given a try on the mound. She responded with a 9–6 record on the year to help the team win the pennant. In 1949 she was moved back to her natural position—second base—and was again the season's best fielder.

The Chicks again turned to "Ziggy" to pitch in 1950. Her three pitches—fastball, curveball and backdoor slider—baffled hitters and she turned in the best winning percentage on the year (.731, 19–7 record). She was honored as the Player of the Year.

Gabby wasn't needed as much in 1951 on the mound and she turned in a 14–8 record. The scrappy hitter turned in the most sacrifices (25) in 1952. In 1953 she was used less on the mound and more at second, where she again was the best fielding second baseman (.954). During the 1953 playoffs, she was called on to manage the team when the manager had been booted out of the game. The Chicks won the game and the championship.

After her long career, she became a court reporter until retiring in 1980. Now an avid golfer, she also delivers meals to the elderly in Los Osos, California. She also attends league reunions.

BATTING

G	BA	AB	H	2B	3B	HR	SB	BB	SO	R	RBI
1154	.173	2621	628	47	8	3	383	641	249	482	239

PITCHING

W–L	PCT	ERA	G	IP	H	R	ER	BB	SO
60–34	.638	1.94	126	839	677	250	181	203	250

FIELDING

PO	A	E	DP	FA
2486	1950	245	306	.950

Ziemak, Frances

Jamaica, New York. Pitcher, Peoria Redwings, 1951.

PITCHING

W–L	PCT	ERA	G	IP	H	R	ER	BB	SO
0–1	.000	6.00	2	9	10	7	6	9	2

Zonia, Violet

Havana, Cuba. Springfield Sallies, 1948.

BATTING

G	BA	AB	H
1	.000	1	0

Zurkowski (Holmes), Agnes "Aggie"

Born: Feb. 21, 1920, Regina, Saskatchewan, Canada. Racine Belles, 1945; Fort Wayne Daisies, 1945.

Agnes Zurkowski played one season in the league but did not enjoy much success. She was inducted into the Saskatchewan Baseball Hall of Fame in 1991.

PITCHING

W–L	PCT	ERA	G	IP	H	R	ER	BB	SO
0–1	.000	5.89	4	12	26	19	17	9	2

Index